# Faculty Work
# and Public Trust

▶

# Related Titles of Interest

**College Teaching Abroad: A Handbook of Strategies for Successful Cross-Cultural Exchanges**
Pamela Gale George
ISBN: 0-205-15767-X

**The Art of Writing for Publication**
Kenneth T. Henson
ISBN: 0-205-15769-6

# Faculty Work and Public Trust

**Restoring the Value of
Teaching and Public Service
in American Academic Life**

**James S. Fairweather**
*The Pennsylvania State University*

**Allyn and Bacon**
Boston • London • Toronto • Sydney • Tokyo • Singapore

*Series Editor:* Stephen D. Dragin
*Editorial Assistant:* Susan Hutchinson
*Manufacturing Buyer:* Aloka Rathnam
*Editorial-Production Service:* Tobi Giannone, Michael Bass & Associates
*Copy Editor:* Carol Ann Sheffield

Copyright © 1996 by Allyn & Bacon
A Simon & Schuster Company
Needham Heights, Massachusetts 02194

*Library of Congress Cataloging-in-Publication Data*

Fairweather, James Steven
    Faculty work and public trust : restoring the value of teaching and public service in American academic life / James S. Fairweather.
       p.    cm.
    Includes bibliographical references (p.      ) and index.
    ISBN 0-205-17948-7
    1. College teachers—United States. 2. College teachers—Tenure—
-United States. 3. Scholarly publishing—United States. 4. College teaching—United States. 5. College teachers—Salaries, etc.–
-United States. 6. College administrators—United States.
7. Universities and colleges—United States—Public services.
I. title.
LB1778.2.F35   1996
378.1'21'0973—dc20                         95-21580
                                             CIP

Printed in the United States of America

10  9  8  7  6  5  4  3  2  1     99  98  97  96  95

*For Linda, my wife and a friend forever, and for Mimi Stearns, also a friend forever.*

# Contents

# Preface

The crescendo of criticism and even outright hostility that increasingly characterizes the environment for American academic institutions in the 1990s has caught many academics unprepared. Are not colleges and universities the repositories of knowledge, the training grounds for youth, the local meeting place for many small towns and large cities? Academic leaders ask, "Why cannot the populace, the politicians, and the pundits see our value and let us get on with our work?"

This era is characterized by miscommunication, lack of credibility, and failure to examine objectively (or at least honestly) the inner workings of academe. When the State of California drastically cuts the budget of the postsecondary sector that trains much of its undergraduates while at the same time calling on academe to devote more time and resources to the training of undergraduates, we have a mismatch between the intent of a policy and its actual consequences. Representative William Clinger of Pennsylvania, in a discussion with Professor Irwin Feller of Penn State University, said that in his many years in the House of Representatives he has never seen research universities (and higher education in general) held in such low esteem. Congresswoman Patricia Schroeder, a long-time advocate of education, has led a congressional committee whose purpose was to criticize colleges and universities for their high cost, lack of emphasis on undergraduate education, and mismanagement of funds.

Although financial abuses, such as the overhead expenditure fiasco at Stanford University and the claims of tuition fixing directed at several elite eastern colleges, contribute to a negative perception of academe, in my view these incidents mask the two largest sources of mistrust. The first is the belief that faculty in American colleges are protected from the vagaries of the marketplace by a tenure system, whereas the rest of the nation must deal with

xi

employment uncertainty and rapid changes in economic conditions. The public perception is that faculty and administrators have created a system to make themselves immune from a rapidly changing economic world, and that such an insulated environment makes it difficult, if not impossible, for faculty and administrators to appreciate the concerns of the populace at large. The source of mistrust here can be broadly cast as concern about the economy of the future. State and federal policy initiatives to encourage more active involvement by colleges and universities in economic development are based on the premise that somehow academic institutions should be key participants in revitalizing an information-based economy. This concern, however, is often poorly understood—how do colleges and universities actually affect the economy?—by both legislators creating policy and by academic administrators who commit their institutions to carry out the policy.

The second source of mistrust centers on perceptions about what faculty do with their time. The perception by the public, politicians, and other outsiders is that faculty in all types of 4-year schools, not just research universities, devote themselves to their own pursuits, which most often fall into publishing research results that have no practical consequences; faculty and administrators are too busy doing their own work to pay attention to anything else. The cost of this devotion to research and publishing is teaching, especially undergraduate instruction, and public service. A basic motivation for public criticism of higher education in this era is the questionable instructional value received for increasingly expensive tuition costs.

Several recent publications have emphasized this point. Books by authors such as Martin Anderson and Richard Huber, the latter a former collegiate administrator, raise questions about the faculty role in creating a privileged status not enjoyed by most people. These authors claim that faculty are motivated primarily by self-interest, which is best served by preserving a status quo increasingly devoted to research and publishing.

I believe that most of these claims are based on a hodgepodge of unrepresentative anecdotes rather than on representative empirical data. The portrayal of the typical faculty member as a highly paid researcher who has little or no interest in the public good or in any endeavor other than self-interest is at best a caricature. One purpose of this book is to set straight the nature of the faculty position (occupation) and the variation in faculty work by type of institution.

Yet the public perception of faculty and their work cannot simply be dismissed as a public relations problem. Once the record has been set straight (i.e., most faculty are not wealthy and spend some of their time with students), the evidence shows that colleges and universities of all types increasingly *do* emphasize research and publishing in faculty assessment. In addition, for most faculty public service, including direct involvement in economic development, continues to represent such a small percentage of their job that it hardly registers. This allocation of effort can lead to a decreased emphasis on undergraduate (and perhaps even graduate) teaching and continued undervaluing of public service, although self-interest alone is not an adequate explanation for this trend. I do not claim that basic research is less valuable than applied research, that all research must have an immediate social benefit, or that public service is the most important activity either for faculty or for their institutions. I do claim that as academics we have invented and reinforced a reward structure and socialization process that increasingly encourages faculty to think more about research than teaching, that stresses publishing volume more than quality, and that treats the publication of research as the principal, perhaps the only, measure by which faculty can claim to have achieved high status.

I recall a speech by David Scott, formerly provost at Michigan State University and now chancellor at the University of Massachusetts at Amherst, in which in a review of his own publication record he found about one-third of the volume could be attributed to promotion criteria or to the desire to present a paper at a conference held in a desirable location. Scott asked whether he might have spent this time more usefully on teaching and public service. Scott also described his role as provost at Michigan State, where to retain a handful of top research-oriented faculty he awarded higher salaries and granted more release time from teaching. Although his rationale was based on a response to the marketplace (i.e., provide incentives to keep the high-profile faculty at Michigan State), Scott admitted that the message given to the rest of the faculty was that devotion to research, spending less time on teaching, and attracting competing job offers based on research productivity were the goals to which they should aspire.

Given these two powerful external pressures on institutions of higher education—to increase the attention paid to teaching and to participate more actively in the economy—how should an academic leader respond? I explore in this book how to enhance the value of teaching in the faculty role. I examine the ways in which academic administrators, knowingly or unknowingly, contribute to a culture based on research productivity, or more accurately research volume, as the basis for faculty rewards. As Trow and Jencks and Riesman found in the past, evidence of a drift toward a publishing-based reward structure exists at all types of 4-year schools, although its depth and the administrative role in promoting such a reward structure is more deeply entrenched than previously thought. I believe that too much has been written about the self-interest of faculty and not enough on the role that administrators play in reinforcing research-oriented performance. I also examine the contribution faculty make to perpetuating a publishing-oriented reward structure, although this is a secondary goal. The purpose is to help administrators, faculty, and the public at large understand the influence of administrative actions in creating and reinforcing one particular role for faculty—

research—which is vital but not alone in its importance as we confront a changing world.

I also explore a second major focus of external pressure on academe, namely efforts to make colleges and universities more productive partners in economic development. To assist academic administrators in making reasoned policy decisions, I examine ways in which colleges and universities, particularly their faculty, make contributions to the economy. Broadly cast under "public service," the roles of the academy in the economy are much more varied than commonly understood.

In my own work, I have found that many administrators, including those committed to enhancing the value of teaching and public service at their institutions, feel powerless to change institutional norms. This assumption is consistent with the view of academe as a work environment where the professors make most of the decisions that affect their work lives and administrators provide the resources to enable faculty to carry out their chosen missions. It is also wrong; the decisions and actions, both intended and unintended, can reinforce the very norms these administrators wish to change. The study of faculty salaries in this book provides ample evidence of the reinforcement of existing norms by administrative action, even if administrators are unaware that the reinforcement is taking place.

Similarly, faculty often feel driven by a system outside their control. Even in master's- and bachelor's-level institutions whose missions are primarily instruction-oriented, surveys by the Carnegie Foundation for the Advancement of Teaching and by Gray, Froh, and Diamond have found that faculty feel pressure to publish and spend time on research. Yet the same faculty participate in promotion and tenure decisions, often voting to emphasize a research-oriented reward system that conflicts with the values they profess.

The key word is "*powerlessness*". In my view, faculty and administrators *can* participate in assessing the fit of the direction academic institutions are heading, help decide if the fit is adequate, and if not, start to redress the mismatch. Such evaluations and decisions are not easy, nor are they immune from external intervention. But they are not impossible; after all, faculty and administrators have been willing participants in the creation and maintenance of the current higher-education structure.

I believe that the fit of a research- and publishing-based model for assessing faculty performance, particularly one based more on internal needs for promotion and pay than on societal needs, is inconsistent with a changing world in at least two areas. The first is internal to academe, the need to enhance the value of teaching in the work lives of many faculty. The second concerns relations with the outside world, the need to respond more directly to the worries and concerns of the public about the economic future of their children. The latter topic I include under the broad heading of public service, although service obviously includes much more than understanding and responding to changes in the economy. I base my discussion, supported by empirical data, on the premise that teaching, research, and public service compete for time within the faculty workweek, and that academic administrators and faculty who want to increase the value of teaching and public service must recognize that some decrease in effort toward research and publishing is needed to reach their goal. I am not arguing that research *per se* is bad, only that we have reached a point in the evolution of American colleges and universities at which restoring a balance to activities that contribute to legitimate social needs must become as important to the faculty work life as activities which have meaning only within the professional reward structure.

I much prefer to have this discussion openly and to encourage academic leaders to develop alternatives for faculty work lives. I encourage policymakers and people from the general public who have an interest in the education of their children to learn about the workings of colleges and universities. I hope that increased understanding will make proposed policy changes more likely to achieve desired goals. Most importantly, unless academics come up with alternatives, state and federal legislators, public funding agencies, and even private philanthropic organizations will prepare their own solutions, ones which may not preserve the best parts of the cultures which historically have allowed American colleges and universities to make such outstanding contributions to society. I am certain that the pursuit of mechanisms to preserve the status quo, to ensure that publishing volume retains a premier place in faculty rewards, and to ignore the economic reality confronting most Americans carries too heavy a penalty; change is coming whether or not we in academe are prepared for it.

# Acknowledgments

Survey data were collected under a contract supported by the National Center for Education Statistics, U.S. Department of Education. Analyses for survey data were supported by grants from TIAA-CREF and from OERI, U.S. Department of Education (as part of the National Center on Postsecondary Teaching, Learning and Assessment). Case study research for Chapter 5 was supported by the National Science Foundation. The views expressed in this book are solely those of the authors.

Thank you to the following reviewers for their useful comments and suggestions: Ellen E. Chaffee, Valley City State University and Mayville State University, and James C. Hearn, The University of Georgia.

On a personal note, I owe a special thanks to Karen Paulson, graduate assistant at Penn State University, for her help in reviewing the manuscript.

# Tables

# Faculty Work
# and Public Trust

# ▶ 1

# Agendas for Change

Academic institutions have played important roles in the development of American society. The traditional emphases on teaching, research, and service have resulted in substantial economic and cultural contributions, including the educated citizenry required to maintain democratic institutions. Academic contributions to local, regional, and national economies are no less important, whether seen as enhancing the social good, as supporting local tax bases and creating jobs, or as "engines" which drive the American research machine.[1] Yet these traditions, which form the core of the debate between factions arguing for major changes in academe and those seeking to maintain the status quo, have evolutionary and, in some instances, even revolutionary beginnings. The teaching function, conceived in its earliest form as one social group seeking to replace itself with another of like background, characterized the colonial period.[2] Not until World War I and especially World War II did American universities, responding to a new national agenda and redirected federal funding, devote their attention wholeheartedly to research.[3] In response to changing national, regional, and local needs, the definition of teaching itself has evolved, today incorporating new technologies and alternative pedagogical approaches to reach older adults and to provide continuing education for professionals.[4] Public service was added to the academic triumvirate along the way,[5] although it has formed a major rationale for community and junior colleges from their inception. The clientele of higher education and the type of institutions established to serve them also have changed over the years. The creation of public 2-year colleges and the establishment in the 1960s of many public regional 4-year colleges and universities reflected a dramatic attempt to increase access to higher education. The Morrill Land Grant Act of 1862 and the GI Bill were indicative of federal efforts to enhance both student access and institutional responsiveness to social needs (i.e., agriculture and technology).

The evolution of academic institutions, their student clientele, and their missions has been influenced strongly by changes in society and in the national agenda.[6] Despite the belief held by many academics that change is initiated through internal debate and introspection, a belief encouraged by the professional mores dominant in most colleges and universities,[7] the historical record shows that change in academe is more often a reactive response to changes in the environment: "initiatives for change and reform of higher education, while they may in some cases come from within the academy, much more frequently and insistently come from these wider [social, economic, and political] contexts."[8] Effective academic institutions have been able to respond to external needs while maintaining a coherent internal professional ethos which is crucial to accomplished teaching, research, and service.[9]

This balancing act is not easy. If academic institutions were completely market-driven, the social costs might exceed the benefits. For example, American economic competitiveness would be far worse today if colleges and universities had closed engineering schools in response to the glut of engineers in the 1950s.[10] Alternatively, the same could be said had colleges and universities refused to add new programs to provide continuing education to professionals or to participate in alleviating adult illiteracy.

One model for explaining this inherent internal/external conflict is resource dependency.[11] Another is to view academic institutions as cybernetic entities whose purpose is self-maintenance.[12] From either perspective, academic institutions can be seen as dependent simultaneously on external sources for support and on the maintenance of existing internal values (e.g., academic freedom, professionalism) to achieve traditional academic goals. Faculty governance and the faculty reward structure are the principal expressions of institutional conservatism, acting to maintain the status quo while the institution attempts, often in more peripheral ways, to respond to social changes. In this reward structure are embedded the traditions of teaching, research, and service—or more appropriately to the current status of academic work, research, teaching, and (perhaps) service. The socialization of faculty to accept the status quo also makes it difficult for faculty, students, and administrators to understand the changing nature of these traditions. In the end, creating substantial changes in faculty and institutional roles to meet changing social and economic needs implies that academic leaders must confront the nature of faculty work and the incentives for maintaining existing faculty norms.

According to Clark Kerr, the autonomy of any academic institution depends on how well the administration carries out its central task, to lead the transformation of the institution in response to changing societal needs.[13]

Such adaptations are crucial when the level of public trust is low and when the societal change itself is seen as fundamental.[14] Today, we have entered such an era. With the end of the Cold War and the dawning of a highly competitive global economy, accompanied by high uncertainty about job security, American citizens and their public servants have questioned the relevance of a system of higher education based at least in part on a mission established during and immediately after World War II. The perceived threat to the United States is no longer based on the ability to keep up with the Soviet Union and Sputnik; more important is the ability to compete in the world economy.

Unlike environmental conditions in the previous three decades, the external pressures on academic institutions at the end of this century and the beginning of the next raise questions about the fundamental component of any academic enterprise, the faculty. Providing increased access to college in the 1960s and surviving the steady state economies of the 1970s and 1980s led to *institutional level* reforms in the shape of new (or expanded) types of institutions and to modified financial and management practices. Recent calls for change—from Congress, state legislatures, and the public—recall the post–World War II and Sputnik eras in their focus on the *faculty role,* in which the emphasis of much federal policy was to enhance the research activity of colleges and universities and their faculty.[15] Today, calls both for a renewed emphasis on teaching and for making academic institutions more actively engaged in the economy imply the need for a fundamental reexamination of faculty work.

In this context, academic institutions today face two primary criticisms, each posing questions about faculty roles and each potentially adversely affecting institutional autonomy. The first is the belief that faculty in American colleges and universities, protected by a tenure system, have little understanding of the vagaries of the marketplace and the anxiety a rapidly changing economy creates for the populace at large. Fair or not, this criticism implies that academic institutions and their faculty should respond more directly to assist the nation and its youth in responding to changes in the economy. Relatedly, the perception of a faculty "elite" who follow self-determined research and teaching agendas has led to criticism about the way in which faculty spend their time. Recent congressional hearings, led by Congresswoman Patricia Schroeder, have codified this criticism as the failure to devote sufficient attention to undergraduate instruction, continuing questions about the lack of access to postsecondary education for many youth, and rising costs.

Not surprisingly, the questions raised in these criticisms have led to new endeavors and to attempts to preserve established practices. The simultaneous acceptance of and resistance to change is not new; it embodies the essence of academic culture. As Alfred and Weissman point out, changing public expectations that antiquate [academic] institutional activity domains and that appear inimical to the professional interests of college faculty and staff have frequently been the focus of institutional efforts to reconfigure activities to match external needs and expectations.[16]

The nature of the debate about the responsiveness of higher education to societal needs is nasty. Richard Huber describes faculty as a self-interested profession pursuing disciplinary norms,[17] whereas Martin Anderson criticizes faculty as a less-than-honorable elite pursuing irrelevant agendas.[18] Relying to some extent on these critical perspectives, state legislatures and federal congressional committees have come to believe that academic institutions must be forced into compliance with specific societal agendas. Yet these agendas themselves conflict. Hence legislative action arises to require faculty to spend more time in the classroom and to mandate faculty workloads while simultaneously demanding more faculty involvement in technology transfer and applied research. Academic leaders who view their role as preserving the status quo and who believe that public relations alone is the appropriate response do not help promote a reasoned conversation about the future directions of American higher education. Instead of the rhetoric of blame and threat all too common today, the current debate should be about the role or roles of higher education in a society which is no longer agrarian or rural in makeup, and which has a distinct set of needs as we move toward the next century.

## CHANGE AND THE NATURE OF ACADEMIC INSTITUTIONS

Academic institutions of all types have been called inherently conservative. Lamenting the inability of colleges and universities to respond effectively to changes in the environment, Ashby noted: "It is a melancholy fact that universities have not devised sufficient built-in mechanisms for change. There are, of course, some virtues in inertia, but not if the inertia is so great that change has to be imposed from the outside."[19] Birnbaum attributes this institutional conservatism to the survival orientation of cybernetic entities whose purpose is to preserve the organization and its cultural mores while responding to changes in the environment.[20] Cohen and March attribute institutional conservatism at least in part to the conflicting messages received from the environment, which is not homogeneous.[21] For example, a state legislature trying to spur investment in high technology may require a different type of response from academic institutions than a local firm needing retraining for its displaced workforce.

A cultural perspective which emphasizes the professional orientation of academe, including self-governance and academic freedom, is another explanation for conservative institutional responses to environmental change.[22] From this viewpoint, the faculty reward structure acts as a mechanism to ensure continuation of academic values across institutions and disciplines.[23] Socialization of new faculty into the profession is accomplished by colleges and universities through mentoring, service on committees, and peer review.

Yet academic institutions remain dependent on public and private support for their survival.[24] As one example, the reliance on external funding for research, which is the most prestigious of academic activities, is longstanding.[25] This resource dependence suggests that resistance to change is not easy, requiring considerable effort to maintain traditional academic values in the face of calls for action. Indeed, it can be argued that the availability of external funding led to expansion of the research mission; that is, academic norms followed changes in the environment rather than preceded them. Moreover, as discussed previously, these traditions have evolved over time. Finally, the continuing drift toward a single research-oriented reward structure by institutions of lower status speaks of constant movement in the academic sector:

> But competition and the accompanying emulation of high-status exemplars by lower-status institutions tend to make for a leveling upward of the whole system toward the characteristics and styles of the leaders; competition accounts for the "drift," noted everywhere, of second- and third-rank institutions and of new institutions and sectors toward the academic forms and styles, the curriculum and standards, of elite institutions.[26]

The crux of the current environmental uncertainty is that academic institutions *are* changing, especially through institutional drift, changes in the demographics of the student population, and budgetary constraints, but not necessarily in ways that constructively respond to societal needs. Alpert[27] and Kerr[28] explain this apparent discrepancy by distinguishing the community responsiveness of an academic institution, which is the responsibility of the administration, from the professional mores which unite faculty within disciplines across institutions. In this hybrid arrangement peripheral structures, such as organized research units or research parks, often are expected to lead the response to societal needs while the core academic functions reflected in the faculty reward structure remain unchanged.[29] This portrait is consistent with Weick's characterization of a "loosely coupled" system.[30]

The challenge for academic leaders is to fulfill traditional functions well, to meet new challenges at the same time, and to accomplish these tasks without losing the managerial authority.[31] Indeed, Clark Kerr went so far as to say that the key to innovation lies in the battleground between administrative leadership and faculty conservatism. He believes that the principal threat to university autonomy is the inability of academic leaders to challenge the conservatism of faculty, who are motivated less by institutional responsiveness to societal needs and more by preservation of the status quo.[32] Ultimately, the challenge is to respond to societal needs in ways that capitalize on the unique capabilities of academe while reinforcing the ability to carry out essential basic missions.

## CHANGING WORLDS

The forces encouraging apparently disparate goals for academe—developing a new economic development role and restoring importance to the instructional mission—are actually related. As I discuss later in the book, the major contribution of higher education to the economy is in human development, that is, the educating and training of youth and adults. This educating and training includes the encouragement of critical thinking and problem solving, both crucial to the long-term economic survival of the nation. Moreover, to achieve at least some form of economic and social equity, youth from underrepresented groups require access to and completion of postsecondary education to obtain useful employment. Although both economic development and instruction are addressed in many ways by the variety of 2- and 4-year institutions that make up American higher education, the most prestigious activity in 4-year schools today is research or, more specifically, research which is valued by academic peers through a peer-review system of publishing and grant awarding. The intense focus on research initially was a response by major universities to a clear national need, expressed by various federal programs during and immediately following World War II.[33] Today, the normative value of research is apparent in all types of 4-year institutions, not just major research universities, including those traditionally devoted to teaching. As I show in this book, this transition is evident in faculty behavior and the concomitant reward structures that encourage its maintenance. It is also evident in the transformation of *research* norms, responding at least in part to societal needs, toward *prestige*, a norm important mainly within the academy:[34]

> Because institutions seem to pay particular attention to those activities that generate prestige, it would not be too much of an exaggeration to argue that resource dependencies to which institutions most closely attend are those that facilitate the pursuit and management of prestige.[35]

From this perspective, enhancing prestige depends on criteria relevant to the academic world. Research and publication are important *within* academe. These criteria are not necessarily valid *external* criteria for assessing academic performance. The ambiguity between internal and external criteria, and between professed institutional missions and actual reward structures, makes assessment of academic effectiveness problematic.[36] In this context, needs of academic institutions that pursue internally relevant goals, such as publication, to enhance prestige may conflict with other, external needs, such as technology transfer, training the workforce, and even providing access to youth from underrepresented groups. Traditional academic activities, such as service and teaching, can be given less attention if their prestige value is low. Even community colleges follow an internally oriented prestige model when giving higher status to the 4-year college transfer function than to vocational preparation courses.

The question today is whether the evolution toward a research-and-prestige model is consistent with the changing needs of society. If so, then the evolution of the American higher education system provides a very strong basis for helping to solve current and future societal needs because, as I argue throughout the book, most 4-year institutions increasingly value faculty research behavior. Yet prestige and internally relevant research behavior are insufficient norms if the match between the performance of academic institutions and evolving societal needs is a poor one. I argue that the match increasingly is poor. Two emerging discrepancies between external needs and internal values are especially important: the changing nature of the economy and the need to enhance the stature of instruction.

## CHANGING NATURE OF THE ECONOMY

The American economy has shifted from an industrial to an information economy.[37] Characteristic of this shift are a dramatic increase in the rate of technological change, increased competitiveness, and the internationalization of the economy.[38] The perception of a national economic crisis has arisen from the declining competitiveness of American industry in the world economy:

> The traditional industrial base has eroded…The United States no longer dominates the production of high technology goods nor the technical disciplines that underlie this production. Instead, Japan, Korea, and others are actively competing for leadership in the forthcoming technologically-oriented economy.[39]

In the "new economy," effective industrial output requires more investment in research and development, a long-term view toward profit, and mechanisms to convert research into commercial products.[40] New jobs are more likely to be generated by small businesses rather than large manufacturing companies.[41] Especially relevant to higher education is the centrality of human capital,[42] including preparing more scientists and engineers; educating more women and minorities (who will make up a larger portion of the population in coming years); upgrading the technical training of the workforce; lifelong learning; and enhancing literacy, remediation, and basic skills training.[43]

The traditional view of the role of academe in innovation no longer applies in an information economy. Technology transfer, in particular, is a complicated and not well understood process. Historically, technology transfer was seen as a simple linear process and research-driven model which started with a major scientific breakthrough and publication of research results. The process progressed through applied research and product development, and ended with industrial manufacturing and marketing. This model of technology transfer presumed that basic research was the domain of the university, and application and product development the responsibility of industry.[44]

This model no longer characterizes technology transfer, if it ever did.[45] Today, technology transfer is seen as highly interactive and market-driven with extensive and synergistic linkages between universities and industry. The lines between basic and applied research are blurred, and the walls between product development and manufacturing and marketing have broken down.[46] In this context, the leading academic institutions in technology transfer have very close ties with industry, including close personal ties between faculty and researchers from industry.[47] For example, some Stanford University engineering faculty speak of their "colleagues" at Intel's Research and Development Center, and often send their doctoral candidates to carry out dissertation research at Hewlett-Packard laboratories.

Universities that succeed at technology transfer seek to understand changing markets, industrial needs, and technological opportunities, using this information to modify the direction of research programs. In these entrepreneurial academic cultures, it is common for university and industrial researchers to work side by side on joint research efforts. These universities have removed traditional institutional barriers and provided incentives for faculty to participate in the research and development process. Modifications to traditional academic organizational structures are common in these institutions, where joint research projects, industrial affiliate programs, small business incubators, and research parks are the norm rather than the exception.

Most important from this perspective is the inadequacy of the traditional dissemination model for economic competitiveness: "When the use of basic research findings in industry involves a gap of up to twenty years it is moot whether one can speak of a university-industry interaction in any meaningful sense."[48] According to such critics, academic institutions must move from a passive stance based on basic research to more active involvement in technology transfer to assist in making the American economy more competitive.[49]

Although the movement to enhance the participation of academe in the economy apparently focuses on institutions, at its base is a fundamental disagreement with existing norms for faculty behavior. Particular concern has been raised about making knowledge and technology transfer a central part of the public service role for faculty, and about enhancing the value of public service in faculty personnel decisions.[50] This criticism is as true of public land grant institutions as it is of private universities: "the pervasive attitude in our land grant universities [is] that applied work is not important; publishing for professional peers and consulting for the highest paying firm or government agency are the priority tasks."[51] The emphasis given by academic leaders and faculty to status and prestige, particularly through publishing within discrete disciplines, has reinforced the perception of uncaring institutions removed from the constraints the rest of society must confront.[52]

To enhance technology transfer and increase the involvement of higher education in the economy, universities are encouraged to participate in public–private partnerships, especially alliances with industry.[53] Federal agencies have supported these alliances through grants such as the National Science Foundation's Engineering Research Centers.[54] State legislatures actively have encouraged ties between industry and higher education.[55] The Thomas Edison program in Ohio and the Ben Franklin Partnership in Pennsylvania, for example, encourage industry–university partnerships to form spinoff companies and to increase technology transfer.[56]

Prior to 1992, the view of industry–university arrangements as fundamental to restored economic competitiveness dominated state technology programs:

> Overall, reservations concerning the appropriateness or effectiveness of closer [industry–university] collaboration have been tabled in the present period of "positive sum" aspiration, specter of long-term economic decline, and programmatic advocacy.[57]

A 1990 survey of state higher education executive officers showed that the greatest concern of state legislatures about higher education was its role in economic development.[58] Recent events, however, point to declining state support for these technology transfer programs because of state budget constraints and because their success in promoting commercialization has not been demonstrated.[59] In particular, with a few exceptions (e.g., Ben Franklin Partnership in Pennsylvania, Thomas Edison program in Ohio), universities simply used state economic development funds as another resource to continue existing activities, particularly nondirected basic research. Faculty behavior, reward structures, and the academic culture, for the most part, remained unchanged.[60] Also, state governments have discovered that retraining the workforce and supporting manufacturing can be more important economic stimuli than investing in high technology research and graduate programs.[61]

In addition to leaders in research universities,[62] academic advocates of increased ties between business and higher education include community college leaders[63] and administrators from regional comprehensive colleges and universities.[64] Many industrial leaders support industry–university alliances.[65] Some national associations and nonprofit research organizations have advocated stronger linkages between business and higher education.[66] The American Council on Education, as one example, formed the Business–Higher Education Forum specifically to promote industry–university cooperation.[67]

Whether or not specific industry–university alliances are effective, the general goal remains the same. Proponents of more direct involvement of academe in the economy, whether they realize it or not, are actually asking for different behavior by faculty and, by implication, a new emphasis within the academy about hiring, rewards, and other personnel decisions. In this new institutional ethos, local and regional economic development are as important to the quality of an academic institution as teaching and research.[68]

## INSTRUCTIONAL QUALITY, ACCESS, AND COST

Although research is the most prestigious activity for faculty in 4-year colleges and universities, the public typically is more concerned with the education of youth. As Hearn points out,

> …it is the instructional function of higher education, not the research and service missions, that most endears higher education to the public. There is no evidence that the public believes the benefits of college are independent of what is taught and learned there.[69]

The status of the instructional mission has come under public scrutiny. Public concern about the cost of higher education and the value received for expensive tuition, anecdotes about attending college to work with renowned professors only to be taught by graduate students, and debates within the academy about curricular content and whether or not faculty have the time to spend on curricular reform add to the lore about the limited role of teaching in the faculty reward structure.[70] In addition, concern about access resulting from increased tuition and declining capacity to enroll students, literacy, and worker retraining, all of which are related to the instructional mission, demonstrate that the debate about the role of academe in the economy is not limited to technology transfer. As one consequence, some state officials have asked colleges and universities to demonstrate the instructional productivity of their faculty.[71]

Reacting to these external criticisms, the American Association of Higher Education set "Reclaiming the Public Trust" as its theme for the 1992 annual conference. Boyer argued that renewing investment in undergraduate education is paramount to restoring this trust.[72] His work echoed the recommendations of the Study Group on the Conditions of Excellence in American Higher Education,[73] which focused on encouraging more active student and faculty involvement in instruction.

At the same time, proponents of the service mission and its instructional components, especially continuing professional education and retraining the workforce, continue to make their case. Schuh and Rattan call for a wider concept of service which includes extending technical knowledge to the private sector and to policymakers, public affairs education, and verifying research results produced in the private sector.[74]

Some proponents of a renewed emphasis on the instructional mission believe that the focus on technology transfer obfuscates the variety of contributions to the economy made by academic institutions through instruction and service.[75] Other proponents fear that faculty involvement in technology transfer will render traditional academic functions ineffective. From this perspective, the separation of the university from the pressures of the marketplace has been crucial to its contributions to society.[76] The emphasis on so-called historical missions and traditional functions can be misleading, however, because it portrays academe as a fixed entity comprising homogeneous institutions and missions rather than an evolving enterprise consisting of widely diverse institutions and aims. Weiner, for example, has shown that questions about industry–university relationships, faculty behavior, and the ethics of patenting began during the "traditional era" in the 1900s, not the 1980s.[77]

## LEADERSHIP AND POLICY ALTERNATIVES

Academic institutions can help meet the needs of an emerging information economy, which is dependent on a well-educated workforce, by increasing access, improving instructional quality, and enhancing student learning. Alternatively, participation in some types of research-based technology transfer activities will require academic leaders and their faculty to make difficult choices between instructional, research, and service missions. In both cases, reliance on the traditional prestige model in higher education with its emphasis on publishing and internally relevant norms can no longer be assumed to meet these changing societal needs.

Fundamental to understanding the roles of academic institutions in society and to making recommendations for change is an appreciation of the underlying cultures and aspirations of faculty and their institutions, and an examination of the myths and behaviors that underly them. To this end I explore the nature of faculty work, the institutional incentives for various faculty endeavors, the relative importance of intrinsic and extrinsic rewards in faculty work, and the role of prestige in perpetuating myths about teaching and research. I also study the changing nature of the economy and how this evolution requires academic institutions of all types to refocus the nature of faculty work.

Beyond studying the development and maintenance of academic cultures, I translate research results into practical policy alternatives for both academic administrators and external policymakers. I attempt to assist academic administrators in understanding the roles they currently play in creating and reinforcing norms for faculty behavior, to help them formulate alternative policies and actions to respond to new societal needs, and to describe appropriate actions that external groups such as state agencies can take to help in this transition. Important here is the internal goal of enhancing the value of instruction in academic work, and the external aim of making public service, particularly as it relates to the economy, a more central part of the faculty work life. Not all situations or recommendations will apply to administrators equally. Some will apply only to administrators whose institutions face pressures to simultaneously promote large-scale technology transfer and enhance the value of undergraduate teaching. Others will apply to administrators who need only to enhance traditional faculty roles in the economy, such as through continuing education. Still others will apply to those who need primarily to encourage faculty involvement in teaching and advising while downplaying expectations for a direct role in economic development.

I emphasize the role of individual faculty and internal academic operations, although relations with external associations and new forms of organizational linkages are part of any comprehensive effort to promote innovation. In examining faculty behavior, although factors such as socialization and prior experience play a part in how faculty view their jobs and how they spend their time, I focus primarily on the roles of administrative action in faculty work. Whether through assignment of work or through direct rewards, this focus on administrative action is meant to help administrators and faculty decide which actions can be used to assist their institutions respond to changes in external environments.

Reexamining the fit among institutional mission, faculty behavior, and national, regional, and local needs is crucial at this junction because change is the operative word today, whether or not academic institutions and their constituencies are ready for it. Better to engage actively in deciding how to respond to changing needs than to be forced to respond to state and federal policies that may not redress perceived inadequacies in the modern college or university. A direct response by academics, whether by clarifying the contributions made to society by various academic endeavors or by conducting serious self-scrutiny aimed at changing the values placed on various activities, may seem impossibly difficult. It is easy for administrators to blame faculty for following self-interested behavior. It is equally easy for faculty to claim that the key to change starts with administrators who set the tone for their institutions. Nevertheless, *both* administrators and faculty, not to mention their students and other valued constituencies, have a vested interest in reexamining their missions and deciding how to respond to emerging societal needs, preserving the strong parts and improving the weak parts, and having an active say in the future evolution of the American college and university. Tackling this difficult assignment directly is not merely an intellectual exercise; it is the key to restoring the public trust in American higher education.

Despite the headlines, few of the claims for or arguments against the involvement of higher education in the economy are supported empirically.[78] Similarly, little is known about faculty involvement in the array of activities which reinforce research norms and potentially detract from teaching. Most data on faculty behavior are either attitudinal or many years old.[79] Baldridge and colleagues' well-respected study,[80] often cited as baseline data for studies of faculty, was published in 1978. Many analyses rely on different Carnegie and Ladd and Lipset surveys of faculty from the early 1970s. Trow may believe that evidence of institutional "drift" is well-documented,[81] and the amount of supporting literature lends credence to his claims, but the anecdotal and attitudinal data he used seem insufficient. I devote the remainder of the book to using the latest empirical data to examine questions which lie at the core of the roles of faculty in academe, in the economy, and in the larger society.

## THE CHAPTERS

The prerequisite for policies designed to enhance faculty involvement in any activity, whether service, technology transfer, teaching, or research, is knowledge about the faculty position. Accordingly, in Chapter 2, Faculty:

The Focal Point, I examine faculty workload and time allocation, seeking additional information about the nature of faculty work and the variation in work patterns by type of institution and academic discipline. Especially relevant are the tradeoff between time spent on one activity versus another and whether faculty behaviors are consistent across types of institution. For this chapter and others based on quantitative data, I used the 1987–88 National Survey of Postsecondary Faculty (NSOPF), sponsored by the National Center for Education Statistics (see Appendix 1 for a description of the survey).

Next, I examine the instructional mission and efforts to increase its value in Part 1, The Internal World: Enhancing the Value of Teaching. The purpose of this section is to examine the variety of factors encouraging faculty to devote time to teaching, research, or public service. Especially important are faculty rewards and the relative importance of extrinsic and intrinsic motivation in faculty behavior. To translate research findings into lessons for policy and practice I also discuss the lessons learned from one attempt to reform undergraduate curricula and reward teaching. I conclude the section with a discussion of the importance of the myths supporting the pursuit of prestige through research and scholarship, and demonstrate that a renewed commitment to teaching and student learning requires making difficult choices between various activities.

Part 1 includes Chapters 3 through 6. Chapter 3, Subtle Messages: The Role of Pay in Faculty Rewards, examines the compatibility between faculty reward structures and various activities, including research, teaching, and public service (which includes consulting and technology transfer). Particular attention is paid to Trow's "institutional drift,"[82] examining the claim of "copycat" behavior by institutions seeking enhanced prestige. I also examine the "balance" claimed by Trow to have been achieved by faculty in research universities.

In Chapter 4, Other Factors Influencing Faculty Teaching, Robert Rhoads and I examine the relative importance of administrative action and socialization in affecting faculty teaching behaviors. Key to our argument about the importance of faculty behavior and rewards is an understanding of whether faculty teaching behavior is primarily a function of socialization, administrative incentives, or a combination of the two. For Chapters 3 and 4, I used national data on faculty compensation, not surveys of faculty attitudes or administrative intent.

In Chapter 5, A Case Study: Administrative Action and Faculty Culture, I supplement survey data with case study data from seven institutions participating in an experiment funded by the National Science Foundation to enhance the quality of undergraduate education. These case study data illuminate how efforts to enhance teaching and curricular reform confront strong resistance by academic cultures. I also examine the possibilities (and limitations) of administrative behavior and faculty rewards in promoting a new, enhanced role for teaching in academic institutions.

In Chapter 6, Accepting the Nature of Tradeoffs, I discuss the implications of survey and case study data for enhancing the value placed on teaching in academe. The nature of tradeoffs among teaching, research, and service is studied, as is the need to make conscious choices between various activities. I discuss the dominant myth in academe, namely that teaching and research are mutually reinforcing. The perpetuation of this myth has direct consequences for efforts to promote the value of teaching.

The three chapters in Part 2, The External World: Enhancing Public Service through Knowledge and Technology Transfer, shift the discussion toward the role of higher education in the economy and discuss the overlap between considerations of meeting knowledge and technology-transfer needs and considerations of improved teaching and learning. Again, faculty are the focal point. In Chapter 7, The New Economy: Consequences for Faculty Behavior and Administrative Action, I discuss the various roles performed by faculty in higher education institutions which affect the economy. These include education and training, research, and technology transfer. Also included is a discussion of the implications of these roles for faculty behavior and rewards.

Chapter 8, Traditional Knowledge and Technology Transfer, again uses survey data to examine the most traditional form of technology transfer in colleges and universities, the faculty consultant, and the potential impact of industry funding on academic research. Geiger argues that traditional technology transfer approaches, such as consulting and carrying out research funded by industry, are consistent with academic mores and should be considered in institutional strategies before proceeding to more commercially oriented endeavors.[83] Tornatzky and Fleisher counter by citing the limited effectiveness of traditional academic strategies in technology transfer.[84] Despite these claims, pro and con, little is known about the potential utility of consulting as an institutional strategy for technology transfer.

Little empirical information exists on the costs and benefits of another traditional form of faculty involvement in technology transfer, industrially supported academic research. Advocates cite the importance of industrial resources for programs in high-technology disciplines, such as biotechnology, both for research[85] and for more meaningful educational experiences for students and better employment opportunities when they graduate.[86] In contrast, critics claim that the involvement of industry in academic research can lessen the time faculty spend on teaching and advising and lower instructional productivity.[87] Particular emphasis has been placed on the consequences for undergraduate education because the focus of most funding from industry is on research and graduate programs.[88]

Little evidence exists to support these competing claims. Blumenthal, Gluck, and colleagues found little credence for this hypothesis in a study of biotechnology faculty, but the study was limited to research universities and to a single field of study.[89] In contrast, Richter found industrial support to affect faculty behavior adversely, but his study was limited to a single institution.[90] I seek answers to these questions by comparing on a national basis faculty who received funding from industry with their colleagues who did not receive funding from industry.

In Chapter 9, Three Case Studies: Leadership, Policy, and Structure, Thomas Chmura and I use case study material from studies of technology transfer policy, biotechnology research organizations, and the impact of higher education institutions on the Baltimore regional economy to examine the influence of institutional policy, structure, and leadership on faculty behavior. Particular attention is paid to leadership, which has been found in previous research to be both an ineffective predictor of institutional responsiveness, overwhelmed by faculty cultures,[91] and crucial to institutional responsiveness through the use of alternative organizational structures and incentives.[92] The findings are provocative, giving an informed answer to the question of how academic institutions can best serve local and regional communities.

Finally, in Part 3, Policy Options, I conclude with a discussion of the implications of research findings for state and federal policymakers (Chapter 10: Reform from Without: Lessons for State and Federal Policymakers) and for academic leaders (Chapter 11: Reform from Within: Lessons for Academic Administrators). Of particular interest is how academic institutions can meet the variety of challenges posed in modern society. These challenges include the juxtaposition of newer roles in knowledge and technology transfer with traditional functions such as teaching.

## NOTES

1. H. R. Bowen, *Investment in Learning: The Individual and Social Value of American Higher Education* (San Francisco: Jossey-Bass, 1977); L. L. Leslie and P. T. Brinkman, *The Economic Value of Higher Education* (New York: ACE/Macmillan, 1988).
2. M. B. Katz, *The Irony of Early School Reform: Educational Innovation in Mid-nineteenth Century Massachusetts* (Cambridge, Mass.: Harvard University Press, 1968).
3. R. L. Geiger, *To Advance Knowledge: The Growth of American Research Universities, 1900–1940* (New York: Oxford University Press, 1986).
4. K. P. Cross,"New Frontiers for Higher Education: Business and the Professions," in *Partnerships with Business and the Professions* (Washington, D.C.: American Association of Higher Education, 1981), 4–7.
5. P. Dressel,"Mission, Organization, and Leadership," *Journal of Higher Education*, 58 (1987): 101–9.

6. J. Ben-David, *Trends in American Higher Education* (Chicago: University of Chicago Press, 1972).
7. D. Alpert, "Performance and Paralysis: The Organizational Context of the American Research University," *Journal of Higher Education,* 56 (1985): 241–81; P. M. Blau, *The Organization of Academic Work* (New York: John Wiley & Sons, 1973).
8. R. M. Millard, *Today's Myths and Tomorrow's Realities* (San Francisco: Jossey-Bass, 1991), 31–2.
9. R. L. Alfred and J. Weissman, *Higher Education and the Public Trust: Improving Stature in Colleges and Universities,* ASHE-ERIC Higher Education Research Report No. 6 (Washington, D.C.: Association for the Study of Higher Education, 1987); C. Kerr, *The Uses of the University,* 3rd ed. (Cambridge, Mass.: Harvard University Press, 1982).
10. J. S. Fairweather, "Academic Research and Instruction: The Industrial Connection," *Journal of Higher Education,* 60 (1989): 388–407.
11. P. R. Lawrence and J. W. Lorsch, *Organization and Environment: Managing Differentiation and Integration* (Boston: Harvard University Press, 1967); J. Pfeffer and G. R. Salancik, *The External Control of Organizations* (New York: Harper and Row, 1978).
12. R. Birnbaum, *How Colleges Work: The Cybernetics of Academic Organizations and Leadership* (San Francisco: Jossey-Bass, 1988), 177–200.
13. Kerr, *The Uses of the University,* 108.
14. D. Bok, "Reclaiming the Public Trust," *Change* (1992): 12–19; G. C. Winston, "Hostility, Maximization, and the Public Trust," *Change* (1992): 20–7.
15. Geiger, *To Advance Knowledge.*
16. Alfred and Weissman, *Higher Education and the Public Trust,* 31.
17. R. M. Huber, *How Professors Play the Cat Guarding the Cream: Why We're Paying More and Getting Less in Higher Education* (Fairfax, Va.: George Mason University Press, 1992).
18. M. Anderson, *Imposters in the Temple* (New York: Simon and Schuster, 1992).
19. E. Ashby, *Adapting Universities to a Technological Society* (San Francisco: Jossey-Bass, 1974), 15.
20. Birnbaum, *How Colleges Work.*
21. M. D. Cohen and J. G. March, *Leadership and Ambiguity* (Boston: Harvard Business School Press, 1974).
22. B. R. Clark, "Faculty Organization and Authority," in *The Study of Academic Administration,* ed. T. F. Lunsford (Boulder, Colo.: Western Interstate Commission on Higher Education, 1963), 37–51.
23. Alpert, "Performance and Paralysis."
24. Lawrence and Lorsch, *Organization and Environment*; Pfeffer and Salancik, *The External Control of Organizations.*
25. R. L. Geiger, "The Ambiguous Link: Private Industry and University Research," in *The Economics of Higher Education,* ed. W. E. Becker and D. R. Lewis (Boston: Kluwer, 1992), 266.
26. M. A. Trow, "The Analysis of Status," in *Perspectives in Higher Education: Eight Disciplinary and Comparative Views,* ed. B. R. Clark (Berkeley, Calif.: University of California Press, 1984), 143
27. Alpert, "Performance and Paralysis."

28. Kerr, *The Uses of the University*.

29. R. S. Friedman and R. C. Friedman, "Organized Research Units in Academe Revisited," in *Managing High Technology: An Interdisciplinary Perspective*, ed. B. W. Mar, W. T. Newell, and B. O. Saxberg (New York: Elsevier, 1985), 75–91.

30. K. Weick, "Educational Organizations as Loosely Coupled Systems," *Administrative Science Quarterly*, 23 (1978): 541–52.

31. Alfred and Weissman, *Higher Education and the Public Trust*, 2; J. A. Perkins, *The University in Transition* (Princeton, N.J.: Princeton University Press, 1966).

32. Kerr, *The Uses of the University*, 122–23.

33. Geiger, *To Advance Knowledge*.

34. D. Garvin, *The Economics of University Behavior* (New York: Academic Press, 1980); Trow, "The Analysis of Status."

35. J. C. Hearn, "The Teaching Role in Contemporary American Higher Education: Popular Imagery and Organizational Reality," in *The Economics of Higher Education*, ed. W. E. Becker and D. R. Lewis (Boston: Kluwer, 1992), 36.

36. K. Cameron, "Measuring Organizational Effectiveness in Institutions of Higher Education," *Administrative Science Quarterly*, 23 (1978): 604–32.

37. D. Bell, *The Coming of the Post-industrial Society: A Venture in Social Forecasting* (New York: Basic Books, 1973); J. Botkin, D. Dimancescu, and R. Strata, *Global Stakes: The Future of High Technology in America* (Cambridge, Mass.: Ballinger, 1982).

38. J. Kreps, "Maintaining the Nation's Competitiveness," in *Issues in Higher Education and Economic Development* (Washington, D.C.: American Association of State Colleges and Universities, 1986), 4–10.

39. J. S. Fairweather, "Academic Research and Instruction," 390.

40. P. Choate, "Business and Higher Education: Imperative to Adapt," in *Issues in Higher Education and Economic Development* (Washington, D.C.: American Association of State Colleges and Universities, 1986), 14.

41. D. H. Swanson, "Transferring Technologies to Industry," in *Issues in Higher Education and Economic Development* (Washington, D.C.: American Association of State Colleges and Universities, 1986), 24.

42. R. Hersh, "Education and the Corporate Connection," *Educational Horizons*, 62 (1983): 6.

43. Public Policy Center, SRI International, *The Higher Education-Economic Development Connection: Emerging Roles for Public Colleges and Universities* (Washington, D.C.: American Association of State Colleges and Universities, 1986).

44. D. F. Noble, *America by Design: Science, Technology, and the Rise of Corporate Capitalism* (New York: Oxford University Press, 1977).

45. L. G. Tornatzky and M. Fleisher, *The Process of Technological Innovation* (Lexington, Mass.: Lexington Books, 1990).

46. L. M. Branscomb, "America's Rising Research Alliance," *American Education*, 20 (1984): 46; G. G. Gold, "Toward Business-Higher Education Alliances," in *Business and Higher Education: Toward New Alliances*, New Directions in Experiential Learning No. 13, ed. G. G. Gold (San Francisco: Jossey-Bass, 1981), 16.

47. G. W. Matkin, *Technology Transfer and the University* (New York: ACE/Macmillan, 1990).

48. E. C. Johnson and L. G. Tornatzky, "Academia and Industrial Innovation," in *Business and Higher Education: Toward New Alliances,* New Directions in Experiential Learning No. 13, ed. G. G. Gold (San Francsico: Jossey-Bass, 1981), 48.

49. Examples include M. Bach and R. Thornton, "Academic-Industrial Partnerships in Biomedical Research: Inevitability and Desirability," *Educational Record,* 64 (1983): 26–32; Business-Higher Education Forum, *Corporate and Campus Cooperation: An Action Agenda* (Washington, D.C.: Business-Higher Education Forum, 1984); T. J. Chmura, D. Henton, and J. Melville, *California's Higher Education System: Adding Economic Competitiveness to the Higher Education Agenda* (Menlo Park, Calif.: SRI International, 1988); D. Dickson, *The New Politics of Science* (New York: Pantheon Books, 1984), 84; E. A. Lynton and S. E. Elman, *New Priorities for the University* (San Francisco: Jossey-Bass, 1987).

50. P. Crosson, *Public Service in Higher Education: Practices and Priorities,* ASHE-ERIC Higher Education Research Report No. 7 (Washington, D.C.: Association for the Study of Higher Education, 1983).

51. G. E. Schuh, "Revitalizing Land Grant Universities: It's Time to Regain Relevance," *Choices,* Second Quarter (1986): 6.

52. Alpert, "Performance and Paralysis."

53. J. S. Fairweather, *Entrepreneurship and Higher Education: Lessons for Colleges, Universities, and Industry,* ASHE-ERIC Higher Education Research Report No. 6 (Washington, D.C.: Association for the Study of Higher Education, 1988).

54. National Research Council, *Engineering Education and Practice: Foundations of Our Techno-Economic Future* (Washington, D.C.: National Academy Press, 1985).

55. I. Feller, "Political and Administrative Aspects of State Higher Technology Programs," *Policy Studies Review,* 3 (1984): 460–6; T. R. Smith and M. Drabenstott, "The Role of Universities in Regional Economic Development," in *The Economics of Higher Education,* ed. W. E. Becker and D. R. Lewis (Boston: Kluwer, 1992), 199–222; C. B. Watkins, *Programs for Innovative Technical Research in State Strategies for Economic Development* (Washington, D.C.: National Governors' Association Center for Policy Research and Analysis, 1985).

56. N. E. Bowie, *University-Business Partnerships: An Assessment* (Lanham, Md.: Rowman and Littlefield Publishers, 1994), 175–82.

57. I. Feller, "University-Industry Research and Development Relationships," paper presented at the Annual Meeting of the Association for Public Policy Analysis and Management, Austin, Tex., 1988, 2.

58. C. S. Lenth, *State Priorities in Higher Education: 1990* (Denver: State Higher Education Executive Officers and the Education Commission of the States, 1990).

59. G. Blumenstyk, "States Re-evaluate Industrial Collaborations Built Around Research Grants to Universities," *Chronicle of Higher Education,* 38 (Nov. 25, 1992): 1, 24–5.

60. Blumenstyk, "States Re-evaluate Industrial Collaborations."

61. Blumenstyk, "States Re-evaluate Industrial Collaborations."

62. R. M. Rosenzweig and B. Turlington, *The Research Universities and their Patrons* (Berkeley, Calif.: University of California Press, 1982).

63. S. G. Katsinas and V. A. Lacey, *Community Colleges and Economic Development: Models of Institutional Effectiveness* (Washington, D.C.: American Association of Community and Junior Colleges, 1989).

64. J. W. Bardo, J. T. Jones, M. Bowden, E. Traynham, and J. Perry, "Economic Development and AASCU Institutions: An Examination of Roles and Critical Questions for State Policy Makers," in *Defining the Missions of AASCU Institutions*, ed. J. W. Bardo (Washington, D.C.: American Association of State Colleges and Universities, 1990), 105–17.

65. J. R. Battenburg, "Forging Links Between Industry and the Academic World," *Journal of the Society of Research Administrators*, 12 (1980): 5–12; T. M. Stauffer, "Expanding Business-Higher Education Cooperation on Research and Development," *Journal of the Society of Research Administrators*, 11 (1979): 41–6.

66. Bach and Thornton, "Academic-Industrial Partnerships."

67. Dickson, *The New Politics of Science*, 87.

68. T. M. Stauffer, "A University Model for the 1990s," in *An Agenda for the New Decade*, New Directions for Higher Education No. 70, ed. L. W. Jones and F. A. Nowotny (San Francisco: Jossey-Bass, 1990), 19–24.

69. Hearn, "The Teaching Role," 21.

70. E. L. Boyer, *College: The Undergraduate Experience in America* (New York: Harper and Row, 1987).

71. R. L. Jacobsen, "Colleges Face New Pressure to Increase Faculty Productivity," *Chronicle of Higher Education*, 38 (April 15, 1992): 1.

72. Boyer, *College*.

73. Study Group on the Conditions of Excellence in American Higher Education, *Involvement in Learning: Realizing the Potential of American Higher Education* (Washington, D.C.: U.S. Department of Education, 1984).

74. G. E. Schuh and V. W. Rattan, "The Research and Service Missions of the University," in *The Economics of Higher Education*, ed. W. E. Becker and D. R. Lewis (Boston: Kluwer, 1992), 69–87.

75. J. S. Fairweather, "Higher Education and the Economy: From Social Good to Economic Development to . . .," paper presented at the Annual Meeting of the Western Interstate Commission on Higher Education, Seattle, Wash., 1991.

76. M. Kenney, *Biotechnology: The University-Industrial Complex* (New Haven, Conn.: Yale University Press, 1986), 246.

77. C. Weiner, "Science and the Marketplace: Historical Precedents and Problems," in *From Genetic Experimentation to Biotechnology—The Critical Transition*, ed. W. J. Whelan and S. Black (New York: John Wiley & Sons, 1982), 123–32.

78. J. S. Fairweather, *Entrepreneurship and Higher Education*, 13–14.

79. Carnegie Foundation for the Advancement of Teaching, *The Condition of the Professoriate: Attitudes and Trends, 1989* (Princeton, N.J.: Carnegie Foundation for the Advancement of Teaching, 1989).

80. J. V. Baldridge, D. Curtis, G. Ecker, and G. Riley, *Policy Making and Effective Leadership* (San Francisco: Jossey-Bass, 1978).

81. Trow, "The Analysis of Status," 143.

82. Trow, "The Analysis of Status."

83. Geiger, "The Ambiguous Link."

84. Tornatzky and Fleisher, *The Process of Technological Innovation*.

85. H. Brooks, "Seeking Equity and Efficiency: Public and Private Roles," in *Public-Private Partnership: New Opportunities for Meeting Social Needs*, ed. H. Brooks, L. Liebman, and C. Schelling (Cambridge, Mass.: Ballinger, 1984), 3–30.

86. J. A. Haddad, "New Factors in the Relationship between Engineering Education and Research," in *The New Engineering Research Centers: Purposes, Goals, and Expectations* (Washington, D.C.: National Academy Press, 1986), 129–36.

87. L. Wofsy, "Biotechnology and the University," *Journal of Higher Education*, 57 (1986): 477–92.

88. National Science Board, *Undergraduate Science, Mathematics, and Engineering Education* (Washington, D.C.: National Science Board, 1986), 1–2.

89. D. Blumenthal, M. Gluck, K. Louis, M. Stoto, and D. Wise, "University-Industry Research Relationships in Biotechnology: Implications for the University," *Science*, 232 (No. 4756, 1986): 1361–6.

90. M. N. Richter, "Industrial Funding of Faculty Research," *Humanity and Society*, 9 (1985): 459–85.

91. K. S. Louis, D. Blumenthal, M. Gluck, and M. Stoto, "Entrepreneurs in Academe: An Explanation of Behaviors among Life Scientists," *Administrative Science Quarterly*, 34 (1989): 110–31.

92. Matkin, *Technology Transfer and the University*.

# ► 2

## Faculty:
### The Focal Point

### THE FACULTY POSITION

When academic leaders pledge to involve their institutions in major research cooperatives with industry, promise to build research parks, encourage technology transfer through consulting, or even promote personnel exchanges between industry and higher education, the involvement of faculty is crucial. Even in major research universities where substantial technology transfer activities involve nonteaching research staff and take place outside of traditional departments, key faculty often play lead roles.[1] Similarly, promises to increase the value of teaching in the academy rely on having faculty pay greater attention to students and to curriculum reform. In sum, the faculty comprise the "raw material" for any academic effort requiring expertise, whether devoted to training students or carrying out research.

Current proposals for restoring the value of teaching and enhancing the role of public service, whether in the shape of a congressional report, a state budget, or the minutes of a college faculty senate meeting, make certain assumptions about the nature of faculty work. Understanding faculty roles and work patterns is fundamental to creating new policies, structures, and procedures designed to help academic institutions respond to changing needs. Before any state legislator or federal policymaker proposes legislation or regulations to codify faculty workloads, and before any academic leader invests time in helping reshape academic values to meet emerging societal needs, let us first examine what faculty actually do with their time.

Faculty have multiple roles. As Gmelch, Wilke, and Lovrich describe, "The plethora of roles (e.g., teacher, adviser, researcher, university citizen, and departmental colleague) and the existence of numerous factions demanding attention produce a multifaceted complex of strains on individuals in the academic role."[2] According to Bowen and Schuster, these roles include instruction, research, public service, and institutional governance and operation (i.e., administration).[3] Yuker argues for including professional development as a separate activity category.[4] Consulting is an accepted part of the academic profession, best studied as a separate activity rather than imbedded in a generic research or service category.[5] Furthermore, each generic activity category contains the distinct concepts of workload, time allocation, and productivity. Measures of instructional activity, for example, might include the number of hours per week spent on teaching (workload); the relative percentage of time spent on teaching activities to other tasks (time allocation); and the number of student contact hours generated (productivity).

The generic behavioral categories also contain a variety of distinct activities. *Instruction* is not limited to classroom teaching. It includes time spent on working with student organizations; formal classroom instruction; independent instruction; noncredit instruction; advising, counseling, and supervising students; and grading papers, preparing courses, and developing new curricula. *Research* includes measures of time spent on research *and* scholarship, including preparing for and conducting research, preparing or reviewing articles or books, attending professional meetings, giving performances in the fine or applied arts, and seeking outside funding for research.

To understand the potential of a variety of institutional activities to effect change, I focus in this chapter on faculty workload (e.g., hours assigned to teach in class), time allocation (e.g., percentage of time spent on teaching, research, and public service), and productivity (e.g., scholarly publications), and examine the profiles of faculty who spend the most time on teaching and research. Results are shown by type of 4-year institution. Based on the Carnegie Foundation for the Advancement of Teaching classification, the types of 4-year schools include: public and private *research universities,* whose faculty train the majority of doctorates in the United States and which house the majority of funded research; public and private *doctoral-granting universities,* whose faculty also train doctoral students and conduct research but whose production of doctorates and research dollars generated are less than found in research universities; public and private *comprehensive colleges and universities,* which focus on liberal arts and professional programs at the undergraduate and master's-degree levels; private *liberal arts colleges;* and *other 4-year institutions,* which in this study were predominately professional schools of engineering and medicine.[6]

**TABLE 2.1    Mean Hours Worked per Week, by Type of Institution**

| Type of Institution | Activities at this Institution | Other Paid Activities | Unpaid Service | Total |
|---|---|---|---|---|
| All 4-Year | 48.84 | 3.20 | 2.64 | 54.68 |
| Research | 51.71 | 3.16 | 2.45 | 57.32 |
| Doctoral | 48.47 | 3.26 | 2.60 | 54.33 |
| Comprehensive | 46.02 | 3.37 | 3.09 | 52.48 |
| Liberal Arts | 48.17 | 2.45 | 2.33 | 52.95 |
| Other 4-Year | 48.77 | 3.39 | 1.82 | 53.98 |

Source: NSOPF 1988

## HOW BUSY ARE FACULTY?

Faculty in 4-year institutions averaged almost 55 hours worked per week in 1987–88 (Table 2.1).[7] Almost 49 of these hours were spent working at their institution; the remainder was about evenly split between other paid activities and unpaid service. Although hours worked per week varies slightly by type of institution, faculty in each type of 4-year institution averaged at least 52 hours per week on the job.

These data are consistent with a review of more than 100 previous studies of faculty workload, which found an average of more than 50 hours per week across the various studies.[8] The NSOPF estimates are higher than those found in 1981 by the National Science Foundation (NSF). Looking only at faculty in the sciences, engineering, and the social sciences, which could account for the difference in estimates, the NSF found faculty across all 4-year institutions spent an average of 45.8 hours per week working at all activities. Faculty in doctoral-granting universities spent 48.2 hours working per week, while their peers in other 4-year schools averaged 42.7 hours per week.[9]

## HOW DO FACULTY SPEND THEIR TIME?

Faculty in 4-year institutions, on average, spent more than half of their time on instruction-related activities in 1987–88. About one-quarter of their time was spent on research, 14 percent on administration, and less than 5 percent each on service, consulting, and professional development (Table 2.2).

Teaching- and research-related activity patterns vary directly by type of 4-year institution. Faculty in research universities and in other 4-year institutions, which are predominantly engineering- and health-science-related in

**TABLE 2.2 Time Allocation, by Type of Institution**

| Type of Institution | Teaching | Research/ Scholarship | Administration | Service | Consulting | Professional Development |
|---|---|---|---|---|---|---|
| | | | **Percent of Time** | | | |
| All 4-year | 53.2 | 22.0 | 14.0 | 2.0 | 4.8 | 4.1 |
| SE | .36 | .30 | .23 | .06 | .17 | .11 |
| Research | 42.6 | 31.4 | 14.6 | 1.6 | 6.1 | 3.8 |
| SE | .55 | .54 | .40 | .10 | .35 | .20 |
| Doctoral | 53.7 | 23.6 | 13.4 | 2.2 | 3.4 | 3.8 |
| SE | .74 | .68 | .54 | .14 | .25 | .22 |
| Comprehensive | 63.8 | 12.6 | 13.4 | 2.4 | 3.6 | 4.2 |
| SE | .53 | .33 | .39 | .10 | .21 | .17 |
| Liberal Arts | 68.0 | 10.5 | 13.8 | 2.3 | 1.6 | 3.8 |
| SE | .96 | .63 | .72 | .19 | .23 | .31 |
| Other 4-year | 39.9 | 27.5 | 15.4 | 1.3 | 10.4 | 5.5 |
| SE | 2.28 | 1.97 | 1.20 | .33 | 1.44 | .93 |

Source: NSOPF 1988
SE = Standard Error

the NSOPF sample, spent the least time on instruction. Faculty in doctoral-granting institutions spent the next lowest amount of time on instruction, followed by their peers in comprehensive and liberal arts colleges, respectively. Faculty who spent less time on teaching invested the hours saved in research. The same pattern described above holds inversely by type of institution; that is, faculty in liberal arts colleges spent the least time on research, their peers in comprehensives the next lowest percentage, and so on.[10]

Time spent on administration and on professional development does not vary by type of 4-year institution. Similarly, although faculty in research universities spent slightly less time on service than their peers in other institutions,[11] in general time spent on service does not vary by type of institution. Faculty in other 4-year institutions spent the most time consulting, followed by their peers in research universities. Faculty in liberal arts colleges spent the least time consulting.[12]

Considering that instruction-related activities are accorded the greatest percentage of time by all faculty, these results are consistent with previous research indicating that faculty felt teaching was their primary activity.[13] The time that faculty allocated to various activities in 1987–88 was remarkably similar to that of 1977–78, although faculty in doctoral-granting institutions spent a bit less time on teaching than they did ten years previously.[14] The finding that faculty in research universities spend less time teaching and more time on research than faculty in other types of institutions is consistent with other studies.[15] However, the finding that faculty in doctoral-granting institutions spend less time on teaching and more on research than their colleagues in comprehensive institutions, and that faculty in comprehensive colleges and universities spend less time on teaching and more on research than faculty in liberal arts colleges, is new.

## Program Area

The pattern of faculty activities varies by program area (Table 2.3). Faculty in agriculture/home economics and the health sciences spent below-average percentages of time on teaching in 1987–88; faculty in business, education, the humanities, the social sciences, and other fields spent above-average percentages of time on this task. Faculty in engineering, the fine arts, and the natural sciences spent average percentages of their time on teaching.[16] Faculty in agriculture/home economics and the natural sciences spent the most time on research and scholarship, whereas their colleagues in education, the humanities, and other fields spent the least time.[17] Faculty in the health sciences spent the most time on administration; faculty in business and in engineering spent the least time on institutional governance.[18]

Faculty in education and other fields were the most likely to spend time on public service in 1987–88, whereas their peers in the humanities and nat-

**TABLE 2.3 Time Allocation, by Program Area: 4-Year Institutions**

| Program Area | Teaching | Research/ Scholarship | Administration | Percent of Time Service | Consulting | Professional Development |
|---|---|---|---|---|---|---|
| Agriculture/Home Economics | 47.6 | 31.6 | 13.6 | 1.8 | 1.6 | 3.9 |
| SE | 1.81 | 1.76 | 1.10 | .23 | .33 | .42 |
| Business | 58.0 | 19.4 | 11.2 | 2.5 | 4.8 | 4.0 |
| SE | 1.51 | 1.24 | .89 | .30 | .65 | .50 |
| Education | 59.6 | 13.6 | 15.9 | 3.4 | 3.6 | 4.0 |
| SE | 1.02 | .68 | .81 | .27 | .38 | .27 |
| Engineering | 56.5 | 22.5 | 11.4 | 1.7 | 4.1 | 3.8 |
| SE | 1.48 | 1.38 | .89 | .26 | .57 | .46 |
| Fine Arts | 55.2 | 19.8 | 12.6 | 2.1 | 4.4 | 5.9 |
| SE | 1.08 | .91 | .83 | .22 | .53 | .49 |
| Health Sciences | 36.1 | 24.5 | 17.3 | 1.7 | 13.3 | 7.0 |
| SE | 1.44 | 1.31 | 1.07 | .23 | 1.23 | .69 |
| Humanities | 63.0 | 17.4 | 14.0 | 1.7 | 1.4 | 2.5 |
| SE | .60 | .46 | .47 | .10 | .14 | .14 |
| Natural Sciences | 54.2 | 26.3 | 12.6 | 1.4 | 2.2 | 3.3 |
| SE | .99 | .97 | .58 | .14 | .24 | .28 |
| Social Sciences | 55.7 | 22.4 | 14.0 | 2.2 | 2.9 | 2.8 |
| SE | .80 | .69 | .56 | .16 | .24 | .19 |
| Other Fields | 59.2 | 18.1 | 13.9 | 2.7 | 3.0 | 3.0 |
| SE | 1.26 | 1.01 | .87 | .25 | .36 | .26 |

Source: NSOPF 1988

ural sciences were less likely to do so.[19] Consulting activity also varies by field: faculty in the health sciences spent above-average amounts of time consulting, whereas their peers in agriculture/home economics, education, the humanities, the natural sciences, the social sciences, and other fields consulted less frequently.[20] Faculty in the fine arts and health sciences spent the most time on professional development, whereas their colleagues in the humanities, natural sciences, social sciences, and other fields spent the least time.[21]

These results are consistent with previous research by Blau, Fulton and Trow, Orlans, and Smart and McLaughlin,[22] which showed that faculty in the natural sciences and social sciences spend more time on research than do faculty in education and the humanities. As discussed in Chapters 3 and 4, however, the allocation of time to task is *not* synonymous with faculty reward structures; i.e., the amount of time spent on teaching is not indicative of its relative importance in the faculty reward structure.

## Academic Rank

Time allocation varies by academic rank (Table 2.4). In 4-year colleges and universities, teaching is inversely related to rank: professors were less likely to spend time teaching than associate professors in 1987–88, and associate professors were less likely to spend time teaching than assistant professors. Professors were the most likely to spend time on research and administration; associate professors spent more time on administration than their junior colleagues. Time spent on service and consulting does not vary by academic rank; professors spent less time on professional development than their junior colleagues.[23]

The results for faculty in 4-year institutions are consistent with work done by Hesseldenz and by Ladd and Lipset,[24] who found that percent of time spent on teaching declines with increases in rank. Hesseldenz also found that time spent on administration increases with rank.[25]

**TABLE 2.4   Time Allocation, by Academic Rank**

| | Percent of Time | | | | | |
|---|---|---|---|---|---|---|
| Rank | Teaching | Research/ Scholarship | Administration | Service | Consulting | Professional Development |
| Professor | 49.8 | 23.0 | 16.8 | 2.1 | 4.7 | 3.6 |
| SE | .54 | .45 | .39 | .09 | .24 | .15 |
| Associate | 53.7 | 21.5 | 13.7 | 1.9 | 4.7 | 4.4 |
| SE | .64 | .54 | .38 | .10 | .30 | .23 |
| Assistant | 56.8 | 22.3 | 9.9 | 1.9 | 5.1 | 4.0 |
| SE | .72 | .62 | .34 | .13 | .40 | .21 |

Source: NSOPF 1988

**TABLE 2.5  Mean Workload and Productivity, by Type of Institution**

| Type of Institution | Teaching | | | | Research | |
|---|---|---|---|---|---|---|
| | Taught Only Undergraduates | Taught Only Graduates | Student Contact Hours | Hours in Class (Week) | Publications, Career | Principal Investigator |
| All 4-Year | 8.4% | 11.7% | 322.3 | 9.4 | 25.1 | 24.7% |
| SE | .41 | .48 | 7.60 | .11 | .63 | .64 |
| Research | 11.3 | 20.1 | 322.9 | 7.7 | 38.4 | 40.2 |
| SE | .82 | 1.04 | 17.67 | .22 | 1.31 | 1.27 |
| Doctoral | 9.1 | 6.5 | 303.5 | 8.8 | 23.4 | 22.3 |
| SE | 1.03 | .88 | 14.08 | .18 | 1.35 | 1.49 |
| Comprehensive | 5.9 | 3.3 | 318.8 | 11.1 | 11.5 | 10.7 |
| SE | .58 | .44 | 7.99 | .15 | .67 | .76 |
| Liberal Arts | 8.3 | NA | 233.8 | 10.6 | 8.1 | 8.5 |
| SE | 1.35 | NA | 8.83 | .26 | .75 | 1.36 |
| Other 4-Year | 3.6 | 32.9 | 495.9 | 9.6 | 45.1 | 34.1 |
| SE | 1.57 | 3.94 | 59.77 | .67 | 4.36 | 3.98 |

Source: NSOPF 1988
NA = Not Applicable

# HOW PRODUCTIVE ARE FACULTY?

Faculty in 4-year institutions averaged 9.4 hours in class per week in 1987–88, generating 322 student contact hours per semester. Most faculty in 4-year institutions taught both undergraduate and graduate students. In 1987–88, the average faculty member in 4-year colleges and universities had 25 career publications; about one-quarter were principal investigators of funded research projects in Fall term 1987 (Table 2.5).

Measures of teaching workload vary by type of 4-year institution, but teaching productivity does not vary substantially. Faculty in research and doctoral-granting universities and in liberal arts colleges were the most likely to teach only undergraduate students; faculty in other 4-year institutions were the least likely. Faculty in other 4-year institutions and in research universities were the most likely to be assigned solely to teaching graduate students. Hours spent in class per week varies directly by type of 4-year institution, with faculty in research universities spending the least time in class and faculty in comprehensives and liberal arts colleges spending the most time in class. Faculty in other 4-year institutions had the greatest number of average student contact hours in Fall term 1987, faculty in liberal arts colleges the least. The student contact hours generated per semester by faculty in research universities, doctoral-granting universities, and comprehensive institutions were virtually identical.[26]

Measures of research productivity vary substantially by type of 4-year institution. Total publications for a career varies directly by type of institution; faculty in research universities and other 4-year institutions (i.e., predominantly engineering and medical schools) have the greatest number of publications, faculty in liberal arts colleges the least. Faculty in research universities, other 4-year institutions, and doctoral-granting universities were the most likely to be a principal investigator on a funded research project in 1987–88.[27]

The 1987-88 findings confirm results in earlier studies, which showed that faculty in more prestigious institutions generate more publications and lead more research projects than faculty in non-doctoral-granting institutions.[28] However, the findings in previous research that teaching loads vary inversely by institutional prestige are only partially supported. According to previous studies, faculty in research universities have the lowest teaching loads, both in the hours spent in class and in student contact hours.[29] In 1987-88, faculty in research and doctoral-granting institutions did spend less time in class per week, but they generated as many student contact hours as their peers in master's-level institutions. This result is a function of the larger class sizes in doctoral-granting and research universities.

**TABLE 2.6   Mean Workload and Productivity, by Program Area: 4-Year Institutions**

| Program Area | Teaching | | | | Research | |
|---|---|---|---|---|---|---|
| | Taught Only Undergraduates | Taught Only Graduates | Student Contact Hours | Hours in Class (Week) | Publications, Career | Principal Investigator |
| Agriculture/Home Economics | 24.9% | 9.7% | 230.2 | 7.7 | 29.3 | 58.7% |
| SE | 3.08 | 2.11 | 20.04 | .40 | 3.00 | 3.51 |
| Business | 4.4 | 4.0 | 295.0 | 8.5 | 10.6 | 4.5 |
| SE | 1.50 | 1.45 | 13.94 | .25 | .95 | 1.53 |
| Education | 5.6 | 6.4 | 227.2 | 9.2 | 17.5 | 14.6 |
| SE | 1.13 | 1.21 | 9.60 | .29 | 1.43 | 1.74 |
| Engineering | 15.8 | 6.4 | 266.8 | 8.5 | 20.2 | 37.6 |
| SE | 2.79 | 1.87 | 19.80 | .39 | 2.33 | 3.71 |
| Fine Arts | 6.5 | 2.9 | 259.7 | 11.6 | 9.0 | 6.1 |
| SE | 1.39 | .94 | 13.31 | .36 | .96 | 1.35 |
| Health Sciences | 7.1 | 30.1 | 488.5 | 12.7 | 30.2 | 38.5 |
| SE | 1.54 | 2.75 | 53.34 | .94 | 2.20 | 2.92 |
| Humanities | 4.0 | 2.8 | 234.5 | 9.5 | 21.1 | 6.5 |
| SE | .58 | .49 | 5.05 | .12 | 1.18 | .73 |
| Natural Sciences | 13.9 | 14.3 | 363.7 | 8.1 | 34.4 | 44.7 |
| SE | 1.49 | 1.51 | 33.45 | .22 | 2.45 | 2.14 |
| Social Sciences | 8.7 | 5.9 | 317.2 | 8.2 | 24.7 | 16.7 |
| SE | 1.01 | .85 | 12.21 | .15 | 1.29 | 1.34 |
| Other Fields | 5.7 | 5.8 | 251.2 | 9.2 | 21.7 | 15.1 |
| SE | 1.28 | 1.29 | 11.60 | .23 | 2.64 | 1.98 |

Source: NSOPF 1988
NA = Not Applicable

## Program Area

Teaching workload and productivity vary by program area (Table 2.6). Faculty in agriculture/home economics, engineering, and the natural sciences were more likely to teach only undergraduates in 1987–88; faculty in business and in the humanities were the least likely to teach only undergraduates.[30] Faculty in the health sciences were the most likely to teach only graduate students; faculty in business, education, engineering, fine arts, the humanities, the social sciences, and other fields had fewer faculty who taught only graduate students.[31] Health sciences faculty generated the most student contact hours; less than average student contact hours were generated by faculty in agriculture/home economics, education, engineering, fine arts, the humanities, and other fields.[32] Finally, faculty in the fine arts and health sciences spent the most time in class, faculty in agriculture/home economics, business, the natural sciences, and the social sciences the least.[33]

Research productivity varies by program area. Faculty in the natural sciences have greater than average number of publications for their careers, whereas faculty in business, education, fine arts, and the humanities publish less often.[34] Faculty in agriculture/home economics, engineering, the health sciences, and the natural sciences were the most likely to head funded research projects in 1987–88; their compatriots in business, education, fine arts, the humanities, the social sciences, and other fields were less likely to lead research projects.[35]

## Academic Rank

In 4-year institutions, number of publications varies directly by academic rank—professors published the most—and senior faculty were the most likely to be principal investigators on research projects (Table 2.7).[36] These results support Fulton and Trow's work, but contradict studies by Hesseldenz and Allison and Stewart which found no relationship between academic rank and number of publications.[37]

TABLE 2.7  Mean Workload and Productivity, by Academic Rank

| | Teaching | | | | Research | |
|---|---|---|---|---|---|---|
| Rank | Taught Only Undergraduates | Taught Only Graduates | Student Contact Hrs | Hours in Class (Week) | Publications, Career | Principal Investigator |
| Professor | 8.8% | 14.8% | 303.7 | 8.8 | 42.9 | 29.2% |
| SE | .64 | .80 | 9.92 | .16 | 1.29 | 1.02 |
| Associate | 9.0 | 7.7 | 372.9 | 9.8 | 17.5 | 24.7 |
| SE | .78 | .72 | 18.75 | .20 | .56 | 1.17 |
| Assistant | 6.7 | 11.4 | 298.4 | 9.7 | 7.0 | 19.6 |
| SE | .78 | .99 | 11.17 | .21 | .31 | 1.24 |

Source: NSOPF 1988

**TABLE 2.8  Profile of Tenure-Track, Full-Time Faculty Who Spend the Most Time on Teaching**

| | Research Universities | | Doctoral/granting Universities | | Comprehensive Universities | | Liberal Arts Colleges | | Other 4-year Institutions | |
|---|---|---|---|---|---|---|---|---|---|---|
| | Top Quartile, Time Spent on Teaching | All Other Faculty (Mean) | Top Quartile, Time Spent on Teaching | All Other Faculty (Mean) | Top Quartile, Time Spent on Teaching | All Other Faculty (Mean) | Top Quartile, Time Spent on Teaching | All Other Faculty (Mean) | Top Quartile, Time Spent on Teaching | All Other Faculty (Mean) |
| *Demographics* | | | | | | | | | | |
| Minority | 9.7% | 10.5% | 3.1% | 8.2%** | 13.1% | 10.7% | 7.2% | 13.5% | 18.2% | 10.0% |
| Male | 79.0% | 82.8% | 67.4% | 80.0%** | 72.8% | 76.7% | 79.4% | 72.1% | 90.2% | 89.4% |
| Age (years) | 50.4 | 47.2*** | 50.9 | 47.1*** | 49.5 | 47.3*** | 48.5 | 45.3*** | 49.3 | 48.9 |
| Years at Current Institution | 15.1 | 12.1*** | 13.2 | 11.6* | 13.7 | 12.2** | 13.3 | 10.8** | 10.3 | 11.9 |
| Highest Degree–Doctorate | 87.4% | 92.7% | 74.6% | 86.9%** | 65.0% | 77.6%*** | 64.3% | 70.0% | 60.8% | 93.8%*** |
| *Teaching* | | | | | | | | | | |
| Student Contact Hours | 399.0 | 314.4 | 326.8 | 298.1 | 356.5 | 293.0*** | 270.4 | 194.8*** | 639.5 | 465.3 |
| Hours in Class/Week | 9.3 | 7.5** | 10.9 | 8.3*** | 12.1 | 10.3*** | 11.2 | 9.8** | 12.3 | 9.0* |

| | | | | | | | | | | |
|---|---|---|---|---|---|---|---|---|---|---|
| Taught Only Undergraduate Students | 13.2% | 11.1% | 3.4% | 10.5%*** | 3.2% | 7.6%*** | 7.2% | 9.4%* | 3.2% | 3.7% |
| Taught Only Graduate Students | 7.0% | 21.4%*** | 1.1% | 7.8%*** | 0.8% | 4.9%*** | NA | NA | 18.3% | 35.8%*** |
| *Research* | | | | | | | | | | |
| Percent of Time Spent, Research | 8.4% | 33.8%*** | 6.7% | 27.7%*** | 5.6% | 17.4%*** | 5.2% | 16.1%*** | 2.3% | 32.5%*** |
| Publications (career) | 25.1 | 39.8* | 11.7 | 26.2*** | 6.7 | 14.6*** | 7.1 | 9.1 | 25.7 | 48.9* |
| Principal Investigator | 20.1% | 42.2%*** | 11.0% | 25.0%*** | 5.9% | 14.0%*** | 4.7% | 12.5%** | 0% | 40.8%*** |
| *Administration and Service* | | | | | | | | | | |
| Percent of Time Spent, Administration | 5.9% | 15.5%*** | 5.6% | 15.2%*** | 5.7% | 18.7%*** | 7.4% | 20.5%*** | 8.1% | 16.8%*** |
| Percent of Time Spent, Service | 0.9% | 1.6%*** | 1.0% | 2.5%*** | 1.4% | 3.1%*** | 1.3% | 3.3%*** | 1.6% | 1.2% |

Source: NSOPF 1988

*** = $p < .001$; ** = $p < .01$; * = $p < .05$.

**TABLE 2.9** Profile of Tenure-Track, Full-Time Faculty Who Spend the Most Time on Research

| | Research Universities | | Doctoral granting Universities | | Comprehensive Universities | | Liberal Arts Colleges | | Other 4-year Institutions | |
|---|---|---|---|---|---|---|---|---|---|---|
| | Top Quartile, Time Spent on Research | All Other Faculty (Mean) | Top Quartile, Time Spent on Research | All Other Faculty (Mean) | Top Quartile, Time Spent on Research | All Other Faculty (Mean) | Top Quartile, Time Spent on Research | All Other Faculty (Mean) | Top Quartile, Time Spent on Research | All Other Faculty (Mean) |
| *Demographics* | | | | | | | | | | |
| Minority | 10.7% | 10.2% | 7.5% | 7.1% | 17.7% | 11.2% | 10.5% | 10.3% | 3.0% | 16.1%** |
| Male | 84.8% | 80.8%** | 86.4% | 74.4%** | 83.1% | 74.5%* | 69.6% | 76.1% | 89.0% | 89.8% |
| Age (years) | 45.7 | 48.8*** | 46.2 | 48.4** | 45.3 | 48.4*** | 43.3 | 47.1 | 49.4 | 48.8 |
| Years at Current Institution | 11.5 | 13.1*** | 10.6 | 12.3* | 10.7 | 13.0** | 10.9 | 12.2 | 10.4 | 12.4 |
| Highest Degree–Doctorate | 96.5% | 89.2%*** | 94.4% | 80.9%*** | 89.5% | 71.2%*** | 77.8% | 66.5% | 95.2% | 84.5%* |
| *Teaching* | | | | | | | | | | |
| Percent of Time Spent, Teaching | 31.8% | 50.6%*** | 36.8% | 60.0%*** | 41.6% | 65.6%*** | 40.9% | 69.5%*** | 21.3% | 50.8%*** |
| Student Contact Hours | 229.4 | 386.6*** | 285.2 | 309.9 | 329.9 | 318.0 | 150.3 | 237.8*** | 571.3 | 454.8 |
| Hours in Class/Week | 5.8 | 8.9*** | 7.0 | 9.5*** | 9.4 | 11.2*** | 7.9 | 10.7*** | 7.2 | 10.9** |

| | | | | | | | | | |
|---|---|---|---|---|---|---|---|---|---|
| **Taught Only Undergraduate Students** | 13.8% | 9.4%* | 14.6% | 7.1%** | 6.2% | 5.8% | 3.6% | 8.5% | 2.8% | 4.1% |
| **Taught Only Graduate Students** | 24.9% | 16.7%*** | 16.3% | 2.9%*** | 4.6% | 3.2% | NA | NA | 55.6% | 20.1%*** |
| *Research* | | | | | | | | | | |
| Publications (career) | 47.9 | 31.7*** | 35.8 | 18.9*** | 26.1 | 10.3*** | 17.4 | 7.6* | 68.2 | 32.0*** |
| Principal Investigator | 57.9% | 27.5%*** | 44.8% | 14.2%*** | 28.3% | 9.3%*** | 29.8% | 7.4%* | 60.0% | 19.4%*** |
| *Administration and Service* | | | | | | | | | | |
| Percent of Time Spent, Administration | 10.2% | 17.8%*** | 7.9% | 15.4%*** | 7.7% | 13.9%*** | 5.7% | 14.2%*** | 13.8% | 16.3% |
| Percent of Time Spent, Service | 0.9% | 2.1%*** | 1.0% | 2.6%*** | 0.9% | 2.6%*** | 0.6% | 2.4%*** | 0.6% | 1.7%* |

Source: NSOPF 1988
*** = p < .001; ** = p < .01; * = p < 05.

Professors were the most likely to teach only graduate students in 1987–88, although assistant professors were more likely than associate professors to do so. Student contact hours produced has a U-shaped distribution with professors generating the least amount on average, associate professors the most, and assistant professors in between the two. Finally, professors spent the lowest average hours in the classroom; assistant and associate professors do not differ significantly on this instruction-related indicator.[38]

## PROFILES: THE TEACHER AND THE RESEARCHER

What characteristics and behaviors distinguish faculty who spend the most time teaching and the most time on research and scholarship? I examine faculty in the top quartile of time spent on teaching and on research, respectively.[39] I compare these faculty with their colleagues, focusing on demographic characteristics, teaching-related activities and productivity, research-oriented workload and productivity, and other activities.

### Teaching Faculty

In all but other 4-year institutions, faculty who spend the most time on teaching are older and have spent more years at their current institutions (Table 2.8). In all but research universities and liberal arts colleges, the most teaching-oriented faculty are less likely to hold the doctorate. In doctoral-granting institutions only, teaching-oriented faculty are more likely to be women and less likely to be members of racial/ethnic minority groups.

Faculty who spend more than three-quarters of their time on instruction are less likely to teach only graduate students. They spend more hours in the classroom per week, on average. However, only in comprehensive and liberal arts colleges do these faculty generate more student contact hours.

In all 4-year institutions, faculty who spend the most time on instruction spend less time on research, administration, and service. At most institutions, they have fewer publications and were less likely to be a principal investigator on a funded research project in Fall term 1987.

### Research-oriented Faculty

In contrast to teaching-oriented faculty, faculty who spend the most time on research and scholarship are more likely to hold the doctorate (Table 2.9). At research, doctoral-granting, and comprehensive universities, these faculty are more likely to be male, younger, and to have spent fewer years at the institution.

At all 4-year institutions, research-oriented faculty spend less hours in the classroom per week and spend less time overall on teaching. Only in research universities and liberal arts colleges do these faculty generate fewer student contact hours, however. At the most graduate-oriented universities, research-oriented faculty are more likely to teach only graduate students.

Not surprisingly, research-oriented faculty are more likely to have published and to have been a principal investigator during Fall term 1987. At most institutions, these faculty spent less time on administration and service than their less research-oriented colleagues.

## SUMMARY

Faculty average more than 50 hours of work per week. For research, publishing, obtaining grants, and consulting, the NSOPF survey results confirm institutional diversity: faculty in research and doctoral-granting institutions spend more time on research, obtain more external funds, publish more, and consult more than their colleagues in master's- and bachelor's-level institutions. Faculty in the latter types of institutions spend more of their time on teaching, although teaching productivity does not vary substantially by type of institution. Time spent on administration, professional development, or public service does not vary substantially by type of institution. Few faculty, even those in institutions with professed public service missions, spend much of their time on service to the community.

For all institutions except research universities, these findings support Fulton and Trow,[40] who found that faculty who spent more time on research did less of other activities. However, these findings contradict Fulton and Trow's claim that faculty at research universities who spent the most time on research did as much teaching and administration as their less research-oriented colleagues. The NSOPF data reveal that in 1987–88 faculty in research universities who focused on research spent *less* time on teaching, administration, and service than their peers. The integrated picture described by Fulton and Trow for research university faculty no longer exists.

## NOTES

1. M. J. Dooris and J. S. Fairweather, "Structure and Culture in Faculty Work: Implications for Technology Transfer," *Review of Higher Education,* 17 (1994): 161–78.
2. W. Gmelch, P. Wilke, and N. Lovrich, "Dimensions of Stress among University Faculty Members: Scope and Depth of Involvement," *Research in Higher Education,* 24 (1986): 267.

3. H. R. Bowen and J. H. Schuster, *American Professors: A National Resource Imperiled* (New York: Oxford University Press, 1986), 15.
4. H. E. Yuker, *Faculty Workload: Research, Theory, and Interpretation*, ASHE-ERIC Higher Education Research Report No. 10 (Washington, D.C.: Association for the Study of Higher Education, 1984), 22–3.
5. J. D. Marver and C. V. Patton, "The Correlates of Consultation: American Academics in the Real World," *Higher Education*, 5 (1976): 319–35.
6. Carnegie Foundation for the Advancement of Teaching, *A Classification of Institutions of Higher Education* (Princeton, N.J.: Carnegie Foundation for the Advancement of Teaching, 1987).
7. The data on estimated number of hours worked per week are self-reported and subject to bias. However, the estimates are consistent across many years of faculty surveys.
8. Interuniversity Council of Ohio, *Faculty Load Study* (Columbus, Ohio: Interuniversity Council of Ohio, 1970).
9. National Science Foundation, *Activities of Science and Engineering Faculty in Universities and 4 Year Colleges: 1978–79* (Washington, D.C.: National Science Foundation, 1981).
10. Percent of time spent on teaching: $t$(research/doctoral) = $-10.86$***; $t$(doctoral/comprehensive) = $-11.01$***; $t$(comprehensive/liberal) = $-3.54$*** [where *** = $p < .001$; ** = $p < .01$; * = $p < .05$]. Percent of time spent on research: $t$(res/doc) = $8.99$***; $t$(doc/comp) = $14.59$***; $t$(comp/lib) = $3.03$**.
11. $t$(res/doc) = $-3.71$***.
12. $t$(other/res) = $2.93$**; $t$(res/doc) = $6.21$***; $t$(comp/lib) = $5.97$***. For a more extensive discussion of consulting activities, see Chapter 8.
13. Carnegie Foundation for the Advancement of Teaching, *The Condition of the Professoriate: Attitudes and Trends, 1989* (Princeton, N.J.: Carnegie Foundation for the Advancement of Teaching, 1989); E.C. Ladd, Jr. and S.M. Lipset, *Survey of the American Professoriate* (Storrs, Conn.: University of Connecticut, 1977).
14. J. V. Baldridge, D. Curtis, G. Ecker, and G. Riley, *Policy Making and Effective Leadership* (San Francisco: Jossey-Bass, 1978).
15. Baldridge, Curtis, Ecker, and Riley, *Policy Making and Effective Leadership*; A. E. Bayer, "Teaching Faculty in Academe: 1972–73," *ACE Research Reports*, 8 (1973): 1–68; E. C. Ladd, Jr., "The Work Experience of American College Professors: Some Data and an Argument," *Current Issues in Higher Education* (Washington, D.C.: American Association of Higher Education, 1979).
16. $t$(agriculture) = $-3.17$*; $t$(business) = $3.23$*; $t$(education) = $6.49$***; $t$(health sciences) = $-12.29$***; $t$(humanities) = $17.95$***; $t$(social sciences) = $3.40$**; $t$(other) = $4.94$**.
17. $t$(agriculture) = $5.63$**; $t$(education) = $-12.37$***; $t$(humanities) = $-10.56$***; $t$(natural sciences) = $4.81$**; $t$(other) = $-3.98$**.
18. $t$(business) = $-3.18$*; $t$(engineering) = $-2.94$*; $t$(health sciences) = $3.22$*.
19. $t$(education) = $5.60$**; $t$(humanities) = $-3.28$*; $t$(nat sci) = $-4.42$**; $t$(other) = $2.95$*.
20. $t$(agriculture) = $-9.16$***; $t$(education) = $-3.14$*; $t$(health sciences) = $7.32$***; $t$(humanities) = $-17.73$***; $t$(nat sci) = $-9.67$***; $t$(soc sci) = $-7.44$***; $t$(other) = $-4.88$**.

21. $t$(fine arts) = 3.86**; $t$(health sciences) = 4.43**; $t$(humanities) = –27.94***;$t$(nat sci) = –3.00*; $t$(soc sci) = –6.94***; $t$(other) = –7.10***.

22. P. M. Blau, *The Organization of Academic Work* (New York: John Wiley & Sons, 1973); O. Fulton and M. Trow, "Research Activity in American Higher Education," *Sociology of Education*, 47 (1974): 29–73; H. Orlans, *The Effects of Federal Programs on Higher Education* (Washington, D.C.: Brookings Institute, 1962); J. C. Smart and G. W. McLaughlin, "Reward Structures of Academic Disciplines," *Research in Higher Education*, 8 (1978): 39–55.

23. Percent of time spent on teaching: $t$(professor/associate) = –4.91***; $t$(associate/assistant) = –3.23***. Percent of time spent on research: $t$(prof/assoc) = 2.14*. Percent of time spent on administration: $t$(prof/assoc) = 5.64***; $t$(assoc/asst) = 7.31***. Percent of time spent on professional development: $t$(prof/assoc) = –2.88**.

24. J. S. Hesseldenz, "Personality-based Faculty Workload Analysis," *Research in Higher Education*, 5 (1976): 321–34; Ladd and Lipset, *Survey of the American Professoriate*.

25. Hesseldenz, "Personality-based Faculty Workload Analysis."

26. Mean comparisons for teaching only undergraduate students: $t$(res/comp) = 5.40***; $t$(doc/comp) = 2.76**; $t$(lib/other) = 2.27*; $t$(doc/other) = 2.96**; $t$(res/other) = 4.35***. Mean comparisons for teaching only graduate students: $t$(res/doc) = 10.07***; $t$(doc/comp) = 3.20**; $t$(res/other) = –3.50***. Mean comparisons for student contact hours per semester: $t$(doc/lib) = 4.19***; $t$(doc/other) = –2.78**. Mean comparisons for hours spent in class per week: $t$(res/doc) = –4.09***; $t$(doc/comp) = –9.40***; $t$(comp/other) = 2.15*; $t$(res/other) = –2.71**.

27. Mean comparison for total publications (career): $t$(res/doc) = 8.00***; $t$(doc/comp) = 7.90***; $t$(comp/lib) = 2.94**. Mean comparison for principal investigator status: $t$(res/doc) = 9.06***; $t$(doc/comp) = 6.90***.

28. Baldridge, Curtis, Ecker, and Riley, *Policy Making and Effective Leadership*; Fulton and Trow, "Research Activity in American Higher Education"; Orlans, *The Effects of Federal Programs*.

29. Baldridge, Curtis, Ecker, and Riley, *Policy Making and Effective Leadership*; Bayer, "Teaching Faculty in Academe"; Fulton and Trow, "Research Activity in American Higher Education"; T. Parsons and G. M. Platt, *The American Academic Profession: A Pilot Study* (Cambridge, Mass.: Harvard University Press, 1968).

30. $t$(agriculture) = 5.56**; $t$(business) = –2.68*; $t$(engineering) = 2.73*; $t$(humanities) = –7.68**; $t$(nat sci) = 4.06**.

31. $t$(business) = –5.41**; $t$(education) = –4.46**; $t$(engineering) = –2.85*; t(fine arts) = –8.87***; $t$(health sciences) = 7.05***; $t$(humanities) = –15.15***; $t$(soc sci) = –6.95**; $t$(other) = –4.59**.

32. $t$(agriculture) = –4.48**; $t$(education) = –8.27***; $t$(engineering) = –2.71*; t(fine arts) = –4.22**; $t$(health sciences) = 3.30*; $t$(humanities) = –10.51***; $t$(other) = –5.42**.

33. $t$(agriculture) = –4.28**; $t$(business) = –3.42**; $t$(fine arts) = 6.24***; $t$(health sciences) = 3.73**; $t$(nat sci) = –5.87**; $t$(soc sci) = –7.30***.

34. $t$(business) = –13.13***; $t$(education) = –5.32**; $t$(fine arts) = 14.80***; $t$(humanities) = –3.90**; $t$(nat sci) = 4.20**.

35. $t$(agriculture) = 9.97***; $t$(business) = –12.52***; $t$(education) = –5.97**; $t$(engineering) = 3.77**; $t$(fine arts) = –13.28***; $t$(health sciences) = 4.93**; $t$(humanities) = –22.34***; $t$(nat sci) = 10.19***; $t$(soc sci) = –5.85**; $t$(other) = –4.98**.

36. Publications (career): $t$(prof/assoc) = 18.07***; $t$(assoc/asst) = 16.26***. Principal investigator status: $t$(prof/assoc) = 2.88**; $t$(assoc/asst) = 3.00**.

37. P. Allison and J. A. Stewart, "Productivity Differences Among Scientists: Evidence for Accumulative Advantage," *American Sociological Review*, 39 (1974): 596–606; Fulton and Trow, "Research Activity in American Higher Education"; Hesseldenz, "Personality-based Faculty Workload Analysis."

38. Taught only graduate students: $t$(prof/assoc) = 6.57***; $t$(assoc/asst) = –3.06**. Student contact hours: $t$(prof/assoc) = –3.26**; $t$(assoc/asst) = –3.23**. Hours in class per week: $t$(prof/assoc) = –3.67***.

39. Top quartile, percent of time spent on teaching: More than 71 percent for faculty in 4-year institutions. Top quartile, percent of time spent on research: More than 33 percent for faculty in 4-year institutions.

40. Fulton and Trow, "Research Activity in American Higher Education."

# ▶ 3

## Subtle Messages:
### The Role of Pay in Faculty Rewards

The high cost of tuition and concerns about the lack of access by students to prominent faculty have raised questions about the traditional roles of faculty, especially the commitment to teaching. National reports by prominent academic groups[1] and state legislative action[2] vie for the lead in asking (or in some cases requiring) colleges and universities to demonstrate the teaching productivity of their faculty. Citing survey evidence that teaching is no longer sufficiently valued in academe, Boyer argued that renewed investment in undergraduate education is paramount to restoring public trust.[3] More recently, Boyer proposed redefining teaching as a scholarly activity to increase its value within academe:

> The work of the professor becomes consequential only as it is understood by others. Yet, today, teaching is often viewed as a routine function, tacked on, something almost anyone can do. When defined as scholarship, teaching both educates and entices future scholars.[4]

Even Clark Kerr, in his spirited defense of research universities, found the lack of emphasis on undergraduate teaching a major shortcoming:

> There seems to be a "point of no return" after which research, consulting, graduate instruction [sic] become so absorbing that faculty efforts can no longer be concentrated on undergraduate instruction as they once were. This process has been going on for a long time; federal research funds have intensified it...How to escape the cruel

paradox that a superior faculty results in an inferior concern for undergraduate education is one of our more pressing problems.[5]

Yet the mechanisms which might enhance the value of teaching are unclear. How should academic leaders in 4-year institutions attempt to encourage faculty to spend more time on teaching and curricular reform, and to value instruction more highly in promotion and tenure decisions? Depending on the type of institution, is the problem increasing faculty time allocated to teaching, creating balance in faculty rewards, or simply understanding better how faculty currently spend their time? The starting point is to understand the cultures and reward structures which influence faculty behavior. Failure to take culture and rewards into account can be costly. Dooris and Fairweather found that individuals who had appointments in academic departments placed more importance on traditional faculty activities than on technology transfer and economic development, even when located in interdisciplinary research units.[6] DeVries found that faculty socialization and self-expectations influenced faculty behavior more strongly than organizational structures.[7] Finkelstein found that the professional orientation of faculty, including the importance which disciplinary peers attach to publishing research findings, is more important to individuals than institutional considerations.[8]

Recommendations for changes in faculty time allocation require an examination of the motivations for faculty behavior, including socialization and the reward structures which have imbedded in them values about the relative importance of teaching, research and scholarship, and service.[9] In Chapters 3 and 4, I first discuss the subtle messages conveyed to faculty by administrators through compensation. Robert Rhoads and I then review the relative importance of administrative action and socialization in faculty teaching and research behaviors.

## FACULTY MOTIVATION

Why do faculty members spend more time on one activity and less on another? Why do they value one accomplishment more than another? Faculty perform a variety of complex roles for a variety of perhaps even more complex reasons. During graduate school faculty learn to adopt many of the values, norms, and beliefs needed to succeed in academe. The training of prospective faculty largely takes place at research and doctoral-granting institutions where faculty mentors are likely to emphasize research over teaching. Hence, socialization into the role of faculty member has an inherent orientation toward research.

*Socialization* is the process whereby individuals acquire the values, attitudes, norms, knowledge, and skills needed to exist in a given society.[10] Graduate training serves as a primary agent of socialization for faculty.[11] From this perspective, practice as a teaching assistant develops early expectations for the role of teaching in faculty work life. Training in research as a graduate assistant provides early clues about expected research performance as a future faculty member. Alpert argues further that the orientation of new faculty toward research is continued with a "publish or perish" emphasis in the promotion and tenure process. Such an emphasis in the ongoing socialization of faculty further enhances the value of nationally visible disciplinary research at the cost of local functions, such as teaching.[12]

Socialization tends to portray faculty behavior primarily as a function of self-interest, in which an individual faculty member follows his or her own path irrespective of decisions made by institutional leaders. This view is consistent with that of an inevitable progression of faculty toward a single behavioral norm, based on research and publishing, incapable of being altered by outside forces. This view is simplistic and ignores the historical evolution of academic institutions of all types; it also seems depressingly self-defeating.

In contrast, many observers claim that reward structures favor research over teaching and thus serve to sway faculty interests for educating students toward research and publishing instead. From this viewpoint, the faculty reward structure acts as a mechanism to ensure continuation of research norms across institutions and disciplines.[13] Bok notes that these incentives apply equally to faculty and administrators.[14] Institutional forces that direct faculty behavior may be seen as *administrative incentives*. Administrative incentives consist of direct *faculty rewards*, such as compensation or promotion and tenure. Administrative incentives also include the allocation of *workload* and work assignment, such as hours assigned to classroom instruction, advising loads, research support, and the amount of support staff. From this perspective, active decision making by administrators (through work allocation and some types of rewards) and by faculty (through other types of rewards, primarily promotion and tenure) influences faculty behavior.

As one example of the focus on rewards, Diamond maintains that institutional forces, namely promotion and tenure, direct faculty interests away from teaching. He focuses on the nature of faculty rewards evident in promotion and tenure policies. Diamond argues that "the faculty reward structure must be modified so as to include a number of features rarely found in present promotion and tenure plans."[15]

In this chapter, I examine one part of administrative incentives—rewards expressed by pay—and study the relationships between this form of faculty reward and behavior. I pay particular attention to the subtle messages conveyed through compensation that express the value of teaching and research to faculty members. In chapter 4, Rob Rhoads and I examine the contribution faculty socialization and other forms of administrative incentive make to faculty time allocation and productivity. These analyses provide the basis in Chapter 10 for identifying strategies that administrators (and faculty) can use to push reform agendas.

## FACULTY PAY AS A REWARD

Most studies of faculty rewards examine promotion and tenure, and the faculty norms which reinforce behaviors, particularly research. This focus is consistent with the conception of academe as a profession in which norms are established and reinforced by peers within specific disciplines. It is supported by research which indicates that many norms are shared across disciplines,[16] and by studies emphasizing the importance of socialization and training in the creation and maintenance of faculty reward structures.[17]

As a consequence, policies meant to change the relative importance of teaching, research, and service (including knowledge and technology transfer) in faculty behavior often emphasize the *faculty* and the part they play in perpetuating the academic culture surrounding promotion and tenure. In particular, the focus has been on decision-making authority of the faculty in promotion and tenure, and on the norms about acceptable behavior expressed through these personnel decisions.

The research on faculty socialization and its role in rewards is primarily attitudinal. Such studies of reward structures typically focus on promotion and tenure, and on faculty and administrator attitudes about the relative importance of teaching and research in promotion and tenure.[18] Bowen and Schuster; Cook, Kinnetz, and Owens-Misner; Gray, Froh, and Diamond; and Peters and Mayfield all found that faculty perceived their rewards to be dependent on research, not teaching, including faculty from institutions with a strong emphasis historically on teaching.[19]

The view of academe as a collection of professionals defining and defending behavioral norms ignores the independent role played by academic *administrators* through work assignment and compensation. Unlike promotion and tenure, which is examined at most three times during the career (promotion to associate professor from assistant professor; tenure, which often is combined with promotion to associate professor; and promotion to full professor), compensation is an annual "reward."

Some theories place the determination of faculty pay outside the scope of administrative influence. Changes in political decisions, such as state funding formulae, have been shown to affect salary trends.[20] Baumol and Bowen attribute increases in average faculty salaries to demographic trends, such as an aging professoriate.[21] Finally, one form of the market-competitiveness model, which attributes macro-level changes in faculty salaries at least in part to supply and demand,[22] focuses on the emergence of a national labor market. Based on prestige generated by research and scholarship, institutions of all types compete for and reward faculty on a similar basis; less prestigious, teaching-oriented schools can attract research-oriented faculty because of a tight labor market for faculty.

More relevant to this discussion, recent research suggests that two perspectives on pay in which administrative action is at the forefront—pay as a means of reinforcing market segmentation and pay as an incentive for faculty behavior—have credibility.[23] Consistent with the commonly accepted norm of institutional diversity in American higher education, some economists and many academic leaders claim that pay reflects market segmentation rather than a national market.[24] Institutions can be distinguished by their appeal—national, regional, local—and by rewards for faculty which reflect these differences.[25] Although different types of institutions share common functions, such as teaching, each can be differentiated by unique missions—liberal arts colleges teaching undergraduates, comprehensive colleges offering master's-level professional education, doctoral-granting schools training Ph.D.'s, and research universities invested heavily in knowledge generation. The principal distinction between the missions of research and doctoral-granting universities, on the one hand, and comprehensive and liberal arts colleges, on the other, is the purported importance of research and scholarship at the former and teaching at the latter. According to Breneman and Youn, colleges and universities with distinct missions select and reward faculty differentially through compensation and other forms of reward: "large research and graduate-training institutions are in the market for different kinds of services than are institutions that emphasize undergraduate teaching...; organizations with an emphasis on research offer a distinctively different form of reward."[26]

Yet another perspective views salaries as a means for administrators to reinforce behavioral norms.[27] For example, dissatisfied with a model of academic strategy which explains compensation and other faculty rewards primarily on the basis of competition for faculty within segmented markets, Levin posited a theory of institutional strategy based on property rights theory. Levin argued that salaries can be viewed as a form of incentive, based on internal norms and values. According to Levin, faculty rewards are a reflection of "the institutional incentives to pursue particular activities" rather than simply a response to external markets.[28]

Existing studies of compensation are inadequate to answer questions about the role of pay as incentive for faculty behavior, which is the viewpoint most relevant to academic administrators attempting to lead their institutions in new directions. Most previous research on faculty compensation is limited, studying only external conditions. The focus has been on the standing of faculty pay relative to inflation and to other occupations,[29] the effect of salary disparities between higher education and industry on potential faculty shortages,[30] discrimination by race and gender,[31] merit pay,[32] mobility,[33] and institutional hiring policies.[34]

The few articles examining the relationships between compensation and faculty behavior are conflicting and inconclusive. Studies of the relationships between compensation and faculty behavior consistently have found that faculty research activity is positively related to promotion and salary,[35] but the relationships between teaching and pay, promotion, and tenure are ambiguous. Teaching has variously been found positively related to salary and promotion,[36] unrelated to salary and promotion,[37] and negatively related to salary and promotion.[38]

Previous research on the relationships among faculty pay, behavior, and productivity also has been limited in scope. Most studies rely on information either about a single discipline[39] or about a single school.[40] These studies also use a small set of explanatory variables because of their availability rather than a more comprehensive model to predict compensation. With two exceptions, the few studies using national data relied on bivariate correlational analyses rather than examining combined relationships between faculty behavior and pay,[41] or failed to look at institutional and disciplinary differences.[42]

The two most comprehensive national studies of the relationships between pay and faculty behavior illustrate the limitations of previous research. Howard Tuckman's research is now quite dated, relying on the 1972–73 American Council on Education survey of faculty.[43] Tuckman used a multivariate (regression) model to estimate relationships between faculty salary and several measures of productivity. Research productivity was measured by number of refereed articles and number of books. However, the only measure of teaching productivity was a dichotomous measure (received a teaching award or not); the measure of administrative productivity was whether or not a faculty member had administrative duties. Tuckman did not include additional measures of workload, activity, or productivity. Most importantly, he did not control for variation by type of institution.

Konrad and Pfeffer, in a 1990 publication, developed a more comprehensive model to predict faculty pay, but applied it to data from the 1969 national survey by the Carnegie Foundation for the Advancement of Teaching. Konrad and Pfeffer examined results separately by type of institution, but the measure used was of limited utility ("university" or "college"). Although Konrad and Pfeffer included demographics as controls and included a measure of teaching productivity (hours in class per week), time spent on public service and administration were excluded.[44]

The different findings about the importance of teaching in faculty rewards from studies about the role of pay in faculty rewards, especially its relationship with teaching productivity, may be a function of these data and analytical limitations. The differences in the years in which data were collected may also be related to differences in research findings.

Previous studies and their data also have been insufficient to compare the relative importance of administrative behavior and faculty socialization in affecting faculty behavior. For example, the recent reviews of the literature on faculty socialization show the dominance of anecdotal information, using small numbers of faculty from one or at most a handful of institutions.[45] Such basic understanding of the motivations for faculty behavior have direct consequences for policy. For example, if faculty compensation is the strongest motivator for research productivity, then specific pay alternatives might be effective in altering faculty behavior. In contrast, if socialization during graduate training and beliefs about the importance of research outweigh the importance of administrative action, then intervention during the training and socialization process will be more important.

This chapter relies on the only national database to date capable of answering questions about the relationships between pay and other administrative actions, faculty socialization, and faculty behavior, the 1987–88 National Survey of Postsecondary Faculty (NSOPF). The analyses reported in this chapter go beyond any work done previously, examining the relationships between pay and faculty behavior by type of institution and discipline using a national sample of faculty. (Further, Robert Rhoads and I provide in Chapter 4 the only empirical study using national data of the relative importance of faculty socialization and administrative behavior in influencing faculty research behavior). The chapter starts with an examination of the relationships between pay and faculty behavior. Included are bivariate relationships between pay and time allocation and pay and productivity. Also studied is a multivariate model to examine the combined relationships between faculty behavior and pay in more detail. In Chapter 4 is another model, namely one to study the relative importance of administrative behavior and faculty socialization in explaining faculty teaching behavior. Through these findings I seek information relevant to forming policy alternatives, discussed in Chapters 10 and 11.

## A Model of Faculty Compensation

The literature on faculty compensation demonstrates the need for a current national portrait of the relationships between how faculty spend their time and pay.[46] A comprehensive model of faculty compensation should include faculty demographics, length of service, activities, workload, and productivity. For this research, the model takes into account relevant human-capital factors, such as seniority and discipline, as control variables. Indicators of faculty behavior are based on the Bowen and Schuster model, in which the faculty role comprises instruction, research, public service, and institutional governance and operation (i.e., administration).[47] Each generic behavioral category contains distinct concepts of workload, time allocation, and productivity.

### Dependent Variable
Basic salary frequently has been used as an indicator of compensation in research on faculty.[48] *Basic salary during the academic year* serves as the criterion for this model of faculty behavior and pay as reported by faculty to the question "For the calendar year 1987, what were your gross earnings before taxes for your basic salary at this institution?" This measure excludes supplemental income, such as summer teaching.

### Demographic Characteristics and Length of Service
Although not directly related to the study of faculty pay and behavior, specific faculty characteristics and experiences are needed as control variables in a study of faculty compensation.[49] According to human-capital theory, experience, seniority, education level, and discipline or program area are assumed indicative of productivity, and hence should be related to faculty pay.[50] Among the specific position-related characteristics found related to pay in previous research are academic rank,[51] discipline,[52] gender,[53] and ethnicity.[54]

Faculty demographic characteristics examined in this research included *years since highest degree awarded, gender, ethnic/racial minority status, highest degree awarded, academic rank,* and *program area*. A respondent was classified as a member of a racial or ethnic minority if she or he was (a) Caucasian of Hispanic descent, (b) Native American, (c) Asian/Pacific Islander, or (d) Black. Program area was the primary field of study in which a faculty member worked: agriculture/home economics, business, education, engineering, fine arts, health sciences, humanities, natural sciences, social sciences, and other fields. An additional variable, *high paying field,* was derived from the ranking of the average pay in each program area relative to the overall national average.[55] Finally, length of service was measured by *time in current rank* (i.e., the number of years since achieving the rank held at the institution in question during Fall term 1987) and the *number of years at the current institution*.

### Faculty Behavior
**Teaching/Instruction.**    Instruction-related measures focused on how faculty spent their time, workload, and productivity. Three measures of instruction-related activities and workloads were used: *percent of time spent on*

*teaching and instruction,*[56] *hours spent in the classroom per week,*[57] and the *type of student taught* (undergraduate, graduate, or both). The percentage of time spent on teaching and instruction included time spent on working with student organizations; teaching, advising, and supervising students; and grading papers, preparing courses, and developing new curricula.

*Total student contact hours* generated during Fall term 1987 was used as a measure of instructional productivity.[58] Student contact hours were estimated by the sum across all courses taught in Fall term 1987 of the number of hours a class met per week times the number of students enrolled in the class.

**Research/Scholarship.** Research and scholarship were examined by one measure of faculty activity—*percent of time spent on research and scholarship*[59]— and two measures of productivity—*total refereed publications during the career* and whether the respondent was a *principal investigator* (or co-principal investigator) on an externally funded research project during Fall term 1987.[60] Percent of time spent on research and scholarship included time spent conducting research, preparing or reviewing articles or books, and attending or preparing to attend professional meetings or conferences; giving performances in the fine or applied arts; and seeking outside funding for research. Total refereed publications for the career included the number of refereed articles, chapters in edited volumes, textbooks, other books, monographs, and reviews of books, articles, or creative works. Being designated as a principal investigator or co-principal investigator meant having at least one research project during Fall term 1987 funded by the federal government, state or local governments, foundations or other nonprofit organizations, or industry.

**Other Activities.** To fill out the picture of the faculty workload, I also included estimates of the *percent of time spent on administrative activities* and on *public or community service.*[61]

## Teaching and Faculty Pay: Contrasting Propositions

The literature on faculty compensation is consistent on the importance of research in faculty rewards, although few analyses by type of institution or discipline exist. The relationship between teaching and pay, however, is ambiguous. Little is known about the relationships between teaching and other behaviors, such as administration and public service. In this chapter, I examine three competing propositions about the role of teaching in faculty pay, as part of a comprehensive study of the relative importance of teaching, research, administration, and service in faculty rewards:

- *Proposition 1*: Teaching is a *positive* factor in faculty compensation. Faculty who spend the most time teaching and whose teaching productivity is high are paid the most. This proposition is consistent with findings by Hoyt; Kasten; Katz; Koch and Chizmar; Rossman; Salthouse, McKeachie, and Lin; and Siegfried and White.[62]
- *Proposition 2*: Teaching is a *neutral* factor in faculty compensation. Faculty whose teaching productivity is high are no more or less likely to be highly paid than faculty who spend little time on teaching. This perspective is supported by Howard Tuckman; Howard Tuckman, Gapinski, and Hagemann; and Howard Tuckman and Hagemann.[63]
- *Proposition 3*: Teaching is *negatively* related to faculty compensation. Faculty who spend the most time on teaching and whose teaching productivity is high are paid the least. This viewpoint is supported by Konrad and Pfeffer and by Marsh and Dillon.[64]

In addition to these three propositions, I examine the relationship between (a) the values expressed by department chairs from distinct types of institutions about the relative importance of teaching and research in faculty rewards and (b) the values expressed through compensation. The NSOPF survey asked department chairs to rate the relative importance of thirteen criteria in granting promotion and tenure, ranging from teaching quality, to number of publications, to research quality.[65] Table 3.1 shows the ranking of criteria based on the percentage of department chairs claiming a criterion was very important in granting tenure or promotion, by type of institution.

Department chairs in doctoral-granting institutions, which include the Carnegie classifications of research and doctoral-granting universities, have higher expectations than their colleagues in other 4-year institutions (comprehensive and liberal arts colleges) for research productivity. The rank-order correlation between the rankings for teaching- and research-oriented institutions was only .38 for this reason. Despite clear differences in the ranking of research and publishing, department chairs in each type of institution rated teaching quality high on their list of criteria (first in teaching-oriented schools, third in research-oriented institutions).

If compensation patterns follow the values expressed by department chairs, research activity and productivity should be highly paid in research and doctoral-granting universities, and teaching should be less highly paid but a positive factor in pay nevertheless. In comprehensive and liberal arts colleges, teaching activity and productivity should be highly paid activities, whereas research activity and productivity should not be related to pay.

## Messages Conveyed through Pay: A First Glance

What messages are conveyed to faculty about the importance of teaching and instruction, research and scholarship, and administration and public service by patterns in compensation?

### Teaching/Instruction

**Percent of Time Spent on Teaching/Instruction.**     For faculty in 4-year colleges and universities, the more time spent on teaching and instruction, the lower the basic salary (Table 3.2). In 1987–88, average basic salary varied from a high of about $56,000 for faculty spending less than 35 percent of their time on teaching, to a low of about $34,000 for faculty spending more than 72 percent of their time on teaching. The same pattern holds for faculty in research universities, doctoral-granting institutions, and comprehensive colleges, although in the latter two types of institutions there is no difference in basic salary between the top two quartiles of time spent on teaching (53–71 percent and 72 percent or more). Time spent on teaching is not related to basic salary for faculty in liberal arts colleges.[66]

**Hours in Class per Week.**     For faculty in 4-year institutions, the fewer hours spent in class, the higher the pay. Average basic salary in 1987–88

**TABLE 3.1     Department Chair Rankings of Criteria for Promotion and Tenure**

|  | Type of Institution | |
| --- | --- | --- |
| Criteria | Doctoral | Other 4-Year |
| Teaching quality | 3 | 1 |
| Highest degree | 4 | 2 |
| Fit with department | 7 | 3 |
| Institutional service | 10.5 | 4 |
| Research quality | 1 | 6 |
| Quality of publications | 2 | 7 |
| Fit with students | 10.5 | 5 |
| Professional reputation | 5.5 | 9.5 |
| Number of publications | 5.5 | 11 |
| Affirmative action | 9 | 8 |
| Community/public service | 12 | 9.5 |
| Ability to obtain ourside $ | 8 | 13 |
| Reputation of individual's graduate school | 13 | 12 |

Source: Russell, Cox, and Buisneii (1990)

**TABLE 3.2    Basic Salary from Institution, by Teaching-Related Variables: 4-Year Institutions**

| | Mean ($) | | | | | |
|---|---|---|---|---|---|---|
| | All 4-Year | Research | Doctoral | Comprehensive | Liberal Arts | Other 4-Year |
| **Percent of Time Spent on Teaching/Instruction** | | | | | | |
| <35% | 56,181 | 57,893 | 46,349 | 50,189 | * | 67,202 |
| SE | 914 | 1,131 | 1,839 | 2,067 | * | 4,639 |
| 35–52% | 42,935 | 47,445 | 39,180 | 37,814 | 30,908 | 54,345 |
| SE | 465 | 709 | 875 | 659 | 1,283 | 4,833 |
| 53–71% | 37,244 | 43,142 | 36,008 | 34,551 | 30,672 | 40,876 |
| SE | 357 | 817 | 716 | 423 | 976 | 2,184 |
| 72% or more | 34,307 | 38,113 | 34,138 | 34,366 | 30,023 | 38,869 |
| SE | 302 | 1,149 | 903 | 379 | 708 | 2,254 |
| **Number of Hours per Week Teaching in Class** | | | | | | |
| <6 | 50,927 | 53,239 | 43,558 | 45,162 | 33,897 | 60,928 |
| SE | 732 | 936 | 1,512 | 1,758 | 2,176 | 3,924 |
| 6–8 | 43,191 | 48,100 | 38,679 | 38,817 | 33,142 | 46,531 |
| SE | 488 | 770 | 823 | 830 | 1,295 | 3,232 |
| 9–11 | 38,060 | 40,845 | 36,706 | 36,181 | 29,708 | * |
| SE | 503 | 927 | 769 | 481 | 1,023 | * |
| 12 or more | 36,793 | 47,542 | 35,263 | 34,251 | 29,139 | 49,180 |
| SE | 433 | 1,612 | 1,092 | 385 | 673 | 4,121 |
| **Number of Student Contact Hours per Semester** | | | | | | |
| <110 | 49,267 | 53,026 | 40,042 | 42,758 | 30,742 | 61,512 |
| SE | 712 | 954 | 1,326 | 1,615 | 1,472 | 3,628 |
| 110–217 | 38,442 | 43,887 | 38,233 | 36,225 | 30,649 | * |
| SE | 378 | 729 | 871 | 513 | 852 | * |
| 218–359 | 37,632 | 45,523 | 36,852 | 35,076 | 29,524 | * |
| SE | 444 | 1,144 | 894 | 416 | 775 | * |
| 360 or more | 43,159 | 51,433 | 38,726 | 36,417 | 32,945 | 54,649 |
| SE | 602 | 1,205 | 1,097 | 583 | 1,662 | 3,833 |

**TABLE 3.2** **Basic Salary from Institution, by Teaching-Related Variables: 4-Year Institutions** *Continued*

| | Mean ($) | | | | | |
|---|---|---|---|---|---|---|
| | All 4-Year | Research | Doctoral | Comprehensive | Liberal Arts | Other 4-Year |
| **Type of Students Taught** | | | | | | |
| Taught Only Undergraduate Students | 44,176 | 48,223 | 42,002 | 42,129 | 31,296 | * |
| SE | 883 | 1,402 | 1,627 | 1,351 | 2,793 | * |
| Taught Both Types of Students | 41,478 | 48,785 | 37,795 | 36,238 | 30,565 | 57,598 |
| SE | 287 | 545 | 533 | 316 | 533 | 3,351 |
| Taught Only Graduate Students | 56,661 | 57,118 | 52,914 | 61,210 | NA | 54,457 |
| SE | 1,365 | 1,742 | 3,072 | 5,824 | NA | 2,495 |

Source: NSOPF 1988
* = Too few cases for reliable estimate.
NA = Not Applicable

ranged from a high of approximately $51,000 for faculty spending the fewest hours in class, to a low of about $37,000 for faculty spending the most time in class per week, although the difference between salary for those spending 9 to 11 hours in class per week versus those spending 12 or more is not significant. This finding conflicts with research by Konrad and Pfeffer, whose study of the 1969 Carnegie survey found hours spent in class unrelated to pay. It is consistent with Marsh and Dillon, who found hours spent in class per week strongly negatively related to pay.[67]

The overall pattern is also found for faculty in doctoral-granting and comprehensive institutions—pay decreases with increased hours spent in class per week. The pattern for faculty in other 4-year institutions and liberal arts colleges demonstrates a dichotomy: those spending less than 6 hours in other 4-year institutions and less than 8 hours per week in liberal arts colleges earned significantly higher salaries. A U-shaped distribution defines the relationship between hours spent in class and compensation for faculty in research universities. The highest salaries were earned by those spending the least time in class, the lowest salaries by those spending between nine and 11 hours in class, and the second lowest salaries being earned by those spending the most hours in class per week.[68]

**Student Contact Hours.**    The relationship between student contact hours generated per semester, a measure of instruction-related productivity, and basic salary is a U-shaped curve. The highest income was earned by those with the least number of student contact hours, dropping to a low point through the mid-range of contact hours, and rising again to the second highest salary for those with the most contact hours. This pattern also holds for faculty in research universities. Similarly, faculty in comprehensive colleges and universities who earned the highest pay had the fewest student contact hours. Student contact hours are not related to basic salary for faculty in doctoral-granting institutions, liberal arts colleges, or other 4-year institutions.[69]

**Type of Students Taught.**    In 1987–88, faculty in 4-year institutions who taught only graduate students were paid the most. This relationship holds true for faculty in research, doctoral-granting, and comprehensive institutions.[70]

*Research/Scholarship*
**Percent of Time Spent on Research/Scholarship.**    For faculty in 4-year colleges and universities, the greater the time spent on research, the higher the compensation (Table 3.3). This finding is consistent with Barbara Tuckman's analysis.[71] In 1987–88, salaries ranged from a high of about $49,000 for those spending the most time on research—34 percent or more—to a low of approximately $37,000 for faculty spending less than 5 percent of their time on research. The same pattern holds for faculty in doctoral-granting universities. For faculty in research universities, comprehensive colleges, and other 4-year institutions, only the faculty most committed to research—34 percent or more of their time—had a significantly higher salary. Time spent on research is not related to basic salary at liberal arts colleges.[72]

**Total Refereed Publications (Career).**    For faculty in 4-year colleges and universities, the greater the career publications (including refereed journal articles, books, textbooks, monographs, chapters in edited volumes, and book reviews), the higher the compensation. In 4-year institutions, faculty with more than 30 career publications earned an average basic salary of about $56,000 in 1987–88, whereas faculty with 2 or fewer publications earned approximately $33,000. This finding is consistent with research by Konrad and Pfeffer, Marsh and Dillon, Barbara Tuckman, and Howard Tuckman.[73]

Examining the average annual number of publications per year, that is, the ratio of total refereed publications to number of years since achieving the highest degree, gives results similar to total career publications. Faculty averaging less than one publication for every five years on the job (a ratio of .20 per year) averaged $35,500, whereas their counterparts averaging two or more publications per year averaged $51,901.

**TABLE 3.3   Basic Salary from Institution, by Research-Related Variables: 4-Year Institutions**

| | Mean ($) | | | | | |
|---|---|---|---|---|---|---|
| | All 4-Year | Research | Doctoral | Comprehensive | Liberal Arts | Other 4-Year |
| **Percent of Time Spent on Research/Scholarship** | | | | | | |
| < 5% | 36,963 | 45,581 | 34,453 | 35,805 | 30,389 | 46,424 |
| SE | 549 | 2,129 | 1,070 | 515 | 943 | 4,946 |
| 5.0–15.9% | 39,638 | 48,384 | 37,249 | 36,974 | 30,281 | 52,394 |
| SE | 475 | 1,220 | 737 | 571 | 789 | 5,356 |
| 16.0–33.9% | 44,062 | 50,990 | 37,799 | 36,711 | 29,615 | 58,935 |
| SE | 588 | 1,043 | 929 | 670 | 1,191 | 4,089 |
| 34.0% or more | 48,711 | 50,060 | 42,825 | 40,044 | * | 60,713 |
| SE | 620 | 736 | 1,326 | 1,220 | * | 4,480 |
| **Number of Refereed Publications (Career)** | | | | | | |
| < 2 | 33,198 | 41,676 | 30,562 | 33,312 | 26,425 | 34,544 |
| SE | 480 | 1,916 | 936 | 619 | 732 | 2,005 |
| 2–10 | 37,401 | 41,783 | 35,066 | 35,679 | 31,626 | 48,678 |
| SE | 355 | 921 | 745 | 402 | 815 | 2,819 |
| 11–29 | 42,869 | 45,519 | 39,415 | 40,466 | 36,922 | * |
| SE | 436 | 740 | 787 | 705 | 1,199 | * |
| 30 or more | 56,183 | 58,082 | 48,465 | 47,057 | * | 67,574 |
| SE | 735 | 894 | 1,329 | 1,390 | * | 4,672 |
| **Average Publications per Year** | | | | | | |
| < .20 | 35,500 | 44,421 | 33,450 | 34,731 | 28,417 | 42,731 |
| SE | 422 | 1,519 | 938 | 512 | 676 | 3,214 |
| .20–.77 | 39,549 | 44,521 | 38,095 | 37,183 | 31,701 | * |
| SE | 414 | 955 | 828 | 515 | 1,106 | * |
| .78–1.96 | 45,451 | 49,383 | 40,613 | 40,239 | 36,496 | 54,064 |
| SE | 508 | 817 | 807 | 852 | 1,455 | 2,811 |
| 1.97 or more | 51,901 | 54,074 | 42,879 | 40,639 | * | 70,609 |
| SE | 833 | 1,001 | 1,551 | 1,281 | * | 6,771 |
| **Status as Principal Investigator on Research Project** | | | | | | |
| Not Principal Investigator | 39,567 | 46,779 | 36,585 | 36,273 | 30,536 | 49,456 |
| SE | 284 | 625 | 478 | 349 | 566 | 2,448 |
| Principal Investigator | 51,517 | 53,980 | 44,973 | 41,364 | 31,572 | 68,240 |
| SE | 761 | 957 | 1,667 | 1,107 | 1,494 | 5,240 |

Source: NSOPF 1988
* = Too few cases for reliable estimate.

Regardless of the measure of publishing productivity, this pattern does *not* vary by institutional type in 4-year schools: publications are as strongly related to compensation for faculty in liberal arts colleges and comprehensive institutions as they are for their compatriots in research and doctoral-granting universities.[74] This finding confirms Konrad and Pfeffer's more limited analysis by institutional type.[75]

**Principal Investigator.**    Pay is positively related to being a principal investigator (PI) on an externally funded research project. In 1987–88, PIs earned about $51,000, whereas their colleagues not having research grants averaged about $40,000. The same pattern holds true for faculty in each type of institution except liberal arts colleges.[76] The overall results are consistent with research by Konrad and Pfeffer and by Marsh and Dillon.[77]

### Administration and Service
**Percent of Time Spent on Administration.**    In 4-year institutions, faculty spending the greatest time on administration earned the highest basic salaries (Table 3.4). This finding confirms patterns from the 1972–73 American Council on Education faculty survey.[78] This relationship between time spent on administration and pay holds true for faculty in research universities, doctoral-granting institutions, and comprehensive colleges. Percent of time spent on administration is only weakly related to compensation for faculty in liberal arts colleges, and is unrelated to compensation for faculty in other 4-year institutions.[79]

**Percent of Time Spent on Public Service.**    Although faculty in 4-year institutions who spent less time on service made slightly higher basic salaries than faculty spending more time on service, the difference is small and disappears when looking at each type of institution.[80]

### Summary
For faculty in most 4-year colleges and universities, bivariate analyses show negative relationships when comparing several measures of teaching activity and productivity with basic salary. Liberal arts colleges are the exception. The relationships between compensation and indicators of research activity and productivity, on the other hand, are uniformly positive. Here, when publishing productivity is examined, the positive relationship with pay holds true even in liberal arts colleges.

The importance of research in faculty rewards in 4-year colleges and universities is consistent with most existing research on faculty compensation.[81] The negative relationships between pay and measures of teaching activity and productivity support previous work by Konrad and Pfeffer and by Marsh and Dillon.[82] They conflict with research indicating teaching is a neutral factor in pay[83] and with studies which found teaching positively related to pay.[84]

## Messages Conveyed Through Pay: A Detailed Look

Although suggestive, bivariate analyses comparing the relationships of faculty demographics, activities, and workload with compensation can be misleading. Relationships between teaching activity and compensation may be influenced, for example, by academic rank. Accordingly, I used multiple regression models to explore the combined relationships between faculty demographics and behavior with compensation.[85] These results focus on type of institution,[86] program area, and academic rank within type of institution. The latter analysis was carried out to control for the effects of seniority. The regression models accounted for the most part for between .30 and .60 of the variance in basic salary across the various analyses.[87] I focus the discussion on the relationships between faculty behaviors and basic salary. The

**TABLE 3.4    Basic Salary from Institution, by Administrative- and Service-Related Variables: 4-Year Institutions**

| | Mean ($) | | | | | |
| --- | --- | --- | --- | --- | --- | --- |
| | All 4-Year | Research | Doctoral | Comprehensive | Liberal Arts | Other 4-Year |
| **Percent of Time Spent on Administration** | | | | | | |
| < 5% | 38,491 | 45,214 | 35,608 | 35,137 | 32,517 | * |
| SE | 489 | 1,118 | 1,002 | 557 | 1,291 | * |
| 5.0–9.9% | 40,410 | 49,569 | 38,257 | 34,154 | 27,012 | * |
| SE | 588 | 1,189 | 1,278 | 546 | 906 | * |
| 10.0–19.9% | 41,720 | 46,200 | 38,830 | 35,522 | 30,782 | 58,716 |
| SE | 466 | 785 | 832 | 538 | 797 | 3,516 |
| 20.0% or more | 48,546 | 56,694 | 41,026 | 42,315 | 32,430 | 62,272 |
| SE | 688 | 1,128 | 1,150 | 910 | 1,288 | 5,733 |
| **Percent of Time Committed to Public Service** | | | | | | |
| < 5.0% | 42,738 | 49,609 | 38,416 | 36,952 | 30,655 | 57,019 |
| SE | 307 | 560 | 565 | 363 | 569 | 2,552 |
| 5.0 % or more | 40,174 | 50,120 | 38,998 | 35,768 | 30,388 | * |
| SE | 731 | 1,669 | 1,464 | 808 | 1,536 | * |

Source: NSOPF 1988
* = Too few cases for reliable estimate.

complete regression equations are shown in Appendices 4, 5, and 6 (institutional type, program area, and academic rank, respectively).

### Scales

For faculty in 4-year institutions, high positive correlations between years since highest degree awarded, time in rank, and years at current institution ($r = .65$ to .68), and a high negative correlation between percents of time spent on teaching and research ($r = -.62$) suggested the need to create composites prior to proceeding with multivariate analyses. A principal components analysis with an oblique rotation was used to create two composite variables or scales. The first was *seniority*, which combined years since highest degree awarded, time in rank, and years at the current institution into a single scale. The second was derived from the finding that time spent on research and on teaching are inseparable—the more faculty spend on one activity, the less they spend on the other. The second composite—*more research/less teaching*—reflected this "exchange" relationship.[88]

### Type of Institution

**Research Universities.** Consistent with their Carnegie classification, highly paid faculty in research universities are first and foremost active publishers (see Table 3.5). In addition to spending more time on administration, highly paid faculty teach only graduate students and overall devote more time to research than teaching. Interestingly, spending more hours in class per week is modestly positively related to higher pay.

**Doctoral-granting Universities.** Highly paid faculty in doctoral-granting universities emphasize research and scholarship, focusing on teaching only graduate students, publishing, obtaining externally funded grants, and spending more time on research and less on teaching. Spending time on administration is also positively related to compensation. This profile is similar to that for faculty in research universities.

**Comprehensive Colleges and Universities.** The strongest predictors of compensation for faculty in comprehensive institutions are similar to the model for research university faculty even though their missions are ostensibly different. Highly rewarded behaviors focus on research, scholarship, and graduate programs. A very small positive relationship between hours in class per week and pay also exists, although it is offset by a stronger negative relationship between spending more time on teaching and pay.

**Liberal Arts Colleges.** Faculty in liberal arts colleges who focus more on research and less on teaching, who publish, and who spend fewer hours in class per week receive the most pay. This profile is inconsistent with the espoused missions of liberal arts colleges.

**Other 4-year Institutions.**   Faculty in other 4-year institutions (i.e., mostly medical and engineering schools in this research) are paid more for publishing, bringing in grant money, and spending time on administration.

**Summary.**   Table 3.6 summarizes the behavioral predictors of faculty salary by type of institution. In 4-year colleges and universities, research and scholarly productivity are the most important behavioral factors in pay. This pattern is as applicable to faculty at comprehensive and liberal arts colleges as it is to faculty at research universities, *despite the differences in professed institutional missions.*

Although no previous studies have examined a model of faculty compensation by a detailed typology of institutions, the overall importance of research productivity in faculty pay is consistent with most previous research.[89] The importance of administrative activity in faculty pay is consistent with data from the 1972–73 American Council on Education faculty survey.[90] Measures of teaching productivity and activity, for the most part, are either unrelated to pay (supporting Proposition 2) or negatively related to it (supporting Proposition 3).

**TABLE 3.5    Behavioral Predictors of Basic Salary, by Type of Institution (standardized regression coefficients)**

|  | Research | Doctoral | Comprehensive | Liberal Arts | Other 4-Year |
|---|---|---|---|---|---|
| *Teaching* | | | | | |
| Hours in Class/Week | .09*** | .05 | .04* | −.11** | −.06 |
| Student Contact Hours | .03 | −.03 | .01 | .09 | −.01 |
| Taught Only Graduate Students | .12**** | .20**** | .23**** | NA | −.26** |
| *Research* | | | | | |
| More Research/Less Teaching | .08*** | .12*** | .08**** | .17**** | .01 |
| Publications, Career | .29**** | .15**** | .14**** | .19**** | .28** |
| Principal Investigator | .02 | .11*** | .01 | −.02 | .23** |
| *Other* | | | | | |
| % Time, Administration | .22**** | .08** | .21**** | .05 | .32**** |
| % Time, Public Service | .03 | .03 | .00 | −.04 | −.08 |

Source. NSOPF 1988
NA = Not Applicable
**** = p < .0001; *** = p < .001; ** = p < .01; * = p < .05.

**TABLE 3.6  Summary of Behavioral Predictors of Basic Salary, by Type of Institution**

|  | Research | Doctoral-Granting | Comprehen-sive | Liberal Arts | Other |
|---|---|---|---|---|---|
| *Teaching* | | | | | |
| Hours in Class/ Week | + | NS | + | – | NS |
| Student Contact Hours | NS | NS | NS | NS | NS |
| Taught Only Graduate Students | + | + | + | NA | – |
| *Research* | | | | | |
| More Research/ Less Teaching | + | + | + | + | NS |
| Publications, Career | + | + | + | + | + |
| Principal Investigator | NS | + | NS | NS | + |
| *Other* | | | | | |
| % Time, Administration | + | + | + | NS | + |
| % Time, Service | NS | NS | NS | NS | NS |

Source: NSOPF 1988
+ = significantly positively related to basic salary.
– = significantly negatively related to basic salary.
NS = unrelated to basic salary.
NA = Not Applicable

### Program Area

To examine faculty rewards across discipline, regression analyses were repeated by type of academic program. Dummy variables indicating type of institution were added to the components described previously for these analyses. The results are compared with those found by Howard Tuckman in his analysis of national faculty data.[91] However limited, Tuckman's article is the only other publication to examine the relationships between faculty pay and behavior by discipline.

**Agriculture/Home Economics.**  Highly paid faculty in agriculture/home economics publish more than their counterparts, obtain externally funded research grants, and spend more time on administration (Table 3.7).

**Business.**  Publishing productivity, the only significant behavioral predictor, is positively related to compensation for business faculty.

**Education.**   Faculty in education who publish more, spend fewer hours in class per week, and generate more student contact hours per semester receive higher pay. These results suggest that teaching a small number of large classes is reflected in higher salaries. Time spent on administration is positively related to pay.

**Engineering.**   Faculty in engineering are rewarded for doing more research and less teaching. They also receive higher pay for publishing and for being a principal investigator on an externally funded grant.

**Fine Arts.**   Faculty in the fine arts who spend more time on administration, publish, teach only graduate students, and obtain grants receive higher pay than their colleagues who spend their time differently.

**Health Sciences.**   The strongest predictor of basic salary for faculty in the health sciences is publishing productivity. Also positively related to compensation are teaching only graduate students and spending time on administration.

**Humanities.**   Having more publications, obtaining research grants, spending more time on research and less on teaching, and teaching only graduate students are positively related to compensation for faculty in the humanities. Spending fewer hours in class per week while generating more student contact hours is positively related to compensation. Spending time on administration is positively related to pay, whereas spending time on public service is negatively related to salary.

**Natural Sciences.**   The graduate-oriented research and scholarship behavioral model is prominent in the reward structure for faculty in the natural sciences. Especially important are publishing, spending time on administration, bringing in funded research projects, spending more time on research and less on teaching, and focusing on graduate instruction.

**Social Sciences.**   Faculty in the social sciences who receive the highest pay follow the same behavioral pattern as their colleagues in the natural sciences. Highly paid faculty publish more, conduct more research while spending less time on teaching, pursue funded research, and spend more time on administration. Spending more hours teaching in the classroom is negatively related to pay.

**Other Fields.**   Publishing, spending more time on research and less on teaching, teaching only graduate students, and spending fewer hours in class

**TABLE 3.7   Behavoral Predictors of Basic Salary, by Program Area (standardized regression coefficients)**

|  | Agriculure/ Home Economics | Business | Education | Engineering |
|---|---|---|---|---|
| *Teaching* | | | | |
| Hours in Class/Week | −.09 | −.11 | −.10* | −.06 |
| Student Contact Hours | −.03 | .03 | .10* | .01 |
| Taught Only Graduate Students | .10 | .06 | .07 | .11 |
| *Research* | | | | |
| More Research/Less Teaching | −.13 | .07 | .03 | .26** |
| Publications, Career | .14* | .38**** | .32**** | .23*** |
| Principal Investigator | .29**** | −.03 | .05 | .15* |
| *Other* | | | | |
| % Time, Administration | .24**** | .01 | .12** | .08 |
| % Time, Public Service | .00 | −.04 | .03 | .01 |

Source: NSOPF 1988
**** = $p < .0001$; *** = $p < .001$; ** = $p < .01$; * = $p < .05$.

while teaching more students are positively related to compensation for faculty in other fields.

**Summary.**   Table 3.8 summarizes the behavioral predictors of faculty salary by program area. Publishing is the only positive predictor of basic salary for each of the ten program areas. Indicators of research activity and graduate program emphasis are positively related to salary in a variety of program areas: more research and less teaching (five fields), being a principal investigator (six fields), and teaching only graduate students (five fields).

In contrast, teaching-related activities typically are either unrelated to salary or negatively related to it. Hours spent in class per week is negatively related to salary in four of the program areas. Time spent on teaching (at the cost of time spent on research) is negatively related to pay in five fields. Although student contact hours generated per semester is positively related to salary in three fields, in each case hours spent in class is negatively related to income. This finding suggests that fewer hours in class spent teaching larger number of students is positively related to income in three fields of study, which is hardly consistent with good instructional practice.[92]

| Fine Arts | Health Sciences | Humanities | Natural Sciences | Social Sciences | Other Fields |
|---|---|---|---|---|---|
| −.05 | .09 | −.19**** | −.02 | −.08* | −.13* |
| .05 | .06 | .14**** | .00 | .03 | .16*** |
| .11* | .24**** | .08*** | .11** | .01 | .13** |
| | | | | | |
| .03 | .00 | .07** | .14** | .09** | .13* |
| .16*** | .42**** | .16**** | .32**** | .23**** | .20**** |
| .10* | .03 | .06** | .12*** | .10*** | .04 |
| | | | | | |
| .18*** | .22**** | .15**** | .25**** | .18**** | .07 |
| .01 | .00 | −.11**** | −.02 | −.03 | .07 |

With one exception, these results do not vary by type of institution. In only one type of program area, other fields, is type of institution significantly related to salary. In the remaining nine disciplines, the significant relationships between pay and faculty behavior do not vary across types of institutions.

The importance of publishing productivity and administrative activity in faculty pay within program area is consistent with Howard Tuckman's analysis of 1972–73 data.[93] In contrast, in 1987–88 substantially more disciplines evidenced a negative relationship between teaching behaviors and pay than in the 1972–73 period.

### Academic Rank: The Junior Faculty Story
The previous analyses leave unaddressed the indirect messages financial incentives convey about the value of distinct activities to the most impressionable faculty, assistant professors.[94] Early socialization into the faculty role may carry long lasting impact. It establishes expectations for behavior and codifies the value of teaching, research, and service in the minds of new faculty. These expectations often are expressed throughout the career in votes on promotion and tenure committees and in hiring decisions.[95] In this

**TABLE 3.8    Summary of Behavioral Predictors of Basic Salary, by Program Area**

| | Agriculture/ Home Economics | Business | Education | Engineering |
|---|---|---|---|---|
| *Teaching* | | | | |
| Hours in Class/Week | NS | NS | – | NS |
| Student Contact Hours | NS | NS | + | NS |
| Taught Only Graduate Students | NS | NS | NS | NS |
| *Research* | | | | |
| More Research/Less Teaching | NS | NS | NS | + |
| Publications, Career | + | + | + | + |
| Principal Investigator | + | NS | NS | + |
| *Other* | | | | |
| % Time, Administration | + | NS | + | NS |
| % Time, Public Service | NS | NS | NS | NS |

Source: NSOPF 1988
+ = significantly positively related with basic salary.
-= significantly negatively related with basic salary.
NS = unrelated to basic salary.

section, I examine the predictors of pay for assistant professors in each type of institution.

As expected, the compensation of assistant professors in research universities suggests early socialization toward research, principally by rewarding publishing. Spending time on administration is the only other significant behavioral predictor of pay (Table 3.9). For assistant professors in doctoral-granting universities, none of the behavioral predictors is significantly related to pay. However, spending fewer hours in class is almost a significant negative indicator of higher pay ($p < .10$). Assistant professors in comprehensive colleges and universities who are paid the most teach only graduate students, spend more time on research and less on teaching, and participate in fewer administrative activities. The highest paid assistant professors in liberal arts colleges publish and spend fewer hours in class teaching larger numbers of students.

| Fine Arts | Health Sciences | Humanities | National Sciences | Social Sciences | Other |
|---|---|---|---|---|---|
| NS | NS | – | NS | – | – |
| NS | NS | + | NS | NS | + |
| + | + | + | + | NS | + |
| | | | | | |
| NS | NS | + | + | + | + |
| + | + | + | + | + | + |
| + | NS | + | + | + | NS |
| | | | | | |
| + | + | + | + | + | NS |
| NS | NS | – | NS | NS | NS |

Patterns of pay for assistant professors indicate the value of research and scholarship, and the relative unimportance of teaching in faculty pay. Assistant professors who produce a substantial publication record and spend more time on research and less on teaching are paid the most at teaching-oriented institutions just as they are at research universities.

### Conclusion
Research, especially scholarly productivity, is very highly valued in pay for faculty in 4-year colleges and universities. Regardless of institutional type or mission and irrespective of program area, faculty who spend more time on research and who publish the most are paid more than their teaching-oriented colleagues. Even in the few cases where teaching productivity is positively related to compensation, the implications for instructional *quality* are not promising. When student contact hours generated is positively related to

pay, it is accompanied by spending less time in the classroom. This finding indicates the financial benefits of teaching larger numbers of students but spending less time with them, not an approach likely to result in higher quality instruction.[96]

These results show very little support for *Proposition 1*, namely that teaching is a positive factor in compensation. Instead, teaching is either a negative factor in pay, as in *Proposition 3* (consistent with Konrad and Pfeffer and with Marsh and Dillon),[97] or as in *Proposition 2* a neutral factor (consistent with Tuckman; Tuckman, Gapinski, and Hagemann; and Tuckman and Hagemann).[98] The reasons for the lack of support for *Proposition 1* are twofold. First, most of the research which found a positive relationship between teaching and pay is based on single institutions;[99] single institution studies of faculty rewards may not be as useful as their popularity suggests. Alternatively, research which found teaching positively related to faculty pay is considerably dated; perhaps the trend away from teaching as a valued activity in the academy simply has accelerated during the past decade or two.

Instead of the institutional diversity so prominent in the academic literature and evident in the NSOPF data on time allocation (Chapter 2), these findings strongly suggest that messages conveyed to faculty by administra-

**TABLE 3.9   Behavioral Predictors of Basic Salary for Assistant Professors, by Type of Institution (standardized regression coefficients)**

|  | Research | Doctoral | Comprehensive | Liberal Arts |
|---|---|---|---|---|
| *Teaching* |  |  |  |  |
| Hours in Class/Week | .02 | −.17 | .03 | −.37** |
| Student Contact Hours | −.02 | −.02 | −.07 | .36** |
| Taught Only Graduate Students | .11 | −.05 | .37**** | NA |
| *Research* |  |  |  |  |
| More Research/Less Teaching | .01 | .13 | .11* | .14 |
| Publications, Career | .21*** | −.06 | .07 | .33** |
| Principal Investigator | −.09 | .13 | −.08 | .05 |
| *Other* |  |  |  |  |
| % Time, Administration | .15** | −.07 | −.13* | −.01 |
| % Time, Public Service | .03 | −.10 | −.03 | −.08 |

Source: NSOPF 1988
NA = Not Applicable
**** = p < .0001; *** = p < .001; ** = p < .01; * = p < .05.

tors, through compensation, about the importance of research productivity is remarkably consistent across institutional type and discipline. This trend is not merely the result of professional mores, in which faculty norms are created in graduate school and enforced by faculty peers through promotion and tenure. Instead, academic administrators reinforce research behavior through salary.

The results indicate an inconsistency between the stated values of department chairs and patterns of pay. Department chair beliefs about the importance of teaching and research in faculty rewards vary along the lines suggested by the Carnegie Foundation typology based on institutional mission. Chairs in comprehensive and liberal arts colleges say that they most value a professor's teaching ability and accord research and scholarly productivity a modest value. Department chairs in research and doctoral-granting institutions value research the most, but also place high value on teaching. However, compensation patterns tell a different story. Teaching is at best a neutral factor in pay. Research and scholarship are more highly valued activities in all types of institutions. Pay, which in part reflects administrative values about faculty activities, does not follow the stated values placed on teaching by department chairs.

Perhaps most ominous for proponents of a renewed investment in teaching, research norms are reinforced early in the faculty career through compensation. Assistant professors in each type of institution except doctoral-granting are encouraged to publish, teach graduate students, and generally spend as little time teaching as possible. In this context, even modest attempts to revitalize undergraduate education by restoring some balance between teaching and research directly confront entrenched faculty reward structures which view research and publishing as the principal activity by which faculty should be judged.

## INITIAL POLICY RECOMMENDATIONS: VALUES, MISSIONS, AND REWARDS

### *Senior Academic Officials*

Senior academic officials (presidents, provosts, vice presidents for academic affairs) in bachelor's- and master's-level institutions are not served well by following a research-oriented model of faculty pay. In tight labor markets, teaching-oriented institutions may attract new faculty from elite research universities, but the consequences of using research-related criteria in selecting the "best" new faculty creates drift toward a research-oriented institutional model. In addition, the inconsistencies between faculty pay and purported mission in comprehensive and liberal arts colleges, especially the lack of a positive relationship between faculty teaching behavior and pay, contributes to the drift away from teaching. Over time, this might discourage undergraduate students from applying to colleges which no longer appear to value teaching.

Especially important is the need to define an alternative concept of institutional prestige for teaching-oriented institutions and for schools serving local and regional needs. Giving pay raises and recognition to faculty for promoting student internships with industry, for example, seems more in keeping with a regional comprehensive institution than giving faculty extra credit for obtaining grants from the National Science Foundation.

For senior administrators at research and doctoral-granting universities, the first step is to recognize the active role of administrators in encouraging faculty research behavior. As Johnathan Cole, provost at Columbia University, says,

> If academic leaders feel that there is currently an imbalance between the time allocated to research and to teaching, it is of their own making ... personal and institutional legitimacy is obtained primarily through research achievements. That is what academic leaders have coveted as much, if not more, than the faculty. Indeed, to a significant degree, enhancing research excellence is a measure of an academic leader's performance in office.[100]

For example, the magnitude of salary discrepancies between top teachers and top researchers is too large to be ameliorated by one-time awards for excellence in teaching. Even when these awards are added to the base salary, the gap between research- and teaching-oriented faculty remains substantial. These awards should be seen as symbolic rather than as actions which lead directly to changes in incentive structures.

More sophisticated concepts of rewards are also needed. The impact of all rewards—promotion and tenure, pay, and other forms of incentives— must be recognized and addressed. When each form of reward points in the same direction—spend less time on teaching—the message to faculty is clear. Giving release time from teaching and travel money to attend conferences, for example, reinforces the incentives in favor of research already imbedded in pay and in promotion and tenure decisions.

## Focus on the Departments

Departments and department chairs are crucial to the implementation of any reforms in faculty rewards. Department chairs translate general policy statements for their faculty, effectively filtering messages from above. Equally important, the pressures on department chairs from mundane tasks such as filling classes and assigning advisees may overwhelm reform-minded rhetoric from above. Finding a part-timer to fill in for a colleague taken ill or for one on sabbatical can take precedence over concerns about teaching quality.

Departments are the best locations to study actual faculty workloads and time allocation. Why not use quality assessment practices as a means to help individual departmental faculty jointly view the emphasis placed by their department on various faculty activities? The department is best suited for trying innovative group-oriented rewards, for making clear that individual faculty actions have consequences for other faculty and students, and for advising new faculty on how to spend their time. Without implementation at the department level, efforts to revitalize instruction in colleges and universities cannot succeed.

## NOTES

1. Association of American Colleges, *Integrity of the College Curriculum: A Report to the Academic Community* (Washington, D.C.: Association of American Colleges, 1985); Study Group on the Conditions of Excellence in American Higher Education, *Involvement in Learning: Realizing the Potential of American Higher Education* (Washington, D.C.: U.S. Department of Education, 1984).
2. R. L. Jacobsen, "Colleges Face New Pressure to Increase Faculty Productivity," *Chronicle of Higher Education*, 38 (April 15, 1992): 1.
3. E. L. Boyer, *College: The Undergraduate Experience in America* (New York: Harper and Row, 1987).
4. E. L. Boyer, *Scholarship Reconsidered: Priorities of the Professoriate* (Princeton, N.J.: Carnegie Foundation for the Advancement of Teaching, 1990), 23.
5. C. Kerr, *The Uses of the University*, 3rd ed. (Cambridge, Mass.: Harvard University Press, 1982), 65.
6. M. J. Dooris and J. S. Fairweather, "Structure and Culture in Faculty Work: Implications for Technology Transfer," *Review of Higher Education*, 17 (1994): 161–78.
7. D. L. DeVries, "The Relationship between Role Expectations and Faculty Behavior," *Research in Higher Education*, 3 (1975): 111–29.
8. M. J. Finkelstein, *The American Academic Profession: A Synthesis of Social Scientific Inquiry since World War II* (Columbus, Ohio: Ohio State University Press, 1984).
9. W. Gmelch, P. Wilke, and N. Lovrich, "Dimensions of Stress among University Faculty Members: Scope and Depth of Involvement," *Research in Higher Education*, 24 (1986): 272; R. R. Hind, S. M. Dornbusch, and W. R. Scott, "A Theory of Evaluation Applied to University Faculty," *Sociology of Education*, 47 (1974): 114–28.
10. R. K. Merton, *Social Theory and Social Structure* (Glencoe, Ill.: Free Press, 1957).
11. J. L. Bess, "Anticipatory Socialization of Graduate Students," *Research in Higher Education*, 8 (1978): 289–317.
12. D. Alpert, "Performance and Paralysis: The Organizational Context of the American Research University," *Journal of Higher Education*, 56 (1985): 241–81.

13. Alpert, "Performance and Paralysis."
14. D. Bok, "Reclaiming the Public Trust," *Change*, 24 (1992): 16.
15. R. M. Diamond, "Changing Priorities and the Faculty Reward System," in *Recognizing Faculty Work: Reward Systems for the Year 2000*, New Directions for Higher Education No. 81, ed. R. M. Diamond and B. E. Adam (San Francisco: Jossey-Bass, 1993), 8.
16. J. Stark, M. Lowther, and B. Hagerty, "Faculty Roles and Role Preferences in Ten Fields of Professional Study," *Research in Higher Education*, 25 (1986): 3–30.
17. R. G. Baldwin and R. T. Blackburn, "The Academic Career as a Developmental Process: Implications for Higher Education," *Journal of Higher Education*, 52 (1981): 598–614; Bess, "Anticipatory Socialization of Graduate Students"; R. Boice, *The New Faculty Member* (San Francisco: Jossey-Bass, 1992).
18. For example, Carnegie Foundation for the Advancement of Teaching, *The Condition of the Professoriate: Attitudes and Trends, 1989* (Princeton, N.J.: Carnegie Foundation for the Advancement of Teaching, 1989).
19. H. R. Bowen and J. H. Schuster, *American Professors: A National Resource Imperiled* (New York: Oxford University Press, 1986); E. P. Cook, P. Kinnetz, and N. Owens-Misner, "Faculty Perceptions on Job Rewards and Instructional Development Activities," *Innovative Higher Education*, 14 (1990): 123–30; P. J. Gray, R. C. Froh, and R. M. Diamond, "Myths and Realities," *AAHE Bulletin*, 44 (1991): 4–7; D. S. Peters and J. R. Mayfield, "Are there *any* Rewards for Teaching?" *Improving College and University Teaching*, 30 (1982): 105–10.
20. W. L. Hansen, "Changes in Faculty Salaries," in *American Professors: A National Resource Imperiled*, ed. H. R. Bowen and J. H. Schuster (New York: Oxford University Press, 1986), 81.
21. W. T. Baumol and W. G. Bowen, *Performing Arts: The Economic Dilemma* (New York: Twentieth Century Fund, 1966).
22. W. G. Bowen and J. A. Sosa, *Prospects for Faculty in Arts and Sciences* (Princeton, N.J.: Princeton University Press, 1989), 145–49.
23. J. S. Fairweather, "Myths and Realities of Academic Labor Markets," *Economics of Education Review*, 14(1995): 179–92.
24. D. Garvin, *The Economics of University Behavior* (New York: Academic Press, 1980), 7–8.
25. M. Getz and J. J. Siegfried, "Costs and Productivity in American Colleges and Universities," in *Economic Challenges in Higher Education*, ed. C. J. Clotfelter, R. G. Ehrenberg, M. Getz, and J. J. Siegfried (Chicago: University of Chicago Press, 1991), 264.
26. D. W. Breneman and T. I. K. Youn, *Academic Labor Markets and Careers* (New York: Falmer Press, 1988), 3.
27. Getz and Siegfried, "Costs and Productivity in American Colleges and Universities," 265–6.
28. H. M. Levin, "Raising Productivity in Higher Education," *Journal of Higher Education*, 62 (1991): 247.
29. American Association of University Professors, "The Annual Report on the Economic Status of the Profession," *Academe*, 75 (1989); K. E. Dillon and H. W. Marsh, "Faculty Earnings Compared with Those of Nonacademic Professionals," *Journal*

*of Higher Education,* 52 (1981): 615–23; S. D. Keister and L. G. Keister, "Faculty Compensation and the Cost of Living in American Higher Education," *Journal of Higher Education,* 60 (1989): 458–74.

30. Bowen and Sosa, *Prospects for Faculty in Arts and Sciences;* G. G. Lozier and M. J. Dooris, *Is Higher Education Confronting Faculty Shortages?* (Houston, Tex.: Institute for Higher Education Law and Governance, 1988).

31. T. Daymont and P. Andrisani, "Job Preferences, College Major and the Gender Gap in Earnings," *Journal of Human Resources,* 19 (1984): 408–28; N. Gordon and T. Morton, "Faculty Salaries: Is There Discrimination by Sex, Race and Discipline?" *American Economic Review,* 64 (1974): 419–27.

32. W. L. Hansen, "Merit Pay in Higher Education," in *Academic Labor Markets and Careers,* ed. D. W. Breneman and T. I. K. Youn (New York: Falmer Press, 1988), 114–37; W. F. Koehler, "From Evaluations to an Equitable Selection of Merit-Pay Recipients and Increments," *Research in Higher Education,* 25 (1986): 253–63.

33. R. Ehrenberg, H. Kasper, and D. Rees, "Faculty Turnover at American Colleges and Universities: Analyses of AAUP Data," *Economics of Education Review,* 10 (1991): 99–110.

34. J. C. Wyer and C. F. Conrad, "Institutional Inbreeding Reexamined," *American Educational Research Journal,* 21 (1984): 213–25.

35. O. Fulton and M. Trow, "Research Activity in American Higher Education," *Sociology of Education,* 47 (1974): 29–73; D. A. Katz, "Faculty Salaries, Promotion, and Productivity at a Large University," *American Economic Review,* 63 (1973): 469–77; A. M. Konrad and J. Pfeffer, "Do You Get What You Deserve? Factors Affecting the Relationship between Productivity and Pay," *Administrative Science Quarterly,* 35 (1990): 258–85; J. E. Rossman, "Teaching, Publication, and Rewards at a Liberal Arts College," *Improving College and University Teaching,* 24 (1976): 238–40; J. J. Siegfried and K. J. White, "Teaching and Publishing as Determinants of Academic Salaries," *Journal of Economic Education,* 4 (1973): 90–8; H. P. Tuckman, "The Academic Reward Structure in American Higher Education," in *Academic Rewards in Higher Education,* ed. D. R. Lewis and W. E. Becker, Jr. (Cambridge, Mass.: Ballinger, 1979), 165–90; H. P. Tuckman, J. H. Gapinski, and R. P. Hagemann, "Faculty Skills and the Salary Structure in Academe: A Market Perspective," *American Economic Review,* 67 (1977): 692–702; H. P. Tuckman and R. P. Hagemann, "An Analysis of the Reward Structure in Two Disciplines," *Journal of Higher Education,* 47 (1976): 447–64.

36. D. P. Hoyt, "Interrelationships among Instructional Effectiveness, Publication Record, and Monetary Reward," *Research in Higher Education,* 2 (1974): 81–9; K. L. Kasten, "Tenure and Merit Pay as Rewards for Research, Teaching, and Service at a Research University," *Journal of Higher Education,* 55 (1984): 500–14; Katz, "Faculty Salaries"; J. V. Koch and J. F. Chizmar, "The Influence of Teaching and Other Factors upon Absolute Salaries and Salary Increments at Illinois State University," *Journal of Economics Education,* 5 (1973): 27–34; Rossman, "Teaching, Publication, and Rewards"; T. A. Salthouse, W. J. McKeachie, and Y. Lin, "An Experimental Investigation of Factors Affecting University Promotion Decisions," *Journal of Higher Education,* 49 (1978): 177–83; Siegfried and White, "Teaching and Publishing."

37. H. P. Tuckman, "The Academic Reward Structure"; Tuckman, Gapinski, and Hagemann, "Faculty Skills and the Salary Structure in Academe"; Tuckman and Hagemann, "An Analysis of the Reward Structure."

38. Konrad and Pfeffer, "Do You Get What You Deserve?"; H. W. Marsh and K. E. Dillon, "Academic Productivity and Faculty Supplemental Income," *Journal of Higher Education*, 51 (1980): 546–55.

39. For example, Siegfried and White, "Teaching and Publishing."

40. For example, Koch and Chizmar, "The Influence of Teaching."

41. For example, Marsh and Dillon, "Academic Productivity and Faculty Supplemental Income."

42. For example, B. H. Tuckman, "Salary Differences among University Faculty and Their Implications for the Future," in *Salary Equity: Detecting Sex Bias in Salaries among College and University Professors*, ed. T. R. Pezzullo and B. E. Brittingham (Lexington, Mass.: C. Heath, 1979), 19–36.

43. H. P. Tuckman, "The Academic Reward Structure."

44. Konrad and Pfeffer, "Do You Get What You Deserve?"

45. W. G. Tierney and R. A. Rhoads, *Faculty Socialization as Cultural Process*, ASHE-ERIC Higher Education Research Report No. 6 (Washington, D.C.: Association for the Study of Higher Education, 1993).

46. K. M. Moore and M. Amey, *Making Sense of the Dollars: The Costs and Uses of Faculty Compensation*, ASHE-ERIC Higher Education Research Report No. 5 (Washington, D.C.: Association for the Study of Higher Education, 1993).

47. Bowen and Schuster, *American Professors*, 15.

48. Dillon and Marsh, "Faculty Earnings"; Gordon and Morton, "Faculty Salaries"; Katz, "Faculty Salaries"; Keister and Keister, "Faculty Compensation"; Siegfreid and White, "Teaching and Publishing."

49. Salary data by type of institution, program area, and demographics of faculty members are shown in Appendix 2.

50. T. L. Parcel and C. W. Mueller, *Ascription and Labor Markets: Race and Sex Differences in Earnings* (New York: Academic Press, 1983).

51. Fulton and Trow "Research Activity in American Higher Education"; J. S. Hesseldenz, "Personality-based Faculty Workload Analysis," *Research in Higher Education*, 5 (1976): 321–34.

52. Gordon and Morton, "Faculty Salaries"; W. L. Hansen, "Salary Differences across Disciplines," *Academe*, 71 (1985): 6–7; J. C. Smart and G. W. McLaughlin, "Reward Structures of Academic Disciplines," *Research in Higher Education*, 8 (1978): 39–55.

53. Gordon and Morton, "Faculty Salaries."

54. Gordon and Morton, "Faculty Salaries."

55. High paying field was scored as follows: 1 = program areas with average salaries above the overall mean (engineering and health sciences), 0 = program areas with average salaries at the overall mean (agriculture/home economics, business, natural sciences), −1 = program areas with average salaries below the overall mean (education, fine arts, humanities, social sciences, other fields). The significant $t$-test values for comparisons between the average salary by discipline and the overall mean salary are as follows: $t$(education) = −10.92***; $t$(engineering) = 3.54**; $t$(fine arts) = −13.95***; $t$(health sciences) = 8.43***; $t$(humanities) = −

16.22***; $t$(soc sci) = −9.24***; $t$(other) = −4.18** [where *** = $p$ < 001; ** = $p$ < .01; * = $p$ < .05].

56. See J. V. Baldridge, D. Curtis, G. Ecker, and G. Riley, *Policy Making and Effective Leadership* (San Francisco: Jossey-Bass, 1978); Fulton and Trow, "Research Activity in American Higher Education."

57. See A. E. Bayer, "Teaching Faculty in Academe: 1972–1973, *ACE Research Reports,* 8 (1973): 1–68; Fulton and Trow, "Research Activity in American Higher Education."

58. See Bayer, "Teaching Faculty in Academe"; Hesseldenz, "Personality-based Faculty Workload Analysis."

59. See Baldridge, Curtis, Ecker, and Riley, *Policy Making and Effective Leadership*; E. C. Ladd, Jr. and S. M. Lipset, *The Divided Academy* (New York: McGraw-Hill, 1975).

60. See E. C. Ladd, Jr., "The Work Experience of American College Professors: Some Data and an Argument," *Current Issues in Higher Education* (Washington, D.C.: American Association of Higher Education, 1979).

61. See Baldridge, Curtis, Ecker, and Riley, *Policy Making and Effective Leadership*; Bayer, "Teaching Faculty in Academe."

62. Hoyt, "Interrelationships among Instructional Effectiveness, Publication Record, and Monetary Reward"; Kasten, "Tenure and Merit Pay as Rewards"; Katz, "Faculty Salaries"; Koch and Chizmar, "The Influence of Teaching"; Rossman, "Teaching, Publication, and Rewards"; Salthouse, McKeachie, and Lin, "An Experimental Investigation"; Siegfried and White, "Teaching and Publishing."

63. H. P. Tuckman, "The Academic Reward Structure"; Tuckman, Gapinski, and Hagemann, "Faculty Skills and the Salary Structure in Academe"; Tuckman and Hagemann, "An Analysis of the Reward Structure."

64. Konrad and Pfeffer, "Do You Get What You Deserve?"; Marsh and Dillon, "Academic Productivity and Supplemental Income."

65. S. H. Russell, R. C. Cox, and J. M. Boismier, *A Descriptive Report of Academic Departments in Higher Education Institutions* (Washington, D.C.: U.S. Department of Education, 1990), 11.

66. All 4-year: $t$(35/35–52) = 12.92***; $t$(35–52/53–71) = 9.71***; $t$(53–71/72) = 6.13***. Research: $t$(35/35–52) = 7.83***; $t$(35–52/53–71) = 3.98***; $t$(53–71/72) = 3.57***. Doctoral: $t$(35/35–52) = 3.52***; $t$(35–52/53–71) = 2.81**. Comprehensive: $t$(35/35–52) = 5.70***; $t$(35–52/53–71) = 4.17***. Other: $t$(35–52/53–71) = 2.54*.

67. Konrad and Pfeffer, "Do You Get What You Deserve?"; Marsh and Dillon, "Academic Productivity and Supplemental Income."

68. All 4-year: $t$(6/6–8) = 8.79***; $t$(6–8/9–11) = 7.32***. Research: $t$(6/6–8) = 4.24***; $t$(6–8/9–11) = 6.02***; $t$(9–11/12) = −4.09***. Doctoral: $t$(6/6–8) = 2.25*. Comprehensive: $t$(6/6–8) = 3.26**; $t$(6–8/9–11) = 2.75**; $t$(9–11/12) = 3.13**. Liberal Arts: $t$(6–8/9–11) = 2.08*. Other: $t$(6/6–8) = 2.83**.

69. All 4-year: $t$(110/110–217) = 13.43***; $t$(218–359/360) = −7.39***. Research: $t$(110/110–217) = 7.61***; $t$(218–359/360) = −3.56***. Comprehensive: $t$(110/110–217) = 3.48***.

70. All 4-year: $t$(both/grad) = −10.89***; $t$(und/grad) = −7.68***. Research: $t$(both/grad) = −4.57***; $t$(und/grad) = −3.98***. Doctoral: $t$(both/grad) = 1.85***; $t$(und/grad) = −3.14**. Comprehensive: $t$(both/grad) = −4.28***; $t$(und/grad) = −3.19**.

71. B. H. Tuckman, "Salary Differences."
72. All 4-year: $t(5/5–15) = 3.61***$; $t(5–15/16–33) = 5.85***$; $t(16–33/34) = 5.44***$. Research: $t(5/34) = 1.99*$. Doctoral: $t(5/5–15) = 2.15*$; $t(16–33/34) = 3.10**$. Comprehensive: $t(16–33/34) = 2.39*$. Other: $t(5/34) = 2.14*$.
73. Konrad and Pfeffer, "Do You Get What You Deserve?"; Marsh and Dillon, "Academic Productivity and Supplemental Income"; B. H. Tuckman, "Salary Differences"; H. P. Tuckman, "The Academic Reward Structure."
74. Total career publications: All 4-year: $t(2/2–10) = -7.04***$; $t(2–10/11–29) = -9.73***$; $t(11–29/30) = -15.78***$. Research: $t(2–10/11–29) = -3.16**$; $t(11–29/30) = -10.83***$. Doctoral: $t(2/2–10) = -3.76***$; $t(2–10/11–29) = -4.01***$; $t(11–29/30) = -5.86***$. Comprehensive: $t(2/2–10) = -3.21**$; $t(2–10/11–29) = -5.90***$; $t(11–29/30) = -4.23***$. Liberal Arts: $t(2/2–10) = -4.75***$; $t(2–10/11–29) = -3.65***$. Other: $t(2/2–10) = -4.09***$; $t(2–10/30) = -3.46***$.

    Average publications per year: All 4-year: $t(.20/.20–.77) = 6.85***$; $t(.20–.77/.78–1.96) = 9.01***$; $t(.78–1.96/1.97) = 6.61***$. Research: $t(.20–.77/.78–1.96) = 3.87***$; $t(.78–1.96/1.97) = 3.63***$. Doctoral: $t(.20/.20–.77) = 3.71***$; $t(.20–.77/.78–1.96) = 2.18*$. Comprehensive: $t(.20/.20–.77) = 3.38***$; $t(.20–.77/.78–1.96) = 3.07**$. Liberal Arts: $t(.20/.20–.77) = 2.53*$; $t(.20–.77/.78–1.96) = 2.62**$. Other: $t(.20/.78–1.96) = 2.65**$; $t(.78–1.96/1.97) = 2.26*$.
75. Konrad and Pfeffer, "Do You Get What You Deserve?"
76. $t$(all 4-year) $= 14.71***$; $t$(res) $= 6.30***$; $t$(doc) $= 4.84***$; $t$(comp) $= 4.39***$; $t$(other) $= 3.25**$.
77. Konrad and Pfeffer, "Do You Get What You Deserve?"; Marsh and Dillon, "Academic Productivity and Supplemental Income."
78. B. H. Tuckman, "Salary Differences"; H. P. Tuckman, "The Academic Reward Structure."
79. All 4-year: $t(5/5–9) = -2.51*$; $t(10–19/20) = -8.21***$. Research: $t(5/5–9) = -2.67**$; $t(5–9/10–19) = 2.36*$; $t(10–19/20) = -7.63***$. Doctoral: $t(5/10–19) = -2.47*$; $t(5/20) = -3.55***$. Comprehensive: $t(10–19/20) = -6.42***$.
80. All 4-year: $t$ (public service) $= -3.23**$.
81. For example, Fulton and Trow, "Research Activity in American Higher Education"; Marsh and Dillon, " Academic Productivity and Supplemental Income"; H. P. Tuckman, "The Academic Reward Structure."
82. Konrad and Pfeffer, "Do You Get What You Deserve?"; Marsh and Dillon, "Academic Productivity and Supplemental Income."
83. H. P. Tuckman, "The Academic Reward Structure"; Tuckman, Gapinski, and Hagemann, "Faculty Skills and the Salary Structure"; Tuckman and Hagemann, "An Analysis of the Reward Structure."
84. Hoyt, "Interrelationships among Instructional Effectiveness, Publication Record, and Monetary Reward"; Kasten, "Tenure and Merit Pay"; Katz, "Faculty Salaries"; Koch and Chizmar, "The Influence of Teaching"; Rossman, "Teaching, Publication, and Rewards"; Salthouse, McKeachie, and Lin, "An Experimental Investigation"; Siegfried and White, "Teaching and Publishing."
85. I used ordinary least square (OLS) estimates, which focus on the total value of each predictor in relation to basic salary. This approach is most useful for administrators who want to understand the relative importance of each predictor in dollar values. An alternative approach, typically used by economists in studies of

labor markets, would employ a semi-log linear analysis (using the log of basic salary) to estimate the percentage increase in salary relative to increases in predictors. Such an econometric study also would examine diminishing returns. See J. S. Fairweather, "Myths and Realities of Academic Labor Markets," *Economics of Education Review*, 14 (1995): 179–92 for a more detailed discussion. A comparison of OLS and log linear estimates shows relatively little difference between the two.

86. *Source of Control* (0 = public, 1 = private) was added to the model to account for within-institutional-type variation in pay. See Appendix 3 for means and variances of study variables.

87. Estimates of regression coefficients were unbiased. A study of residuals showed no evidence of heteroskedasticity or for the need to transform variables. The analysis of residuals showed no evidence of interaction effects or for the need to explore quadratic or other polynomial equations.

88. Contact the author for a complete description of the principal components analysis. In essence, with the exception of the two scales—seniority and more research/less teaching—the composites are simply standardized versions of the original indicators.

89. For example, Fulton and Trow, "Research Activity in American Higher Education"; Konrad and Pfeffer, "Do You Get What You Deserve?"; H. P. Tuckman, "The Academic Reward Structure."

90. B. H. Tuckman, "Salary Differences"; H. P. Tuckman, "The Academic Reward Structure."

91. H. P. Tuckman, "The Academic Reward Structure."

92. W. J. McKeachie, *Teaching Tips: A Guidebook for the Beginning College Teacher*, 8th ed. (Lexington, Mass.: D.C. Heath, 1986).

93. H. P. Tuckman, "The Academic Reward Structure."

94. The number of respondents in other four-year institutions was insufficient to carry out analyses by rank within type of institution.

95. Boice, *The New Faculty Member*.

96. McKeachie, *Teaching Tips*.

97. Konrad and Pfeffer, "Do You Get What You Deserve?"; Marsh and Dillon, "Academic Productivity and Supplemental Income."

98. H. P. Tuckman, "The Academic Reward Structure"; Tuckman, Gapinski, and Hagemann, "Faculty Skills and the Salary Structure"; Tuckman and Hagemann, "An Analysis of the Reward Structure."

99. For example, Koch and Chizmar, "The Influence of Teaching."

100. J. R. Cole, "Balancing Acts: Dilemmas of Choice Facing Research Universities," *Daedalus*, 122 (1993): 23–4.

► 4

# Other Factors Influencing Faculty Teaching

**JAMES S. FAIRWEATHER**

**ROBERT A. RHOADS**
*PENNSYLVANIA STATE UNIVERSITY*

Although pay and promotion and tenure are related to teaching and research behaviors, albeit not in the same manner, left unanswered is the relative importance of financial incentives and other administratively controlled actions vis-à-vis the internal values and interests faculty bring with them to the job. Are faculty motivated to spend their time on research because of tangible rewards, or are they, as Van Maanen suggests, socialized through a different process to pursue research?[1] How much can administrators expect to affect faculty behavior through administrative action?

Researchers who study faculty behavior imply the importance of direct administrative action and faculty reward structures in reinforcing research norms, serving to sway faculty interests for educating students toward research and publishing.[2] Institutional forces that direct faculty behavior may be seen as *administrative action*. Administrative action consists of direct faculty rewards, such as compensation or promotion and tenure, for which either a dean or department chair (or in some cases the chief academic officer) has some say. Administrative action also includes the allocation of workload and work assignment, such as hours assigned to classroom instruction, advising loads, and the amount of support staff. In most cases, the locus of control for work assignment lies with department chairs.

Levin argues that faculty salaries are a form of institutional incentive, a mechanism to reinforce internal norms and values.[3] Kasten's review of the literature found faculty research productivity consistently positively related to promotion and tenure and to salary.[4] The focus on incentives and rewards is also the major component of reform proposals[5] and of advocates for using rewards to enhance the campus teaching environment.[6]

In addition to pay and other forms of reward, some authors argue that administrative support for teaching or for research is expressed through control of workload and assignment of duties, and through making resources such as instructional development widely available.[7] In this context, administrative behavior creates or at least strongly reinforces the prestige of research activities.[8]

Academic cultures and the relative value they place on teaching and research and public service, however, are not merely a creation of administrative action.[9] Administrators cannot create and maintain a culture without the consent and participation of the faculty: "the deadliest devaluation of the teaching role lies in the widespread belief, shared by administrators as well as faculty, that scholarship keeps the mind supple whereas teaching deadens and rigidifies."[10] From this perspective, faculty are socialized at an early stage in the career to value research more than teaching, through direct and indirect messages about the relative value of research and teaching in promotion and tenure.[11]

Socialization, as previously stated, is the process whereby individuals acquire the values, attitudes, norms, knowledge, and skills needed to exist in a given society.[12] Graduate training serves as an initial agent for faculty socialization.[13] Practice as a teaching assistant, for example, may develop early expectations for the role of teaching in faculty work life.

Alpert, Baldwin and Blackburn, Boice, Jarvis, Reynolds, and Turner and Thompson claim that the socialization experiences during the faculty career also shape attitudes toward teaching and research.[14] Alpert argues further that the orientation of new faculty toward research is reinforced by a publish-or-perish emphasis in promotion and tenure.[15] Such an emphasis in the ongoing socialization of faculty enhances the value of nationally recognized disciplinary research at the cost of local functions, such as teaching.

*Self-motivation* also plays an important role in faculty behavior. Individuals who choose faculty careers value achievement, autonomy, and intellectual satisfaction.[16] The "intrinsic rewards" of faculty work lives often are cited as the principal reason for high job satisfaction among the professoriate.[17]

Studies about the relative importance of socialization, self-motivation, and administrative action in faculty behavior rely mostly on anecdotal data gathered from a small number of institutions; none use a national sample of faculty.[18] The limitations of these data are problematic because of the need to control for academic discipline and type of institution in the study of faculty behavior.[19]

## POLICY PERSPECTIVES

In this chapter, we examine the relative importance of faculty *socialization and self-motivation*, both during graduate training and during the faculty career, and *administrative action*, represented by both work allocation and specific rewards, in predicting the time faculty spend on teaching and instruction, using NSOPF data. We compare four policy perspectives on enhancing the value of teaching: early intervention, fit with institution, work allocation and workload, and rewards.

### Perspective 1: Early Intervention

Bess claims that the time to change the way faculty think about teaching is during graduate training, not afterwards.[20] Graduate school is a period when values toward teaching are shaped.[21] Examples of intervention strategies during graduate training include involving students meaningfully in curriculum development and providing active learning experiences.

### Perspective 2: Fit with Institution

Socialization experiences during the faculty career, especially in its early stages, shape and reinforce attitudes toward teaching and research.[22] Intrinsic rewards derived from activities as a faculty member influence the commitment to teaching or research.[23] The first policy consequence here is to focus during the hiring process on the fit between individual interest and institutional mission. Secondly, academic leaders should recognize that socialization does not stop with the hiring, but continues with mentoring and advice from colleagues.[24]

### Perspective 3: Work Allocation and Workload

Austin, Boice, and Jarvis assert that administrative support for teaching is strongly implied by the allocation of work responsibilities, such as hours assigned to classroom instruction.[25] Assigning fewer hours in class and granting more release time for research means less time spent on teaching.

## Perspective 4: Rewards

Diamond claims that faculty are more likely to emphasize teaching or research behaviors in response to direct rewards and incentives.[26] Faculty who believe that their institutions reward research more than teaching behave accordingly.

## THE MODEL

The criterion we examined was the *percent of time spent on teaching and instruction*. This measure includes the components both of work assignment and of personal commitment to teaching. The latter is reflected in the extra time a faculty member devotes to instructional activities. The model to predict time spent on teaching contains four principal parts. *Early socialization* consists of experiences during graduate school. *Current socialization and self-motivation* contains measures of beliefs and attitudes about teaching and research. Administrative action contains *work allocation* and *rewards*.

Early socialization was measured by the *highest degree awarded* and the *prestige of the institution* awarding the degree (1 = no doctorate, 2 = doctorate from a nonresearch university, 3 = doctorate from a major research university). Early socialization was also measured by whether or not the faculty member was *a teaching assistant in graduate school* (0 = no, 1 = yes).

Current socialization/self-motivation was measured by four indicators: the degree of *satisfaction with the mix of teaching, research, and service activities* (scale from 1 = very dissatisfied to 4 = very satisfied), the degree of *satisfaction with time to work with students* (scale from 1 = very dissatisfied to 4 = very satisfied), the extent of *agreement with using research publications as the principal criterion for promotion and tenure* (scale from 1 = strongly disagree to 4 = strongly agree), and if a faculty member were to leave the current position *what would be the importance of reduced pressure to publish?* (scale from 1 = not important to 3 = very important).

As stated, administrative action contained work allocation and rewards. Work allocation was assessed by *hours in class assigned per week* and whether or not the faculty member was *assigned only to graduate classes* (0 = no, 1 = yes). Direct measures of faculty rewards included the faculty member's assessment of *whether the institution rewarded research more than teaching* (scale from 1 = strongly disagree to 4 = strongly agree) and *basic salary during the academic year*.

Finally, we included several control variables to reflect more accurately the relationships between predictors and time spent on teaching. Individual-level control variables included *gender, race/ethnicity*, and *time in rank* (measured in years). *Type of institution* (teaching- or research-oriented) was included as an institutional-level control.

The analytical focus was on the statistical significance of the relationships between predictors and time spent on teaching derived from multiple regression analyses, and on the relative proportion of unique variance contributed by measures of early socialization, current socialization/self-motivation, work allocation, and rewards in explaining commitment to teaching. We examined the model separately for junior (assistant professor) and senior (associate and full professors) faculty to take into account potential time effects.[27]

## COMMITMENT TO TEACHING: INFLUENCES

Neither the prestige of the institution where the professor received the degree nor experience as a teaching assistant (TA) are significantly related to time spent on teaching (see Table 4.1). Moreover, this pattern does not vary meaningfully by academic rank: early socialization has as little influence for new faculty as it does for faculty who have been in place for many years. Although we would expect some dissipation in effects over time, these results suggest that socialization experiences in graduate school may not have long lasting importance even for new assistant professors.

Although early socialization indeed may not influence later teaching behavior, an alternative explanation is that experiences such as being a TA are not designed to enhance commitment to teaching. Employing TAs as a cost-saving measure to enable faculty to spend more time on research and failing to provide substantial training to TAs in instructional practices convey a message to prospective faculty that teaching is less important than research: "For those who plan careers as college or university faculty members, the TA role can be considered as an internship or training period. The skills, behavior, and attitudes developed while one is a TA are important determinants of one's future faculty role."[28]

Motivation and beliefs and the concurrent socialization related to them, on the other hand, strongly influence the amount of time that junior and senior faculty devote to teaching. Both junior and senior faculty who believe that publishing should be the most important criterion in promotion and tenure spend less time on teaching. On the other hand, professors who are likely to leave their positions to reduce the pressure to publish spend more time on instructional activities. The latter relationship is slightly stronger for senior than for junior faculty. This finding signals the importance of finding a fit between a faculty member's interests and skills and the mission of the institution. New professors who prefer teaching over research may not be well-suited for research universities even if they receive their training in them. Faculty who prefer research to teaching may not find satisfaction working in a comprehensive or liberal arts college.

**TABLE 4.1    Socialization and Administrative Action Part 1: Time Spent on Teaching, by Academic Rank**

| | Assistant Professor | | Associate/Full Professor | |
|---|---|---|---|---|
| $R^2$ | .31 | | .28 | |
| $N$ | 837 | | 2597 | |
| *Controls* | Standardized Beta | Delta $R^2$ | Standardized Beta | Delta $R^2$ |
| Doctoral Institution | −.20**** | .023 | −.15**** | .014 |
| Male | −.08** | .006 | −.07**** | .005 |
| Minority | .06* | .004 | .00 | .000 |
| Time in Rank | .08* | .005 | .10**** | .009 |
| *Early Socialization* | | | | |
| Highest Degree/ Prestige | −.02 | .000 | .02 | .000 |
| T.A | −.05 | .002 | .03 | .001 |
| *Current Socialization/ Self-Motivation* | | | | |
| Satisfied with Activity Mix | .01 | .000 | −.04* | .001 |
| Satisfied with Time for Students | .05 | .002 | .04* | .001 |
| Publications should be Criterion for Promotion | −.13*** | .012 | −.09**** | .006 |
| Leave to Reduce Pressure for Publishing | .12 | .011 | .18**** | .024 |
| *Work Allocation* | | | | |
| Hours in Class/Week | .15**** | .018 | .23**** | .045 |
| Taught Only Graduate Students. | −.15**** | .020 | −.14**** | .017 |
| *Rewards* | | | | |
| Research Rewarded More than Teaching at Institution | −.12*** | .010 | −.07*** | .004 |

Source: NSOPF 1988
**** = $p < .0001$; *** = $p < .001$; ** = $p < .01$; * = $p < .05$.

**TABLE 4.2** **Socialization and Administrative Action Part 2: Basic Salary, by Academic Rank**

|  | Assistant Professor | | Associate/Full Professor | |
|---|---|---|---|---|
| $R^2$ | .10 | | .09 | |
| $N$ | 837 | | 2597 | |
|  | Standardized Beta | Delta $R^2$ | Standardized Beta | Delta $R^2$ |
| % Time, Teaching | −.66**** | .103 | −.60**** | .094 |

Source: NSOPF 1988
**** = $p < .0001$.

Irrespective of rank or seniority, the more hours assigned to classroom instruction, the greater the percentage of time spent on instruction-related activities. Being assigned to teach only graduate courses, often in the faculty member's area of research expertise, goes hand in hand with spending less time on teaching. The belief that research is rewarded more than teaching in promotion and tenure is strongly negatively related to time spent on teaching. Finally, Table 4.2 shows that time spent on teaching is strongly negatively related to basic salary for both junior and senior faculty.

Table 4.3 summarizes these results by variable category. The time devoted to teaching by junior and senior faculty appears little influenced, at least directly, by experiences in graduate school. In contrast, current socialization and motivation, especially beliefs about the importance of scholarship, are related to time spent on teaching. Early socialization may play an *indirect* role here by influencing attitudes about faculty work, which is

**TABLE 4.3** **Unique Variance Explained, Socialization and Administrative Action**

|  | Assistant Professor | Associate/Full Professor |
|---|---|---|
| Early Socialization | .002 | .001 |
| Current Socialization/ Self-Motivation | .025 | .032 |
| Work Allocation | .038 | .062 |
| Rewards[a] | .113 | .098 |

[a] Includes variance in basic salary explained by percentage of time spent on teaching.

reflected in faculty values rather than directly in faculty time allocated to teaching.[29] Work assignment is strongly indicative of how faculty spend their time. When the relationship between pay and percent of time spent on teaching is included, rewards appear the strongest influence of all on faculty teaching behavior.

The importance of faculty rewards is clear. When faculty believe that the institution rewards research more than teaching they spend more time on research. The negative relationship between time spent on teaching and pay indicates that faculty beliefs about institutional priorities are fairly accurate.

## Conclusion

Although Bess claims that the place to start emphasizing the importance of teaching is during graduate training,[30] these findings suggest that early socialization has at best an indirect relationship with commitment to the teaching role. Intuitively, one expects that the graduate student experience *should* have a long lasting effect. Yet either the experience itself is ineffectual, or it is outweighed by later factors such as faculty rewards and work allocation.

In contrast, the congruency between organizational culture and the culture of orientation of the faculty member—the institutional fit—is related to commitment to teaching. Our research confirms Finnegan's finding that recruitment and selection are crucial to developing and encouraging a culture which values teaching.[31] In addition, ongoing socialization experiences and the concomitant motivation that goes with them continue to shape values, norms, and beliefs about faculty roles. These results suggest that ongoing efforts in faculty development and mentoring may help overcome incompatibility between institutional missions and faculty beliefs.

The finding that work allocation, especially hours assigned to the classroom, is positively related to time spent on teaching is hardly surprising. We have included the relationship because of the trend to consider mandatory classroom hours for faculty.[32] Yet factors such as the type of class (and students) taught and especially rewards are equally if not more important influences on faculty teaching behavior. Our findings clearly indicate that research is rewarded more than teaching. Although faculty reward structures are not controlled entirely by individual institutions or by academic administrators—disciplinary peers, funding agencies, and the labor market all exert significant influence—administrative action is not irrelevant. To increase faculty commitment to teaching, it is imperative that academic administrators increase the value of instruction through the reward structures over which they do have control.

# INITIAL POLICY RECOMMENDATIONS: SOCIALIZATION AND WORK ASSIGNMENT

## *The Earliest Teaching Experiences*

The apparently limited effect of graduate student experiences on later commitment to teaching suggests that rethinking early exposure to the teaching experience is in order. Too often the graduate student is exposed to a teaching assistantship whose goal is to relieve faculty from teaching, to do so without much assistance or training, and to teach classes without interfering with the student's own research work. Alternatively, experience as a research assistant simply reinforces dominant research norms; research assistantships are not renowned for exposing students to the joys and benefits of teaching. Recent research results imply that commitment to teaching can be enhanced by making undergraduate "student interns" part of the instructional process. Many of these interns claim that direct involvement in teaching, including preparing materials and teaching other students, has led them to consider preparing for a career in teaching, an option that previously did not attract them.[33] Why not make the teaching assistant role for graduate students equally meaningful, using the experience to prepare future faculty members in useful instructional practices?

## *Hiring and Early Faculty Experiences*

The hiring process—especially making clear the expectations for new faculty and determining the fit between institutional missions and faculty preferences—has implications beyond enhancing institutional status. Treating teaching as an important part of the faculty role during the hiring process and requiring demonstration of teaching effectiveness for new hires is fundamental to improving college and university teaching. Yet the hiring process may be less important than the messages given (often indirectly through senior faculty) about the relative importance of teaching, research, and public service. Our results suggest that early interventions to influence new faculty member expectations may be more influential in their future commitment to teaching than the biases which they bring to the job with them. Leaving the shaping of expectations to vague horror stories communicated in hidden ways is harmful to generating commitment for teaching. To stress the importance of teaching, college and university administrators should develop a coordinated orientation program that makes clear to new faculty the expectations for teaching and identifies the resources available to help faculty become better teachers.

## *Teaching Undergraduates*

For many undergraduate students today, the primary focus of the early stages of the degree program is to fulfill general-education requirements. Many of these courses are in the humanities and fine arts; some are in the natural and social sciences. The data on faculty pay and rewards suggest that irrespective of type of institution, few faculty in these disciplines are encouraged to devote their time to teaching lower-level undergraduates in general education courses. Yet one key to improving the undergraduate student experience may be to involve the very faculty who currently are discouraged from (or who have no interest in) teaching the most impressionable group of students on campus. Whether pay is the primary incentive for faculty or whether faculty respond more to disciplinary norms and self-interest, the fact remains that pay reinforces the limited value of general education in the work lives of many faculty. We suggest that making instruction of undergraduates—at least one course per year—an expectation for each faculty member regardless of type of institution or discipline would go far in restoring the value placed by faculty and administrators on undergraduate instruction.

## NOTES

1. J. Van Maanen, "Doing New Things in Old Ways: The Origins of Socialization," in *College and University Organization: Insights from the Behavioral Sciences*, ed. J. L. Bess (New York: New York University Press, 1983), 211–47.
2. H. R. Bowen and J. H. Schuster, *American Professors: A National Resource Imperiled* (New York: Oxford University Press, 1986); E. L. Boyer, *College: The Undergraduate Student Experience in America* (New York: Harper and Row, 1987).
3. H. M. Levin, "Raising Productivity in Higher Education," *Journal of Higher Education*, 62 (1991): 241–62.
4. K. L. Kasten, "Tenure and Merit Pay as Rewards for Research, Teaching, and Service at a Research University," *Journal of Higher Education*, 55 (1984): 500–14.
5. E. L. Boyer, *Scholarship Reconsidered: Priorities of the Professoriate* (Princeton, N.J.: Carnegie Foundation for the Advancement of Teaching, 1990).
6. R. M. Diamond, "Changing Priorities and the Faculty Reward System," in *Recognizing Faculty Work: Reward Systems for the Year 2000*, New Directions in Higher Education No. 81, ed. R. M. Diamond and B. E. Adam (San Francisco: Jossey-Bass, 1993), 5–12; M. F. Green, "Why Good Teaching Needs Active Leadership," in *How Administrators Can Improve Teaching*, ed. P. Seldin (San Francisco: Jossey-Bass, 1990), 45–62; P. Seldin, "Academic Environments and Teaching Effectiveness," in *How Administrators Can Improve Teaching*, ed. P. Seldin (San Francisco: Jossey-Bass, 1990), 3–22.
7. A. E. Austin, "Supporting Junior Faculty through a Teaching Fellows Program," in *Developing New and Junior Faculty*, ed. M. D. Sorcinelli and A. E. Austin (San

Francisco: Jossey-Bass, 1992), 73–86; R. Boice, *The New Faculty Member* (San Francsico: Jossey-Bass, 1992); D. K. Jarvis, *Junior Faculty Development: A Handbook* (New York: Modern Language Association of America, 1991).

8. Seldin, "Academic Environments and Teaching Effectiveness."
9. W. G. Tierney and R. A. Rhoads, *Enhancing Promotion, Tenure and Beyond: Faculty Socialization as a Cultural Process,* ASHE-ERIC Higher Education Research Report No. 6 (Washington, D.C.: Association for the Study of Higher Education, 1993).
10. H. W. Sheridan, "Ichabod Crane Dies Hard: Renewing Professional Commitments to Teaching," in *How Administrators Can Improve Teaching,* ed. P. Seldin (San Francisco: Jossey-Bass, 1990), 172–3.
11. R. G. Baldwin and R. T. Blackburn, "The Academic Career as a Developmental Process: Implications for Higher Education," *Journal of Higher Education,* 52 (1981): 598–614; Boice, *The New Faculty Member*; A. Reynolds, "Charting the Changes in Junior Faculty: Relationships among Socialization, Acculturation, and Gender," *Journal of Higher Education,* 63 (1992): 637–52.
12. R. K. Merton, *Social Theory and Social Structure* (Glencoe, Ill.: Free Press, 1957).
13. J. L. Bess, "Anticipatory Socialization of Graduate Students," *Research in Higher Education,* 8 (1978): 289–317.
14. D. Alpert, "Performance and Paralysis: The Organizational Context of the American Research University," *Journal of Higher Education,* 56 (1985): 241–81; Baldwin and Blackburn, "The Academic Career as a Developmental Process"; Boice, *The New Faculty Member*; Jarvis, *Junior Faculty Development*; Reynolds, "Charting the Changes in Junior Faculty"; C. S. V. Turner and J. R. Thompson, "Socializing Women Doctoral Students: Minority and Majority Experiences," *Review of Higher Education,* 16 (1993): 355–70.
15. Alpert, "Performance and Paralysis."
16. M. J. Finkelstein, *The American Academic Profession: A Synthesis of Social Scientific Inquiry since World War II* (Columbus, Ohio: Ohio State University Press, 1984), 64–5.
17. B. R. Clark, *The Academic Life: Small Worlds, Different Worlds* (Princeton, N.J.: Carnegie Foundation for the Advancement of Teaching, 1987), 222.
18. Tierney and Rhoads, *Enhancing Promotion, Tenure, and Beyond.*
19. B. R. Clark, *The Higher Education System* (Berkeley, Calif.: University of California Press, 1983); J. W. Cresswell and R. Roskens, "The Biglan Studies of Differences among Academic Areas," *Review of Higher Education,* 4 (1981): 1–16.
20. Bess, "Anticipatory Socialization of Graduate Students."
21. Clark, *The Academic Life.*
22. Alpert, "Performance and Paralysis"; Baldwin and Blackburn, "The Academic Career as a Developmental Process"; Boice, *The New Faculty Member.*
23. Clark, *The Academic Life.*
24. Tierney and Rhoads, *Enhancing Promotion, Tenure, and Beyond.*
25. Austin, "Supporting Junior Faculty"; Boice, *The New Faculty Member*; Jarvis, *Junior Faculty Development.*
26. Diamond, "Changing Priorities and the Faculty Reward System."
27. We used a two-stage least squares multiple regression procedure to estimate time spent on teaching and instruction. Time spent on teaching was first regressed on all predictors except basic salary. Basic salary was then regressed on time spent

on teaching. In addition, estimating the unique variance required calculating the partial $r$-square for each predictor. To check for possible variation by discipline, we tested the assumption of homogeneity of variance for program area (defined as arts and humanities, natural science, social science, health science, other professional fields, and other fields). The hypothesis of homogeneity of variance for program area was rejected (Chi-square = 11,008; 600 d.f.; $p < .0001$). Accordingly, the pooled within-groups covariance matrix was estimated (based on within-program-area groups) and used in the regression analyses. Additional tests showed no evidence of multicollinearity or heteroskedasticity, nor were there indications of substantial interaction effects. Means and variances for study variables are shown in Appendix 7.

28. A. Q. Staton and A. L. Darling, "Socialization of Teaching Assistants," in *Teaching Assistants Training in the 1990s,* New Directions for Teaching and Learning No. 39, ed. J. D. Nyquist, R. D. Abbott, and D. H. Wulff (San Francisco: Jossey-Bass, 1989), 16.

29. Some evidence of a potential indirect relationship exists. The correlation between prestige of institution where the faculty member received the degree and belief about the importance of publishing in promotion and tenure is modest but positive for both junior ($r = .26$) and senior ($r = .16$) faculty.

30. Bess, "Anticipatory Socialization of Graduate Students."

31. D. E. Finnegan, "Academic Career Lines: A Case Study of Faculty in Two Comprehensive Universities," unpublished doctoral dissertation (University Park, Penn.: Penn State University, 1992).

32. R. L. Jacobsen, "Colleges Face New Pressure to Increase Faculty Productivity," *Chronicle of Higher Education,* 38 (April 15, 1992): 1.

33. See S. B. Millar and J. S. Fairweather, *NSF Coalition: Report on the Second Year of Activities: 1991–92* (University Park, Penn.: Center for the Study of Higher Education, Penn State University, 1992).

# ▶ 5

## A Case Study:
### Administrative Action and Faculty Culture

Faculty socialization, administrative action, and direct rewards increasingly combine to place high prestige value on research and publishing. Recent survey work by Boice suggests that this trend manifests itself in the experience of new faculty regardless of discipline or type of institution.[1] For new faculty, the path toward tenure is often ambiguous, full of stress, and increasingly dependent on research productivity. Relatedly, Gray, Froh, and Diamond found that faculty attitudes toward teaching, especially the belief that teaching is undervalued, is remarkably consistent across disciplines.[2] Ongoing Carnegie Foundation surveys continually show the interest in the professoriate in teaching regardless of type of institution or discipline; the principal identification of the faculty role in the Carnegie surveys is as a teacher even when the faculty member is from a scientific discipline in a research university.[3]

Yet these survey findings do not automatically convey policy alternatives. Survey results convey a set of relationships but do not imply cause and effect. More detailed exploration using an alternative form of data collection and analysis is needed to attach "stories" to the connections implied in the survey results. Especially important are the real life experiences of faculty and administrators attempting to change academic cultures, to reexamine long-held beliefs about the faculty role and institutional missions.

In this chapter, I examine in detail the first three years of one major project to enhance teaching and instruction across a range of academic institutions, faculty, and students, namely an effort to revitalize undergraduate engineering education. I use this case study not as an examination of engineering per se, but of the larger issues involved in reorienting faculty toward teaching. Case study methodology is ideal for this type of analysis, having a long history of deriving general principles from a small number of cases.[4] The sites examined here are made more generalizable by the longitudinal perspective employed (three years of study), the large number of faculty and administrators interviewed (more than 300), and the variety of institutions studied (ranging from teaching-oriented schools to research universities).

## BACKGROUND

Since 1985, the effectiveness of undergraduate engineering programs has been questioned by leaders in industry and government. Attention has been paid to the low retention rate of engineering majors and the content of the engineering curricula, particularly the lack of exposure to teamwork and design.[5] In 1990, the National Science Foundation (NSF) undertook a major effort to fund several consortia of American universities whose principal goal was to revitalize undergraduate engineering education. These consortia have focused on incorporating more design activities into courses, encouraging the use of more interactive teaching techniques, and emphasizing more active student involvement in their own education.[6]

In funding these consortia, NSF assumed that the combination of external funding from a prestigious agency and pressure from industry would encourage curricular reform and enhance the value placed by academic institutions and their faculty on teaching and instruction. The underlying belief was that the interdependence between industry and colleges of engineering was sufficiently embedded in the culture of engineering faculty to lead to reform. In effect, NSF asked these consortia to behave like engineers and make the changes needed to ensure the betterment of their discipline.

In taking this approach, the NSF hoped to encourage curricular change that could not be achieved through appeals to institutional loyalty. This belief is consistent with Alpert's argument that faculty respond more to disciplinary mores than to institutional loyalties.[7] The interdependence between industry and colleges of engineering also held the possibility for eventual improvement of the economy through a more appropriately trained workforce, and through graduating greater numbers of women and minorities who increasingly will make up the workforce in coming years.

In this chapter, I examine the influence of faculty cultures and reward structures on curricular change at one NSF coalition, entitled ENGINEER,[8] to determine whether or not a single reward structure emphasizing research over instruction supercedes the appeals even to disciplinary loyalty. I also examine the effect of the faculty culture in engineering on curricular change and improvement in teaching.

## THE ENGINEER COALITION

The ENGINEER coalition, established in 1990, consists of seven institutions: Big Rural University, a large research university in a rural location in the mid-Atlantic region; Big Suburban University, a similar institution located in a suburban setting; Comprehensive University, a historically black institution offering bachelor's and master's degrees; Prestige Institute, an internationally recognized engineering-oriented research university in the Northeast; Specialized University, a prestigious historically black research university; Urban College, a 4-year doctoral-granting university whose principal clients are commuting students from diverse ethnic backgrounds; and Western University, a large research university on the West Coast. The coalition accounted for 5.3 percent of undergraduate degrees awarded in engineering nationwide, and 6.3 and 7.9 percent, respectively, of degrees awarded to women and underrepresented minorities.

ENGINEER received a 5-year grant from NSF to improve undergraduate engineering education and to enhance the retention rates of engineering students, including women and underrepresented minorities. ENGINEER proposed to expose students to engineering at a much earlier stage than normal by creating courses for first-year students. The coalition proposed to reform engineering curricula by incorporating design experiences in classes and by reforming the teaching process through use of curricular modules, new technology, and faculty development. ENGINEER proposed to enhance outreach and retention programs for underrepresented groups of students. Liaisons with industry were proposed to ensure that curricular reforms were consistent with future workforce needs.

ENGINEER formed a hierarchical organization to carry out project tasks. The *Director*, a dean at one of the coalition schools, is in charge of the overall coalition. He is supported by two advisory councils, the external *Advisory Board* and the *Council of Deans*. Reporting to the director are two chief administrators, one in charge of programs and the other responsible for technical support. Both are faculty members at coalition schools. Three associate directors, all faculty, report to each administrator. *Outreach, Curriculum Development*, and *Teaching/Learning Innovation* report to the *Director of Programs*. *Dissemination, Technical Support*, and *Evaluation* report to the *Director of Technical Support*. Task leaders then report to each associate director. In addition, each school has a *Principal Investigator* to manage local activities.

## THE TRADITIONAL UNDERGRADUATE ENGINEERING EXPERIENCE

With the exception of architecture and nursing, engineering is alone among the professions in using the baccalaureate degree to prepare (and unofficially certify) students for practice. The majority of coursework for all engineering degrees, including the doctorate, is taken during the undergraduate years. An "engineering student" is typically a "science and mathematics" student until the sophomore or junior year. Students take prerequisites in physics, chemistry, calculus, and so on to make them eligible for engineering courses, followed by an additional sequence of courses in the major. The heavy courseload means that the traditional 4-year baccalaureate degree is actually a 5-year program for most students in many institutions. Engineering curricula offer little flexibility for nonrequired courses. Electives tend to be choices among specialty classes in the engineering major rather than, say, a course in liberal arts or the humanities.

The emphasis on science and mathematics and the determination to limit the undergraduate degree to five years has led many engineering schools to eliminate practical courses on design and to minimize exposure to real world experiences. One student eloquently described the lack of continuity between engineering education and practice:

> Let's say the goal is to design a house. What engineering education does is teach you to use a saw, slide ruler, sander, etc. It does not relate any of these tools to the design problem, namely building a house. At a really good school, you learn to design and build a saw! You still don't relate the activity to building a house.

The common approach of introductory science and mathematics courses and of engineering courses is to weed out weaker students. As an example, at one ENGINEER institution at least 50 percent of the students fail *remedial* mathematics courses. The focus is on finding the "best" students, meaning students who are most likely to be suitable for graduate work. For many faculty, the primary interest is in preparing students for doctoral work rather than preparing students for the workplace, even though few engineering students obtain the Ph.D. Little attention is placed on occupational reality. At Prestige Institute, for example, the faculty in electrical engineering assume that most master's candidates will pursue the doctorate and do not require practical experience in the curriculum. Only one-third of these master's candidates, however, actually continue for the doctorate; the remainder go into the workforce.

Another illustration of the dominance of the graduate/research orientation of faculty, even in schools which have far more undergraduates than graduate students, is the dissociation of curricular content from the workplace. As one dean described, faculty "download their research into their undergraduate classes. These classes have become much more theoretical than is warranted, given student and employer needs."

Teaching styles also hinder learning in engineering. Students immersed in an intense, often foreign, curriculum need interaction with faculty.

Instead, they are often left to find the answers in textbooks. Evaluation is based on achieving correct answers on problem sets rather than on what students have learned. As one student described, the engineering curriculum is "theory, problem sets, tests, take your grade, and move on." Most engineering faculty approach teaching as information transmittal, not engagement.

The barriers to successful degree completion are even greater for women and underrepresented minorities. Retention programs for women are more likely to focus on remaining in engineering, whereas for many minority students, particularly those from low-income families, the focus is on keeping them in school. Women students are confronted by a largely male faculty, many of whom are insensitive to the effects of behaviors such as referring to engineering students only as "he," and by limited support structures (only two of the seven coalition schools have an Office for Women in Engineering). Women and minority students often feel out of place because of the small number of women and minorities in engineering courses. School performance is often inhibited by lack of confidence, which requires strong support from faculty to overcome.

## IMPLEMENTING CURRICULAR REFORM

Interview data strongly confirm the need for colleges of engineering to incorporate design experiences in their curricula, enhance faculty teaching and advising skills, and pay more attention to the actual employment needs of students. The coalition elected to treat curricular reform as a collection of distinct tasks, including adding first-year preparation courses, incorporating design across the curriculum, and developing instructional modules. Unfortunately, this disaggregated approach has distracted faculty from focusing on the total undergraduate student experience. The short-term goal may be completing a module or developing a new course, but the long-term goal is to use engineering preparation programs for first-year students, new ways of presenting course material, and design to improve the curricula and to enhance the student learning experience.

The focus on faculty activity rather than on the total student experience and the overall curriculum has had adverse consequences. Only two institutions have completed a review of existing curricula, and only one, Comprehensive College, is undertaking a restructuring of the entire curriculum. Little attention has been paid to the logistics of curricular changes, including credit equivalency for new courses, the university approval process for new courses, and class size. Relatedly, the fit between each curricular innovation and existing course structures and degree requirements is largely unexamined. Because traditional engineering programs do not have room for additional courses, decisions about which courses to leave out are as important as those concerning which courses to add.

In this section, I explore the achievements and failures of ENGINEER in achieving several goals. I examine coalition efforts to establish new classes for first-year students. Next, the attempts of ENGINEER coalition members to incorporate design into the curriculum and to restructure engineering curricula are examined, as are approaches to improve teaching and learning. Finally, I analyze attempts to retain women and underrepresented minorities.

## First-Year Preparation

Except for Prestige Institute, which has a fixed first-year curriculum for all students, each ENGINEER institution either created or restructured existing programs for first-year students. The common theme was to use hands-on experiences to expose students to engineering principles and to the engineering profession. Two schools had substantial success with large-scale implementation. Urban College, which previously did not have engineering classes for first-year students, developed a two-semester course. In 1991, about 30 students participated, all but one of which stayed for the second semester; the retention rate in the course was remarkably high for engineering. Half of the departments in engineering were to make the first-year course a requirement for 1992–93. Big Suburban University offered five sections of a revised course for first-year students during 1991–92. Emphasizing design and product development, Big Suburban attracted about 20 students in each section. The college of engineering was to expand the experiment to all first-year students in 1992–93.

Student evaluations and interviews with faculty and students were invariably positive about the courses for first-year students. Particularly effective were hands-on experiences, which led to greater student/faculty interaction. The design orientation required faculty to use more interactive teaching styles, which improved learning and created interest in engineering as a field of study. Particularly successful was the "faculty as consultant" model used at three schools. In this approach, a faculty member and a teaching assistant acted as consultants while students tried to solve design problems. This allowed faculty to view the ways in which students were absorbing the material, and to modify design experiences to demonstrate relevant principles. As one faculty member said, "groups in a lab who have access to consultants can accomplish in a 50-minute lab what it would take nine lectures to present."

Although faculty and students are enthusiastic about first-year, design-oriented courses, a central problem remains. Faculty have found more effective ways to enhance learning, but each method is labor-intensive. Developing and incorporating design experiences, having open-ended answers which are not in standard textbooks, and engaging students actively have been effective techniques in ENGINEER. These approaches also require substantial faculty investment in time and energy, which has led to faculty burnout, fears about potential effect on professional careers, and questions about the likelihood that such smaller, successful experiments can be implemented on a larger scale.

## Design across the Curriculum

"Design across the curriculum" is a major goal of ENGINEER, shared by participants at all coalition institutions. Yet the definition of design and the activities meant to encourage its implementation vary widely. Definitions of effective implementation range from getting faculty to emphasize creativity without making major changes in the current curriculum, to adding a "design piece" to a course, to creating a single design project which runs the length of the student's degree program. Each of these approaches to design invokes distinct implementation issues. A comprehensive 4-year design course requires going through the concomitant college and university regulations for achieving such change. Other definitions require less drastic curricular change but more radical changes in the way faculty teach students.

Most participants recognize that implementing design across departments is more difficult than integrating design across four years within a single department. The limited involvement of electrical engineering in coalition efforts makes implementation of design across departments especially problematic. Even so, interview data and student evaluations suggest that experience with teaching design is exciting to faculty and students, and that exposure to teaching design may itself be a vehicle to promote the integration of design across departments.

Three of the seven institutions have made substantial progress in incorporating design into their curricula. The curriculum in civil engineering at Prestige Institute is replacing its research-only theme with one based on design. Western University successfully restructured three lower-division courses in materials science to incorporate design. At Big Rural University, faculty in aerospace engineering created a large-scale design course to develop a sail plane over the 4-year engineering curriculum. Students enroll in the course and move from simple design exercises to actual construction by their senior year. The emphasis on teamwork has been so effective that students have taken over their own learning; that is, older students make sure that the newer students have a good experience.

Faculty who have adopted design projects in their courses have become converts: "Students need opportunities to use their imagination and to design projects out of everyday materials. Engineering needs to be taken out of the textbook setting." On their part, students learned more in courses using hands-on design experiences than in traditional classes. Often the amount of learning was not apparent to students until they took subsequent courses.

Although well-received, the emphasis on design has run into problems. The integration of design across the curriculum has not happened. Instead, design has become a theme in a few courses, particularly classes for first-year students. Despite the obvious educational benefits to faculty and students, the time required of faculty to develop a series of design exercises for each of their courses has become a barrier to large-scale implementation.

Student expectations also contribute to the limited adaptation of design. Socialized to analyze discrete problems, not open-ended ones, many students find the lack of a single appropriate answer a frightening experience. Ironically, the discomfort in an open-ended educational experience has not decreased learning. The design experience appears a powerful mechanism for learning engineering.

## Curriculum Restructuring

Only one of seven institutions in ENGINEER devoted substantial time to curriculum restructuring. Although three others focused on changing a sequence of courses or, in one case, a department (civil engineering), faculty and staff at Comprehensive College chose to develop a new "phenomenon-driven" curriculum. The focus is on selecting phenomena which can unite teaching in engineering, arts, the humanities, and the social and natural sciences. Comprehensive College is the only school in the coalition which has engaged faculty outside of engineering in its curriculum development efforts.

In the experimental program, 25 first-year students enrolled in a summer program to design and build a solar-powered automobile. Instruction in English, mathematics, and several sciences was modified to adopt the automobile as a theme. Students took all classes together. Faculty worked together closely, often team teaching. Faculty at Comprehensive College currently are developing an entire undergraduate curriculum based on distinct phenomena.

## Improving Teaching and Learning

ENGINEER has shown that experienced faculty can learn better teaching techniques, but that large-scale implementation and institutionalization of these innovations is problematic. One faculty member in electrical engineering did not believe that first- and second-year students could understand design concepts. Challenged to try open-ended design problems in his course, he discovered that students could understand design and, more importantly, that general principles could be taught more effectively by using hands-on methods. In general, faculty who try more interactive techniques are greatly rewarded by the amount of student learning and the enthusiasm of students who are more engaged in their own education. Moreover, this finding transcends departments and even institutions. Not all faculty have adopted an open mind about new instructional techniques, however. Some faculty do not have interest in students nor high expectations for them. Others continue to use textbooks, some of which have been used for 30 years.

More troubling is the long-term experience of faculty who have tried interactive teaching methods and open-ended design exercises. According to Millar and Fairweather,

> Faculty who have changed their approaches to teaching consistently report that teaching this new way is more work than they expected. Furthermore, they report that teaching open-ended problem-solving with innovative student assessment techniques (such as journals) does not become more efficient over time. As one professor put it, "It's like teaching a new course, each and every time."[9]

Coalition progress toward enhancing teaching practice has been inhibited by failing to distinguish the goals of instruction from its tools, particularly the favorite coalition vehicle, the instructional module. Module development, for the most part, has focused on stand-alone units driven by advanced technology. Modules range from a highly interactive multi-media tutorial for materials to simple hands-on projects using paper and pencil. Faculty have not focused on broader instructional practices, such as using new pedagogies to attract and interest women and minorities or displaying and involving students in real problems. Because few faculty who develop modules have adopted this larger focus, the potential exists for an even *less* integrated instructional experience than is true now. If current trends continue, the coalition may generate 50 modules in mechanical engineering, two or three in electrical, and a handful in civil and aeronautical. This is not a recipe for comprehensive curriculum change nor for a pedagogically consistent experience for students:

> A plan for modules is meaningless unless the modules are a subset of a larger plan for curricular change and the integration of design. Since there's no plan for integration of design, there cannot be a plan for modules. Faculty working on modules don't have a larger vision of how the modules could be used by others and across courses.[10]

## Retaining Women and Ethnic Minorities

The coalition has spent less effort on retention programs than on curricular change. Faculty involvement has been particularly lacking, and coalition institutions have relied almost exclusively on ongoing institutional and collegiate programs for women and minorities. Faculty often assume that retention lies outside their sphere of influence. Although precollege experiences and financial aid affect retention, so do classroom experiences in college.[11]

# FACTORS ENCOURAGING CHANGE

The primary factor encouraging change in the ENGINEER coalition is the commitment of a core group of faculty and their deans. This core group is convinced that change in the undergraduate engineering experience is long overdue, and that reorienting student experiences toward design is crucial.

## *Faculty Commitment*

The coalition leadership realized that large-scale change depends on faculty support. Leadership to date has focused on attracting as many faculty as possible to participate. This approach has been a resounding success. ENGINEER has helped unite the engineering faculty at Comprehensive College and to clarify the mission of an emerging engineering school. Urban College has seen "unprecedented communication" between departments since the onset of the coalition. A faculty member from Prestige Institute is running a local outreach program despite being on sabbatical. In all, the coalition has been successful in attracting about 18 percent of all engineering faculty in the seven schools to participate in one way or another, which is impressive irrespective of the actual activities of these individual faculty members and staff.

The extent of faculty involvement demonstrates widespread support for the most widely understood premise of ENGINEER among participating faculty, a commitment to undergraduate education. Less certain are the implications for doing the work, which may require concentrating funds on fewer individuals and activities. Consider the experience at Specialized University, where the principal investigator shifted his focus from involving all faculty to focusing on a more manageable number of individuals who had the time and commitment to carry out activities.

More problematic is the commitment to the variety of goals in the coalition, most of which are not well understood by individual faculty participants. At each institution, only a core group of faculty having leadership responsibilities understand the totality of coalition goals. Faculty developing modules, for example, understand that ENGINEER promotes changes in the content (or method of delivery) of courses but do not know about (or necessarily agree with) the goals for increased recruitment and retention for underrepresented groups, curriculum restructuring, or even the integration of design.

## *Deans of Engineering*

ENGINEER was started by a coalition of deans of engineering. Convinced that the undergraduate engineering experience needed a dramatic overhaul, each dean identified a set of believers among the faculty who were placed in charge of coalition activities. This core group wrote the proposal, established the coalition management structure, and set goals. The deans stepped aside to allow faculty to run the coalition, an astute maneuver which recognized both the impossibility of a full-time administrator running a major research project and the importance of faculty's having a sense of ownership for the coalition to succeed. The Council of Deans serves as an advisory board to the coalition.

Each dean of engineering signed a letter to the faculty indicating support for faculty involvement in curricular innovation. The letter strongly stated that the dean would treat involvement in ENGINEER favorably in promotion and tenure reviews. Faculty have appreciated the stated support of the deans for participation in curricular (i.e., nonresearch) activities. Faculty *belief* in the importance of this support is ambivalent. In the first two years, only twice did a dean intervene with a department chair and a faculty promotion and tenure committee to push for promotion for a coalition participant. In both cases the direct action had much more effect on faculty beliefs about the commitment of their administration to reward teaching than did the symbolic action of the letter of support. Faculty in colleges where the dean did not take direct, concrete action to support ENGINEER participants continue to believe that research and publication are more crucial to tenure and promotion than involvement in teaching and curricular change. Even in schools where deans intervened directly, however, faculty are reluctant to commit too much effort to teaching; they recognize that research is still the coin of the realm. Perhaps most telling, the letter from each dean did *not* ask faculty to spend less time on research and publishing, only to add time to teaching. The failure to accept the exchange relationship between teaching and research makes the symbolic claim of support by the deans seem hollow.

## IMPEDIMENTS TO IMPROVING UNDERGRADUATE ENGINEERING EDUCATION

Based on the ENGINEER experience, three impediments stand in the way of large-scale, long-term improvement in undergraduate engineering education. The first is faculty workload, which makes the addition of a curricular-change agenda to an already full schedule problematic. Second is the lack of training in and rewards for project management. Finally, and most important, the research-oriented reward structure which dominates each school works against continued faculty involvement in curricular change.

## Faculty Workload

Spreading resources over 200 or so faculty at seven institutions means that few faculty get sufficient resources to obtain release time from other activities. Instead, most faculty in the coalition receive only tiny amounts of release time; some receive none at all. In this context, coalition activities simply become an additional load on top of existing commitments. As one respondent said, "It's not that I'm not interested. It's that to add anything new means you have to take something else away. You can't just keep adding more stuff all the time." The extensive involvement of faculty despite these funding problems reflects favorably on the ability of ENGINEER to obtain faculty commitment. Signs of burn-out, however, are apparent and may have dire consequences for institutionalizing change.

To succeed, the coalition eventually must place its activities within the normal workload. As discussed later, this requires enhancing the stature of teaching and instruction in the faculty reward structure. It also means that deans and provosts must be willing to permit faculty to replace part of their research burdens with time spent on curricular change. These findings are consistent with survey results in Chapter 4, which show the strong relationship between administrative allocation of work load and time spent on teaching.

*Coalition-related* activities have even less status for participants, including those with leadership roles. Coalition jobs are second in priority to institutional tasks, which themselves have low status in a research-oriented reward structure. As a consequence, coalition management is ineffective and coalition-wide communication suffers.

## Project Management

Academics are noted for their research and teaching skills, not their administrative expertise.[12] The ENGINEER experience shows that project management is unrecognized in the faculty reward structure, and that colleges and universities are unprepared to assist faculty to learn how to manage complex activities. Faculty socialization and concomitant rewards which reinforce research underly the inattention given to project management. Principal investigators (PIs) see themselves first and foremost as faculty members. They view developing a module or teaching a course as fundamental faculty activities, whereas administrative and leadership roles are accorded less stature. Yet who else but the PI at each school can make sure that faculty understand the full range of coalition goals, work with faculty and staff to determine how to achieve goals, and provide the information needed for participants to do their work effectively?

Because they operate in an academic environment, not an industrial one, PIs who use management techniques consistent with academic mores are the most likely to succeed. Two styles dominated. The directive model emphasized autocratic decision making, secrecy in budgeting and in allocating resources, and attempts to restrict faculty access to department chairs and other administrators. This approach backfired, engendering hostility and decreasing faculty commitment to the project. The decentralized, faculty-led model was in tune with traditional academic values, encouraging faculty to take responsibility and accomplish tasks when they felt like it. This style did not conflict with departmental operations, but it was ineffective in getting faculty to place greater value on curricular change and to obtain needed support from departmental chairs.

In ENGINEER, one PI adopted an "inclusive" leadership style to gain faculty cooperation. In this model, faculty were involved in making decisions but agreed that once a decision was reached they were obligated to carry out tasks. Symbolic activities, such as devoting a part of a room or building for ENGINEER gatherings, were crucial to this style of leadership.

Another measure of failed management was the tendency by PIs to assign task leader roles without delineating specific tasks or responsibilities. Task leaders were left to figure out what to do on their own. This approach failed when the task fell outside the collective substantive expertise of faculty, such as in instructional development, the use of technology in instruction, and faculty participation in retention programs for women and underrepresented minorities.

Ineffective project management also means failed internal communication. At three institutions, several faculty and staff could not identify activities supported by the coalition. Some participants also did not know whether or not their salary was covered by ENGINEER funds, or the nature of their responsibility to the project. Finally, staff responsible for ongoing college services, particularly those working with women and minority students, seldom were included in decision making.

## Faculty Rewards and the Research Culture

The results of this study indicate that faculty and administrative commitment can lead to improved instruction and curricular change in particular cases, but suggest that the reward structure and academic culture work against large-scale enhancement of teaching and learning and long-term change. The deterrents to improving undergraduate engineering education embedded in an academic culture which values research above all include the value of research and publication (or the lack of value attached to teaching), separation from society, and specialization and departmentalization.

### Research, Publish, and Get Individual Credit

Value in academe is placed on what faculty do, especially research and publishing, and on how they do it. Rewards focus on the individual, not the group. Individual faculty, not departments or colleges, receive (or do not receive) promotion and tenure. As a group activity, ENGINEER runs counter to prevailing academic norms. As one consequence, said one respondent, many faculty decline to participate in curricular reform sponsored by the coalition: "When you get your own grant, you do the work, and you get the credit, but with ENGINEER, the PI can't do all the work, but he gets much of the credit. So there are no obvious rewards for faculty who participate."

Consistent with survey findings and with national surveys of faculty attitudes,[13] faculty in all seven coalition schools, including those whose mission historically has focused on teaching, said that research was the *primary* factor in their department, college and institution: "Colleagues always ask about my research activity, never about my teaching activity." Undergraduate education in particular is undervalued: "There should be room for people who are average researchers and superb teachers. As it is, they are killing off people who really are excellent with undergraduates."

Despite letters of support from each dean and the obvious commitment of each dean to improving undergraduate education, faculty believe that assistant professors who devote time to teaching and curricular reform are at risk. Department chairs consistently warned assistant professors to stay out of coalition activities in spite of the commitment by deans. Coalition efforts to enhance collaborative work and newer forms of scholarship, such as developing innovative software to enhance learning, are even less valued than time spent on teaching. Symbolic action, such as letters of support from a dean, may be sufficient for senior faculty, but junior faculty (and even many senior faculty) require evidence of the value of participating in educational innovations before they stake their careers and compensation on these experiments. Typical comments from faculty showed that promotion and tenure criteria used by departmental and college review committees had not changed despite the efforts of deans to enhance undergraduate teaching:

> ENGINEER faculty who have redesigned courses and changed to a more interactive mode of teaching believed that they are alone in understanding the workload demands—and the overall social and pedagogical value—of what they are doing. They believe they are at risk of not being formally rewarded for very significant and difficult work. One interviewee's view was that, to the degree that ENGINEER objectives don't mesh with the reward structure, ENGINEER is asking faculty to take time away from the activities that get rewarded—and is providing no alternative reward beside the intrinsic pleasure of watching students flourish. Even tenured faculty

complained of not being rewarded—and of not even being acknowledged for the ENGINEER work they do.[14]

### Separation from Society

Faculty respondents agreed in general that physics-based engineering curricula which discard design, remove hands-on learning experiences, and disdain student exposure to engineering practice are partly responsible for the declining economic stature of the U.S. in the global economy. The scientific accomplishments of U.S. engineering programs are superb; the translation of science into engineering practice, particularly design and manufacturing, has been lacking. Engineering faculty even agree that their disciplines are not "pure sciences" but are inherently tied in to the eventual use of research.

Yet engineering curricula do not reflect the practical nature of engineering nor the societal needs to enhance design and technology transfer. Instead, theoretical science has become the mainstay of engineering curricula and research has become the standard by which faculty are judged. Employers claim that a consequence of the separation of education and practice is that graduates of engineering programs require about two years of additional practical training and socialization to perform on the job. As one faculty member noted, the student learning experience and engineering practice inevitably suffer in a curriculum divorced from practice: "But that's [science classes] not how you learn engineering. You learn by seeing the differences in designs, by how designs are used, by considering users' perspectives, and financial and material constraints that must be included in the design." Put another way, "the common sense of how you deal with constraints and opportunities is what has been missing in the engineering curriculum . . . has been pushed out of regular education from kindergarten up."

### Specialization and Departmentalization

Academic organization and faculty reward structures are based on discipline-oriented departments. Department chairs often see themselves as preservers of the discipline, ensuring that dominant mores continue. In the modern college and university, valued faculty behaviors focus on research and publication and on minimizing the time devoted to undergraduate instruction. The very structure which ensures maintenance of the disciplines works against faculty involvement in teaching and learning and against developing a more successful undergraduate curriculum.

The importance of obtaining support of department chairs cannot be overestimated. Department chairs must approve matching funds, provide release time, and hire replacements so faculty can participate in ENGINEER activities. Department chairs play a crucial role in promotion and tenure; their support of ENGINEER activities sends a message to faculty committees about the importance of ENGINEER to the department. The support of the chair is required to get uninvolved faculty to go along with innovations sponsored by ENGINEER. Illustrative of the power of department chairs is the statement by one untenured faculty member that he withdrew from active participation in ENGINEER on the advice of his department chair despite having a personal interest in the project and despite the support of the dean.

The success of each institution in involving department chairs is mixed. At least one and usually two department chairs in each institution are strongly supportive of ENGINEER. In no case were *all* department chairs actively engaged, with the exception of Comprehensive College, which has only 15 engineering faculty. One consequence is the uneven involvement of faculty across various engineering disciplines in ENGINEER. The lack of electrical engineering faculty throughout the coalition may threaten the ability to institutionalize change at a later date because of the large number of faculty and students in this discipline at each campus.

The disciplinary orientation of faculty also works against interdisciplinary cooperation, particularly outside engineering disciplines. Engineering by its nature, however, is interdisciplinary, dependent on mathematics and science faculty to provide essential training for students. At six of the seven coalition institutions, participating faculty have not attempted to change the content of or teaching practices used in science and mathematics courses because of the resources required and the political deterrents to such efforts. Yet change in science and mathematics is as crucial to enhancing the undergraduate engineering experience as change in the engineering curriculum. Efforts to change the first-year engineering experience, retool the junior and senior courses to include design, and focus on retention within the major will fail if concomitant changes are not made in science and mathematics. The dominant student experiences in mathematics and science courses include exposing students to large, impersonal classes; tough and often unfair grading (consistent with a philosophy of weeding out sufficient numbers to meet engineering enrollment demands); and little student/faculty interaction. Most engineering students will spend about two years in mathematics and science confronted by the very experiences which ENGINEER has declared detrimental to student involvement in learning and to retention! At the very least, this argues for making faculty from mathematics and science aware of the goals of ENGINEER. More active cooperation would be much more useful.

## LESSONS FOR ENHANCING TEACHING

ENGINEER has demonstrated that a core group of faculty in engineering strongly supports paying more attention to undergraduate education. One benefit of the coalition is the discovery by faculty that individuals in other institutions feel the same way about the problems with existing curricula. The combination of commitment by faculty and deans, and the emphasis by NSF on improving the discipline rather than on supporting a particular institution has resulted in some impressive improvements in engineering education.

The progress demonstrated to date indicates the importance of a national agenda supported by highly visible organizations, such as NSF, to curricular change.[15] As claimed by Boyer[16] and many others, specific, demonstrable changes in faculty rewards appear at least somewhat effective in changing faculty attitudes toward teaching. Symbolic action without the attendant behavior is unconvincing to faculty.

Although these signs are positive, evidence suggests that the prospects for institutionalization are remote without changing the academic culture, the rewards which reinforce current norms, and the criteria used to hire faculty in the first place. Regardless of faculty commitment to teaching and to the needs of the profession, signs of faculty burn-out, continued emphasis on research in the reward structure, and lack of support by departmental chairs indicate the entrenched nature of the current academic culture and its ability to modify an innovation to fit existing norms. In the next chapter, I explore one key for academic administrators trying to enhance the value of teaching in conservative academic cultures: accepting and acting on the trade-offs between teaching and research.

## NOTES

1. R. Boice, *The New Faculty Member* (San Francisco: Jossey-Bass, 1992).
2. P. J. Gray, R. C. Froh, and R. M. Diamond, "Myths and Realities," *AAHE Bulletin*, 44 (1991): 4–7.
3. Carnegie Foundation for the Advancement of Teaching, *The Condition of the Professoriate: Attitudes and Trends, 1989* (Princeton, N.J.: Carnegie Foundation for the Advancement of Teaching, 1989).
4. For example, M. B. Miles and A. M. Huberman, *Qualitative Data Analysis: A Sourcebook of New Methods* (Beverly Hills, Calif.: Sage, 1984); R. K. Yin, *Case Study Research: Design and Methods* (Beverly Hills, Calif.: Sage, 1984).
5. J. A. Haddad, "New Factors in the Relationship between Engineering Education and Research," in *The New Engineering Research Centers: Purposes, Goals, and Expectations* (Washington, D.C.: National Academy Press, 1986), 129–36; National Research Council, *Engineering Education and Practice in the United States: Foundations of our Techno-economic Future* (Washington, D.C.: National Academy Press, 1985).
6. S. B. Millar and J. S. Fairweather, *NSF Coalition: Report on the Second Year of Activities: 1991–92* (University Park, Pa.: Center for the Study of Higher Education, Penn State University, 1992).

7. D. Alpert, "Performance and Paralysis: The Organizational Context of the American Research University," *Journal of Higher Education*, 56 (1985): 241–81.

8. The names of the coalition and participating institutions have been changed to preserve confidentiality. The study was based on interview data gathered from 138 and 195 faculty, students, and administrators during Spring term 1991 and Spring term 1992, respectively. Documentation was also obtained from each of the seven participating ENGINEER institutions, including student evaluations of courses. The role groups interviewed included *local personnel:* principal and co-principal investigators; deans of engineering; program and task leaders; other faculty and staff identified as formal participants; students organized into groups according to whether or not they had ENGINEER experiences and according to sex; former faculty participants; informal institutional players, including administrators and faculty whose cooperation is deemed essential to the success of ENGINEER; and outsiders, such as supporters from industry. Also included were *coalition personnel*: executive officers, associate directors, task leaders, and student advisory board members. Interview staff developed and pretested an interview protocol to assess the progress of implementation of ENGINEER. Teams of two researchers carried out site visits over a 3 to 4 day period. The length of interviews varied from 20 minutes to up to two hours, averaging slightly more than one hour.

9. Millar and Fairweather, *NSF Coalition*, 65.

10. Millar and Fairweather, *NSF Coalition*, 67.

11. E. T. Pascarella and P. T. Terenzini, *How College Affects Students* (San Francisco: Jossey-Bass, 1991).

12. G. Keller, *Academic Strategy* (Baltimore: Johns Hopkins University Press, 1983).

13. Carnegie, *The Condition of the Professoriate*; Gray, Froh, and Diamond, "Myths and Realities."

14. Millar and Fairweather, *NSF Coalition*, 18.

15. H. W. Sheridan, "Ichabod Crane Dies Hard: Renewing Professional Commitments to Teaching," in *How Administrators Can Improve Teaching*, ed. P. Seldin (San Francsico: Jossey-Bass, 1990), 165–80.

16. E. L. Boyer, *Scholarship Reconsidered: Priorities of the Professoriate* (Princeton, N.J.:Carnegie Foundation for the Advancement of Teaching, 1990).

# ▶ 6

# Accepting the
# Nature of Trade-Offs

## THE TEACHER-SCHOLAR

Despite the increased emphasis on research and publishing evident in faculty attitude surveys and in compensation patterns at nearly all 4-year institutions, academic leaders and faculty continue to claim allegiance to teaching as the principal function of college and university life.[1] The basis for this claim is the mythology central to academic life, namely that the pursuit and reinforcement of scholarship invariably enhances teaching.[2] This tenet holds that active scholars are better able to modify curricula in response to changes in the literature, incorporate research findings into classes, and provide better learning opportunities for graduate students through research projects. Even Boyer, in his landmark work *Scholarship Reconsidered*,[3] felt that an effective way to enhance the value of instruction was to label various instructional activities as alternative forms of scholarship (e.g., the "scholarship of instruction"), thereby avoiding the old teaching-versus-research debate.

Recent efforts to enhance teaching are not merely rhetorical.[4] The NSF commitment of substantial funds to undergraduate education is a positive sign. Funds provided by the Fund for the Improvement of Postsecondary Education, NSF, and various foundations, and efforts by the American Association of Higher Education and various disciplinary groups are leading to the identification and construction of networks of faculty members who share an interest in teaching. Last but not least, faculty continue to view themselves as teachers first, researchers second.[5]

The long-term effects of reform efforts, however successful in the short term, rely on fundamental cultural change, visible changes in faculty rewards, active administrative support, and altered expectations for new faculty. Intensive faculty involvement in curricular change for two or three years can lead to positive instructional outcomes *and* to burn-out. Successful curricular and classroom change often is not institutionalized once the particular faculty member returns to the "normal" faculty work life.[6]

Influenced by the belief that teaching and research are mutually reinforcing and that choices do not need to be made between the two, academic leaders often try to improve teaching at the margin. This fine tuning, in which the balance of faculty activities is not effectively altered, is evidenced by such practices as giving excellent teachers a modest boost in salary as a reward for their efforts rather than making substantial increases in pay.[7] It is evidenced by deans attempting to enhance teaching without saying to faculty that less research productivity is an acceptable trade-off for successful curricular reform. Fine tuning is also at play when instructional development services are made available to faculty as an option but not as a requirement. By keeping such support services at the periphery of faculty work life, the likely impact on faculty behavior is diminished.[8]

By accepting the view of research and teaching as mutually supportive, however accurate or inaccurate, academic leaders and their faculty have avoided a rational discussion about the choices faculty must make in the allocation of their time. This view has allowed academics to gloss over the manner in which faculty rewards emphasize the discreteness, not the mutuality, of teaching and research. Most importantly, the acceptance of teaching and research as part of the same greater whole has permitted academic leaders and their faculty to avoid addressing the fundamental trade-offs involved if the academy is to restore teaching as a highly valued function.

## Teacher-Scholar: The Mythology

The teacher-scholar long has been accepted as the ideal in American higher education.[9] Teaching and research are seen as mutually reinforcing. From this perspective, the best scholars are the best teachers: the best teacher is a scholar who keeps abreast of the content and methods of a field through continuing involvement in research and who communicates knowledge and enthusiasm for a subject to students.[10]

Feldman found that the claim that teaching and research are mutually reinforcing has several tenets.[11] The first set of premises can be categorized under Linsky and Straus' "spillover effect."[12] This effect is evidenced by the following:

- Research may help faculty keep current with their discipline and may increase intellectual interest.[13]
- Faculty who conduct research may be more likely to introduce new materials into their classes.[14]

- Research work requires skills in organizing materials, which may assist faculty in better organizing materials for presentation in class.[15]
- Research may socialize faculty to expect more from their students and to challenge students intellectually.[16]
- Research-oriented faculty may be more likely to instill an enthusiasm for scholarship among students.[17]
- Highly productive researchers may be the most stimulating teachers.[18]
- Research productivity may enhance faculty interest in course subject matter.[19]

Crimmel adds another commonly held premise about the "spillover" between research and teaching:

- Faculty who are actively engaged in research may serve as better role models for students than less research-minded faculty.[20]

Research and teaching productivity may also be part of a larger construct of general intelligence or ability.[21] If both good teaching and productive research are a function of general ability, the two should be positively related.

Surveys of faculty indicate widespread acceptance of the belief that teaching and research are mutually reinforcing.[22] A survey of faculty in the natural sciences found that 95 percent agreed that keeping abreast in the discipline through research is fundamental to effective instruction.[23] Peer ratings of teaching effectiveness and research productivity indicate a perceived positive relationship between the two.[24] The National Academy of Sciences ratings of doctoral program quality showed a strong positive relationship between peer ratings of overall program quality (including quality of students and of instruction) and research productivity across disciplines.[25]

The teacher–scholar mythology has two important policy and administrative consequences. First, it requires that each faculty member who desires promotion, tenure, and large salary increases follow the same behavioral pattern encompassing both research and teaching. The volume of research productivity and amount of teaching will vary by type of institution, but both are required. Excellent teaching alone is insufficient; both research and teaching are (purportedly) needed. This concept is consistent with the general-ability tenet, in which both teaching and research are indicators of an individual's overall ability. Second, the presumption of a benefit to teaching from research activity permits heavy emphasis by faculty and administrators on the importance of research. Consistent with Linsky and Straus' spillover effect,[26] since both teaching and research purportedly benefit from the research function, the reasoning goes, faculty who spend the most time on research enhance institutional prestige and visibility *without cost* to the instructional function. That is, the best researchers make the best teachers.

## *Teacher-Scholar: The Evidence*

Despite the general acceptance of the teacher–scholar concept, Crimmel asserts that "this claim is usually presented…not as an empirically verified hypothesis, but as a self-evident truth."[27] Some critics believe that research activity actually detracts from instructional quality primarily by reducing the time faculty spend with students: "The time expended to become a productive scholar and do research is taken away from teaching activities, such as classroom participation, close contact with students, and intellectual supervision of them."[28]

To examine both the dominant teacher–scholar ideology and the contrasting view of the negative influence of research on teaching, Feldman completed a meta-analysis of published work on the relationship between teaching and research quality.[29] Across several studies, he found only a minimal relationship between student ratings of teaching effectiveness and faculty research productivity (an average correlation of .12). This relationship was small regardless of the measure of faculty productivity used (i.e., publishing, obtaining research grants). Measures of the quality of research publications based on citation indices were found unrelated to teaching effectiveness ($r = -.002$).

Feldman also examined the distinct components of the teaching-enhances-research ideology. He found modest support (average correlation about .20) for the beliefs that research helps faculty keep abreast of their disciplines and increases intellectual interest, and that research can assist faculty in better organizing their class presentations and syllabi. Feldman found little, if any, support for the ideas of research socializing faculty to expect more from their students, research-oriented faculty being more likely to instill an enthusiasm for scholarship among students, highly productive researchers being the most stimulating teachers, faculty who engage in research bringing new material into classroom instruction more frequently than less research-oriented faculty, or research productivity enhancing faculty interest in course subject matter. Feldman concluded by stating: "An obvious interpretation of these results is that, in general, the likelihood that research productivity actually benefits teaching is extremely small or that the two, for all practical purposes, are essentially unrelated."[30] Centra adds:

> No one would question the need for teachers to keep up with current knowledge in their fields. But whether they must actually carry on research in order to do so is questionable. Reading and discussing current findings in their discipline as a whole may do as much to help some teachers keep up-to-date as if they focused on a narrow research problem.[31]

Feldman found no support for research productivity being negatively related to teaching effectiveness. Yet Crimmel argued that the emphasis on research has led to a culture which denigrates teaching and harms instruction:

The myth of the "teacher-scholar" is rationalized by a web of false beliefs. Chief among these are the empirically mistaken belief that publication benefits teaching and the conceptually mistaken belief that publication is one of the essential responsibilities of the teacher in the liberal arts college.[32]

I explore the cultural implications of the teacher–scholar myth next.

## TEACHING AND RESEARCH: REINFORCING OR IN COMPETITION?

Most faculty can cite examples of how teaching and research, whether through funded grants or publishing, are mutually reinforcing. Stories about the benefits to students accruing from having their teachers up-to-date with their disciplines and about teachers benefiting from involving students in research projects remain conventional wisdom in academe. Faculty who have no research interests and who do not keep up with their fields are held as negative examples because they are said to be doing a disservice to their students.

The purported symbiotic relationship between teaching and research continues because both faculty and administrators have a vested interest in its continuation. By investing in research instead of teaching, administrators can pursue enhanced prestige (and fiscal benefits) while purportedly assisting instruction. The social utility of research *for the academic profession*—enhanced prestige and potential fiscal benefits—has led academic leaders and faculty to continue supporting the dominant ideology about teaching and research.

In this larger cultural context, the emphasis on research can adversely affect teaching by detracting from efforts to enhance instruction directly. The evidence increasingly points to teaching and research as discrete activities having less in common than accepted in conventional academic lore. Effective teaching and effective research share a common feature: both are labor-intensive.[33] Using student journals to track shifts in analytical thinking and substantive knowledge is more effective for this task than paper-and-pencil tests given only at the end of the term. Changing undergraduate engineering courses to provide more real-world experiences for students increases retention and learning. Transforming dull text-oriented courses to interactive learning environments makes students more active participants in their own learning.[34] Each of these successful innovations, however, requires substantial faculty time; pursuing research and scholarship alone will not "naturally" lead to improved student learning experiences.[35]

Faculty participating in ENGINEER, for example, recognize that the question is one of trade-offs. When the deans of engineering wrote letters of support for participation in curricular reform without stating that research and publishing requirements would be reduced, in the absence of evidence of behavioral intervention (such as in the two cases where deans intervened in the promotion and tenure process), faculty understood the unstated message: the effective reward structure remained unchanged. Whether faculty and administrators are willing to make this choice is a separate issue.

The 1987–88 NSOPF survey data confirm the competition between time spent on teaching and research for faculty in all types of 4-year institutions. An analysis of faculty time allocation shows that administration and public service are independent dimensions of the faculty work load. Teaching and research, however, are highly inversely related ($r = -.62$) (see Table 6.1). In effect, the more time faculty spend on research, the less they spend on teaching, and vice versa. Since effective teaching requires substantial faculty effort, and because the increased effort must come from time spent on research, the implication for faculty and administrators is clear: improvement in teaching requires faculty to spend less time on research and publishing.

**TABLE 6.1    Dimensions of Faculty Activities**

| | *Component (rotated loadings)* | | |
|---|---|---|---|
| | **More Research/ Less Teaching** | **Percent Time, Administration** | **Percent Time, Service** |
| % Time, Teaching | −.83 | −.41 | −.11 |
| % Time, Research | .95 | −.30 | −.08 |
| % Time, Administration | −.05 | .99 | −.04 |
| % Time, Service | −.01 | −.03 | .99 |
| | *Correlations between Components* | | |
| | **1** | **2** | **3** |
| 1  More Research/Less Teaching | 1 | .13 | −.06 |
| 2  Percent Administration | | 1 | .06 |
| 3  Percent Service | | | 1 |

Source: NSOPF 1988

Table 6.2 presents the correlations between two measures of research productivity—number of refereed publications in the past two years and being a principal investigator on a funded research project—with time spent on teaching and instruction. The results are similar: the percentage of time faculty devote to teaching and instruction is inversely related to both measures of research productivity, overall and for each type of institution.

## Who Teaches Whom?

To incorporate research results into teaching practice, faculty involved in research must at some point spend time in the classroom. The claim that the highly experienced researcher brings a "special something" to his or her classroom requires that these researchers teach. Yet recent trends show the opposite. As shown in Chapter 2, hours spent in the classroom by full-time faculty have declined in the past two decades. Faculty in nonresearch universities now spend more time on research than in previous years. In addition, colleges and universities of all types increasingly rely on part-time faculty and teaching assistants to handle a major part of the instructional load.[36] This policy allows full-time faculty to spend more time on research. Unverified data from state agencies suggest that in some major research universities full-time, tenure-track faculty may teach as little as one-quarter of undergraduate courses.[37]

## Faculty Rewards

Junior faculty seeking promotion and/or tenure must prepare a dossier indicating their accomplishments. The format of promotion-and-tenure dossiers reveals the lack of connection between teaching and research productivity in

**TABLE 6.2   Correlations between Research Productivity and Time Allocated to Teaching**

| Refereed Publications during Previous 2 Years | | Principal Investigator, Funded Research Project | |
|---|---|---|---|
| All 4-Year | −.34 | All 4-Year | −.36 |
| Research | −.26 | Research | −.28 |
| Doctoral-Granting | −.36 | Doctoral-Granting | −.30 |
| Comprehensive | −.16 | Comprehensive | −.16 |
| Liberal Arts | −.20 | Liberal Arts | −.19 |
| Other 4-Year | −.22 | Other 4-Year | −.48 |

Source: NSOPF 1988

faculty rewards. At many 4-year colleges and universities, each faculty member being judged for promotion and/or tenure is asked to list activities separately. The section on "research and scholarship" contains published articles, books, monographs, and research grants. A separate chapter on "teaching and instruction" delineates courses taught and the student ratings of them. An elaboration of contributions to "service" defines the faculty member's contributions to the university and the profession. In preparing dossiers, faculty seldom are asked to describe how teaching and research are mutually reinforced. Rather, the use of discrete categories of job performance allows differential weights to be used for each category of work.

These findings indicate why "fine tuning" is an ineffective approach to improving the value of teaching in faculty rewards. Data on faculty salaries and surveys of faculty[38] indicate that rewards in all types of 4-year schools increasingly support research and scholarship rather than teaching and instruction. Minor adjustments to such a strongly entrenched system, whether through rhetoric or through small pay increments for teaching performance, are simply not enough to strike a meaningful balance in how faculty spend their time.

Beyond the entrenchment of research norms in faculty and administrative cultures is the declining conflict between *institutional* or locally important behaviors, such as teaching, and *national* norms, which rely on the visibility of research. The traditional viewpoint is that disciplinary norms, which emphasize research and national prestige, conflict with institutional values, which stress teaching and service.[39] Gaff and Wilson summarize this purported value conflict as follows:

> One's national advancement rests on publishing in a specialty, being active in a professional society, and being visible and respected by specialists at other schools. One's advancement locally ... depends on one's contribution to the school by teaching, counseling, administration, and, if the school values national prominence, one's national professional standing.[40]

The NSOPF data strongly suggest that institutional and national norms have merged or are merging in academe, and that the conflict between the two has diminished. Both the NSOPF results and work by Bieber, Lawrence, and Blackburn in their longitudinal case study of faculty suggest that publishing and research productivity are the single most important behavioral components of faculty rewards at most 4-year colleges and universities.[41] To enhance teaching, the conflict between local activities, such as teaching, and national norms must be reintroduced.

# THE NATURE OF TRADE-OFFS

These findings indicate why we must revisit the teaching-versus-research debate, informed by how effectively academic cultures have reinforced the conflict between, not the mutuality of, teaching and research. Academic administrators and faculty must make conscious choices between these activities rather than assuming that one simply reinforces the other. As Crimmel says, "surely the reasonable response to the desire to further teaching is to reward teaching excellence, not to reward some other activity whose causal relationship to teaching is less than certain."[42]

Academic leaders will not find making these choices easy. To emphasize teaching, or even to enhance its value slightly, may mean asking a faculty member to discard a grant opportunity or to write fewer articles. This exchange has a potential cost to prestige—at least as currently accepted—but it has the value of honesty and, as important, the potential to start the difficult process of changing institutional norms. As these new norms become clear to the public, which every day is making its interest in teaching and learning more visible, the possibility of enhancing prestige through an avenue other than research grows. In the end, academic leaders must confront the difficult *trade-offs* between teaching and research, and reconsider how best to encourage improving both the teaching and research missions.

# NOTES

1. S. H. Russell, R. C. Cox, and J. M. Boismier, *A Descriptive Report of Academic Departments in Higher Education Institutions* (Washington, D.C.: U.S. Department of Education, 1990).
2. D. Bok, "Reclaiming the Public Trust," *Change*, 24 (1992): 12–19.
3. E. L. Boyer, *Scholarship Reconsidered: Priorities of the Professoriate* (Princeton, N.J.: Carnegie Foundation for the Advancement of Teaching, 1990).
4. T. A. Angelo and K. P. Cross, *Classroom Teaching Techniques: Handbook for College Teachers*, 2nd ed. (San Francisco: Jossey-Bass, 1993).
5. Carnegie Foundation for the Advancement of Teaching, *The Condition of the Professoriate: Attitudes and Trends, 1989* (Princeton, N.J.: Carnegie Foundation for the Advancement of Teaching, 1989); P. J. Gray, R. C. Froh, and R. M. Diamond, "Myths and Realities," *AAHE Bulletin*, 44 (1991): 4–7.
6. For example, S. B. Millar and J. S. Fairweather, *NSF Coalition: Report on the Second Year of Activities: 1991–92* (University Park, Penn.: Center for the Study of Higher Education, Penn State University, 1992).
7. H. M. Levin, "Raising Productivity in Higher Education," *Journal of Higher Education*, 62 (1991): 241–62.
8. M. Weimer, *Improving College Teaching: Strategies for Developing Instructional Effectiveness* (San Francisco: Jossey-Bass, 1990).

9. H. H. Crimmel, "The Myth of the Teacher-Scholar," *Liberal Education,* 70 (1984): 183–98.

10. J. G. Gaff and R. C. Wilson, "The Teaching Environment," *AAUP Bulletin,* 57 (1971): 477.

11. K. A. Feldman, "Research Productivity and Scholarly Accomplishment of College Teachers as Related to their Instructional Effectiveness: A Review and Exploration," *Research in Higher Education,* 26 (1987): 227–98.

12. A. S. Linsky and M. Straus, "Student Evaluation, Research Productivity, and Eminence of College Faculty," *Journal of Higher Education,* 46 (1975): 89–102.

13. J. A. Centra, "Research Productivity and Teaching Effectiveness," *Research in Higher Education,* 18 (1983): 379–89; Crimmel, "The Myth of the Teacher-Scholar"; R. J. Friedrich and S. J. Michalak, Jr., "Why Doesn't Research Improve Teaching? Some Answers from a Small Liberal Arts College," *Journal of Higher Education,* 54 (1983): 145–63.

14. R. D. McCullagh and M. R. Roy, "The Contribution of Noninstructional Activities to College Classroom Teacher Effectiveness," *Journal of Experimental Education,* 44 (1975): 61–70.

15. Friedrich and Michalak, "Why Doesn't Research Improve Teaching?"

16. Friedrich and Michalak, "Why Doesn't Research Improve Teaching?"

17. Centra, "Research Productivity and Teaching Effectiveness"; J. Harry and N. S. Goldner, "The Null Relationship between Teaching and Research," *Sociology of Education,* 45 (1972): 47–60.

18. Centra, "Research Productivity and Teaching Effectiveness"; Linsky and Straus, "Student Evaluation, Research Productivity, and Eminence."

19. Centra, "Research Productivity and Teaching Effectiveness"; Friedrich and Michalak, "Why Doesn't Research Improve Teaching?"

20. Crimmel, "The Myth of the Teacher-Scholar," 184–5.

21. Centra, "Research Productivity and Teaching Effectiveness," 380–1; M. A. Faia, "Teaching and Research: Rapport or Mésalliance," *Research in Higher Education,* 4 (1976): 235–46.

22. Gaff and Wilson, "The Teaching Environment."

23. L. R. Jauch, "Relationships of Research and Teaching: Implications for Faculty Evaluation," *Research in Higher Education,* 5 (1976): 1–13.

24. Centra, "Research Productivity and Teaching Effectiveness."

25. For example, L. V. Jones, G. Lindzey, and P. E. Coggeshall, eds., *An Assessment of Research-Doctorate Programs in the United States: Biological Sciences* (Washington, D.C.: National Academy Press, 1982).

26. Linsky and Straus, "Student Evaluation, Research Productivity, and Eminence."

27. Crimmel, "The Myth of the Teacher-Scholar," 184.

28. Gaff and Wilson, "The Teaching Environment," 477.

29. Feldman, "Research Productivity and Scholarly Accomplishment."

30. Feldman, "Research Productivity and Scholarly Accomplishment," 275.

31. Centra, "Research Productivity and Teaching Effectiveness," 388.

32. Crimmel, "The Myth of the Teacher-Scholar," 192.

33. T. A. Angelo, ed., *Classroom Research: Early Lessons from Success* (San Francisco: Jossey-Bass, 1991); Weimer, *Improving College Teaching.*

34. Millar and Fairweather, *NSF Coalition.*

35. The NSF officially recognizes this conflict. A recent grants announcement offers incentives for faculty researchers to spend time making their research findings available in instructional settings. Apparently, the NSF believes that research-oriented faculty do not have the time (or the incentive) to make this connection without release time from their regular work load.

36. J. M. Gappa and D. W. Leslie, *The Invisible Faculty: Improving the Status of Part-timers in Higher Education* (San Francisco: Jossey-Bass, 1993).

37. R. L. Jacobsen, "Colleges Face New Pressure to Increase Faculty Productivity," *Chronicle of Higher Education*, 38 (April 15, 1992): 1.

38. For example, Carnegie Foundation for the Advancement of Teaching, *The Condition of the Professoriate*.

39. D. Alpert, "Performance and Paralysis: The Organizational Context of the American Research University," *Journal of Higher Education*, 56 (1985): 241–81.

40. Gaff and Wilson, "The Teaching Environment," 477.

41. J. P. Bieber, J. H. Lawrence, and R. T. Blackburn, "Through the Years—Faculty and Their Changing Institution," *Change*, 24 (1992): 28–35.

42. Crimmel, "The Myth of the Teacher-Scholar," 188.

# ► 7

---

# The New Economy:

## Consequences for Faculty Behavior and Administrative Action

The uncertainty about the economic future of the nation, especially the employment consequences for individuals and families who can no longer count on a particular job or career even existing a decade from now, has placed additional pressure on academic institutions. On the surface, state efforts to involve colleges and universities in technology transfer, federal programs to encourage industry–university research alliances, and the like appear to add one more factor competing for time in an already full faculty schedule. If college administrators must confront the trade-offs between teaching, research, and other activities, do not the calls for increased faculty involvement in economic development exacerbate the nature of the trade-offs? Not necessarily. The most highly visible direct contributions to the economy—research alliances between large corporations and major research universities—account for only a tiny portion of the impact of higher education on the economy. Many, perhaps most, of these contributions are made by colleges and universities and their faculty through traditional endeavors such as teaching, continuing education, and research. I review the broad array of contributions made by higher education to the economy in this chapter.

## HIGHER EDUCATION AND THE ECONOMY

The multimillion dollar research agreements between a few elite research universities and major international corporations, developed in the 1980s, have come for many to symbolize the involvement of higher education in the economy. For many individuals, the liaison between Washington University and Monsanto Corporation and the high-technology consortia at Stanford University and at the University of Texas, to name but a few, have defined the manner in which colleges and universities contribute to the American economy. The emphases in these relationships are on research, technology transfer, and placing the leading scientists from academe and industry together in the pursuit of breakthroughs in high technology for the benefit of the economic competitiveness of the nation.

Many state governments have backed these alliances enthusiastically. Some state economic development plans now focus heavily on the encouragement of high technology through industry–higher education partnerships.[1] The number of colleges and universities pledging to enhance economic development through partnerships with industry has expanded dramatically.[2] Federal support through the National Science Foundation's Engineering Research Centers and other mechanisms continue to encourage industry–university collaboration in high technology ventures.

Yet these highly visible research partnerships are not representative of the full range of roles of different kinds of higher-education institutions in the economy, nor do they accurately portray the involvement of different types of industry in academe. Industry support of university research did not start with the collaborative research agreements in the 1980s. Industry has supported academic science since the early 1900s, primarily to gain access to faculty expertise, to have a window on new technology, and to locate potential employees. The pursuit of research by academic institutions always has been dependent on external sources; industry is simply one source among many which college and university faculty turn to for support.[3] Beyond funding, these research agreements account for only a small portion of college and university involvement in the economy (although increasingly important in an era of declining federal funding for research).[4] The portrayal of applied research and technology transfer as the principal contributions of industry–higher education liaisons to the economy is oversimplified. It ignores the multifaceted nature of economic development and technology transfer, and the complex roles that colleges and universities and industry play in them. It also ignores other economic contributions made by colleges and universities which are not aimed directly at economic development.

The evolutionary, or perhaps revolutionary, change that *does* characterize recent academic endeavors is the shift in outcomes from research productivity toward commercialization:[5]

> Colleges and universities are in the business of educating students and producing knowledge. The pursuit of commercial activities is a fundamental strategy change and must be seen in that way. For ex-

ample, developing a college-owned asset because of its revenue potential or entering into a joint venture with a corporation for the purpose of generating a profit is not a "business as usual" activity.[6]

Geiger claims that this shift reflects the resource dependence of academic institutions, primarily research universities, which must find additional revenues for research as federal support declines.[7] Equally likely, however, is simply the continued motivation to enhance prestige by increasing research funding even if the endeavor is carried out under the guise of economic development. If true, the pursuit of prestige would explain the increasing number of nonresearch colleges and universities seeking partnerships with industry.[8]

The pursuit-of-prestige hypothesis also seems supported by research on the effectiveness of industry–university collaboration in achieving positive economic benefits. Using publication and faculty research productivity as criteria, the partnerships between business and higher education have been successful.[9] If economic development through commercialization is the criterion, industry–university research partnerships have had little success.[10] Highly touted technology transfer mechanisms such as research parks have spotted histories.[11] Even in the few cases where commercial benefits can be shown, industry–university partnerships do not appear cost-effective.[12]

In this chapter, I examine the economic development agenda for colleges and universities. Next, the various types of academic activities related to economic development are described. I conclude with a discussion of the types of institutions involved in economic development, and a summary of the various roles of higher education in the economy.

## THE ECONOMIC DEVELOPMENT AGENDA

I refer to the economic development agenda for colleges and universities as activities meant to enhance visibly and directly the economy of a particular region or locality, or in the case of elite institutions the economy of the nation, *which require some involvement by faculty*. Typically, these efforts are in concert with participants from industry.[13] Broadly speaking, the "economic development agenda" for academic institutions, whether initiated by institutional leaders or envisioned by state officials, is not an agenda at all. The illusion of careful planning engendered by state economic development plans, such as the Ben Franklin Partnership in Pennsylvania, confronts the reality of academic institutions serving multiple purposes, responding to competing external demands, and competing with other institutions for resources. Critics of the apparent inertia of academe, including individuals and groups concerned with the urgent need to respond to a new economic world, often assume that academic institutions constitute a "system" that can be strategically aimed to accomplish straightforward goals. Instead, colleges and universities compete for resources and struggle to meet societal expectations while simultaneously achieving the professional goals of faculty.[14]

This misconception can lead to unwarranted expectations and inappropriate criteria for success. Many state strategic investment plans that encourage colleges and universities to participate actively in technology transfer and product development assume that benefits will accrue to the immediate locality, region, or state. This view of a "localized economy" is ill conceived and can lead to great disappointment. Consider the recent example of the biotechnology center at Michigan State University, which was established in the early 1980s with state funds earmarked specifically for technology transfer and product development.[15] The center was successful in attracting qualified faculty and in decreasing the time between the basic research discoveries and actual product development for pharmaceuticals. Because knowledge is not geographically bound and because manufacturing capacity is as crucial as product development to achieve economic benefits, the primary beneficiaries of the Michigan State center's research findings were in other states, namely New Jersey, Indiana, and Illinois, which house the majority of the pharmaceutical industry. Finding the biotechnology center a failure in terms of *state* economic development, the legislature decreased funding. The center today is primarily a real estate investment, housing a restaurant and other service enterprises.[16]

In part, recent strategies to enhance economic development, particularly by states, have been limited by visions of big payoffs from investments in high risk industry–university research ventures. This perspective ignores the complexity of economic development and the limited role of academic institutions in it. State policymakers—and universities themselves—must recognize that economic development is a complex process in which academic institutions contribute only part of the necessary elements for success. For example, the development of high technology start-up companies in a region requires a source of high-quality science, vehicles to translate science into commercializable technology, quality management and technical talent, seed and venture capital, affordable commercial and industrial space, a network of specialized support services (e.g., patent attorneys, marketing specialists), and perhaps most important, a culture of entrepreneurship.

Colleges and universities are (or can be) excellent sources of scientific and human talent. They cannot be expected to provide many of the other ingredients essential to high technology start-up companies. It is the lack of a complete package of talents and services that explains the failure of many state and local governments, indeed of colleges and universities, to replicate Silicon Valley or Route 128. In sum, disappointment in college or university involvement in economic development can be a function of naive economic analysis and strategy by state and local policymakers, and/or academic institutions promising more than they can deliver to attract additional revenue.

Beyond questions of capacity are the narrow conceptions of the roles of colleges and universities and their faculty in local and regional economies. In particular, the contributions of higher education encompass far more than high technology start-up companies and multimillion dollar research agreements. The wide array of contributions of academe to the economy encompasses *education and training*, *research*, and *technology transfer*.

## CONTRIBUTIONS TO THE ECONOMY

### Education and Training

**Traditional Functions**

Postsecondary institutions of all types, ranging from community colleges to elite universities, contribute to economic development through substantive training and certification, both of which are required for entry into the workplace. In addition to the more prestigious degree programs in science and engineering, education and training also focus on basic skills in writing and mathematics, which are the foundation of any trained workforce. Preparation in more advanced skills such as critical thinking and problem solving increasingly are required for the majority of positions in industry, regardless of degree.

Although largely unrecognized by individuals charged with hiring technical professionals, traditional liberal-arts degree programs are increasingly relevant to the modern economy. Training in foreign languages and cultural understanding is fundamental to competitive success in a global economy. Adding liberal arts courses to degree programs for students in technology fields, such as engineering, may enhance the development of creative problem-solving abilities.[17]

The preparation of youth for adulthood, whether through skills enhancement or through broad exposure to different sources of knowledge, is inevitably tied to the future of the economy. In this context, the dependency between higher education and the economy can only grow, as increased societal complexity requires a workforce able to think creatively, make independent judgments, solve problems, and use advanced technologies.

Learning does not stop with degree completion, however. Original degree programs often are inadequate preparation for a career, particularly in a global, knowledge-based economy where occupations change radically over time. The changes in electrical engineering from dependence on vacuum tubes to microchips exemplify "half-life" in the educational context; that is, the preparation in the original degree program is sufficient only for a few years until the discipline evolves. Even in library sciences, once associated solely with cataloguing books, the ability to use word processing and operate computerized data bases have become standard skills. In this context, academic institutions make important contributions to the economy through continuing professional education.

Continuing education seems an ideal meeting ground for industry and higher education.[18] Colleges make courses and degree programs available to employed individuals, while industry often includes personnel exchanges for faculty and students as part of collaborative components of research agreements.[19] Yet for the most part, 4-year colleges and universities have relegated continuing education to the periphery or have attempted to make continuing education a traditional formal degree program.[20] The evolution of continuing education at the University of California–Berkeley is a typical example, in which the service mission has been partially sacrificed in favor of postgraduate "certificate" programs to attain credibility for continuing education programs.[21] Left to its own devices, industry has sought alternative sources for continuing education, including national associations, proprietary schools, individual consultants, and corporate "universities."[22] Industry also has expanded its internal capacity for education and training: at least 18 corporations now offer accredited degree programs. Often these programs are seen as more sophisticated than comparable ones in universities.[23]

### Emerging Functions

Additional educational and training needs, each with distinct economic and social implications, confront postsecondary education in the coming decades. These include (a) literacy and the elementary/secondary–higher education connection, (b) demographic shifts and access, and (c) the increasing pace of change in workforce skills and its implications for postsecondary curricula.

### Literacy and the Elementary/
### Secondary–Higher Education Connection

Although less prestigious than research alliances with industry, a primary contributor to healthy local and regional economies is a literate workforce, particularly in service-industry jobs.[24] Many high-technology initiatives emphasize the development of doctoral programs in a handful of elite institutions, addressing a highly trained but relatively small proportion of the workforce. Even continuing professional education programs typically address retraining for well-educated but out-of-date professionals. Yet economic needs are not always fully met by improvements in high technology or in traditional education and training functions alone. The State of Maryland initiated high-technology initiatives in the mid–1980s that emphasized adding specialty research programs in engineering and technology to spur growth in the state. Universities and special research institutes, particularly those that had achieved or aspired to research greatness, received the majority of funding under this plan. The economy of the major metropolitan region in the state, however, was in many respects more threatened by the lack of a literate workforce in its service industry than by the lack of a highly trained workforce in engineering, science, and technology. The inner-city school system and local community college upon which local industry relies has been ineffective in increasing the literacy rate among inner-city youth. A more effective and relevant strategy for maintaining economic health might have been to focus on increasing literacy, either through the secondary schools or through community colleges, neither of which was targeted for significant enhancement in the original state efforts.[25]

In this context, the relationships between elementary/secondary schools and their postsecondary counterparts need reexamining. To what extent can postsecondary institutions resolve remedial problems while simultaneously providing graduate education and training in advanced thinking skills? Is it sufficient for a college or university to "adopt a school," or must postsecondary institutions play more active roles in the transition from high school to colleges and universities? The latter question is particularly important for the highest-risk groups, for which the traditional assumption that high school completion leads to college attendance does not seem to hold true.[26] It is especially important to remember that colleges and schools of education train virtually all elementary/secondary teachers. How well colleges and universities perform this training task directly affects the quality of learning in earlier grades.

### Demographic Shifts and Access
Youth from racial and ethnic minority groups, many of which are at risk in the postsecondary system, will make up a larger percentage of the population and the workforce in the near future.[27] In California and Texas, the so-called minorities already constitute the *majority* of elementary school children.[28] Economic survival depends as much on bringing these youth into the mainstream of the educational system as it does on research and technology transfer.

### Change in Workforce Skills: Curricular Implications
Educational programs, whether offered by industry or by higher education, must prepare students with the skills needed for the economy of the future. Simply offering traditional education and training is not sufficient. Instead, revising curricula to meet changing needs and rapidly changing technologies is required. The feedback mechanisms between industry and higher education and the ability of colleges and universities to adapt curricula in light of the changing economy are weak. As an example, IBM has offered a one-year

course for computer science graduates, not to train them as new employees but to add crucial knowledge that should have been part of their undergraduate coursework.[29] Indeed, IBM offered computer science training in the corporate workplace long before any college or university established a computer science degree program.

In professional fields, the combination of having too much material to place in a four- or even five-year curriculum creates student overload and prevents all but the smallest of curricular changes. In engineering, for example, in spite of faculty approval in principle, reintroducing design into the curriculum has proved a major difficulty because agreement is lacking on what to leave out. Today it is possible to graduate with a degree in computer engineering without having practical design experience with computers.[30]

## Research

Research receives more publicity as a component of economic development than education and training: "Although the majority of industry–education relationships deal with education and training, the majority of industrial funds universities receive go to academic research."[31] This emphasis is partly a function of the higher prestige of research in academe, and partly a result of the high visibility of the industry–university alliances promoted by state and federal policies. Industry-funded academic research typically emphasizes *applied* rather than *basic* research.[32] Industry–higher education research agreements emphasize arenas most likely to show commercial benefit, including agriculture, biotechnology, chemistry, computer science, engineering, and medicine.[33]

Although contributing a small piece of the total investment in academic research and development—6.6 percent in 1989—industry has doubled its investment since 1975.[34] The investment in particular academic disciplines is much greater.[35] About half of all companies that work in biotechnology have a research arrangement with universities, accounting for about one-quarter of all university funding for biotechnology.[36]

The most common form of technology agreement between industry and higher education is not an agreement between institutions but an arrangement with individual professors to consult. Industry also funds grants and contracts. More recent research arrangements include multidisciplinary research centers and institutes.[37]

## Technology Transfer Mechanisms

According to Tornatzky and Fleisher, technology transfer, not education and training or basic research, is the key to effective commercialization and the health of the economy.[38] Consistent with this perspective, many state programs envision a more active role for academe in economic development through alliances with industry.[39] Some academic leaders counter by claiming that faculty involvement in publishing, conferences, extension programs, and advisory councils for industry contributes to technology transfer, but these approaches are not consistent with an interactive, market-driven model.[40] Other technology transfer mechanisms, now well-established, include industrial affiliate programs in which corporations contribute funds to gain access to university research and talent, and research parks.[41]

With the exception of a handful of institutions which have adopted an entrepreneurial culture and where other ingredients for technology transfer are present, these traditional technology transfer programs have not adequately enhanced product development, according to Tornatzky and Fleisher.[42] Many academic institutions have responded with more active approaches to commercialization.[43] According to Fairweather,

> These innovations include the use of industrial incubators to develop new companies; private patent companies to secure rights for sale; expanded university research offices to monitor and promote licensing of technology to industry; research and development limited partnerships where a university contracts with a particular corporation to develop products from faculty research findings; nonprofit organizations (e.g., Wisconsin Alumni Research Fund, Brown University Research Fund); independent for-profit entities originated by universities (e.g., Michigan Research Corporation); for-profit joint ventures, often including participation by venture capital firms; and wholly-owned subsidiaries (e.g., Washington University Technology Associates, Case Western University Technology Inc.).[44]

Despite the appeal of active participation in technology transfer through commercialization, the economic benefits of these programs is not proved.[45] The DOME Corporation at Johns Hopkins University provides an example of the difficulty of these "bridging mechanisms" in promoting economic development. DOME was created by Johns Hopkins University and Johns Hopkins Hospital to manage the business aspects of the university and hospital, ranging from parking and home health care to technology transfer and a research park. DOME established TRIAD Ventures to promote technology transfer. TRIAD sought to develop a venture capital fund to commercialize Johns Hopkins technology through a process called "discovery management." The goal was to promote the commercialization of academic research without threatening traditional academic functions. The staff of TRIAD were to examine research findings produced by faculty, determine which research findings had commercial potential, secure the investment required, and take responsibility for commercialization either through licensing or by recruiting a team to organize a new company. In this manner, faculty researchers would be somewhat removed from the commercialization process, enabling them to continue with their university responsibilities without conflict of interest.

Although DOME initially was viewed as an ideal mechanism for preserving academic integrity while promoting technology transfer, it failed. The venture fund had difficulty attaining capital, and the skills required to make the bridging mechanism work were in short supply. Above all, the failure of DOME and TRIAD Ventures illuminates the inappropriateness of a university's attempting to take on a highly specialized for-profit business function, namely venture capital investment and new company formation. The desire of the university to protect its integrity and traditional functions made commercialization impractical.[46] Fortunately, the leadership at Johns Hopkins has restructured TRIAD, turning it over to private sector management. New policies were established to recognize the reality of conflict between academic and commercial interests, and to establish reasonable processes for managing this conflict. Today, TRIAD is much better situated to take advantage of the original promise of DOME than the earlier manifestation.

## Fit with Institutional Incentives and Faculty Rewards

Technology transfer, the process for converting knowledge into a product or service, is a prerequisite for achieving utility in academic research. In this context, the success of the contribution by higher education to technology transfer depends largely on the involvement of faculty.[47] Whether achieved through consulting, scientific invention, or assisting in product development, faculty are the key academic resource in making technology transfer work. One hypothesis for the limited demonstrable success to date of higher education in technology transfer, particularly when commercialization of products is the outcome, is the inadequacy of the mechanism. Tornatzky and Fleisher, Lynton and Elman, and the Office of Science and Technology Policy among others view the reliance of academics on consulting and publishing as being inadequate to decrease the time between idea, invention, and production.[48] From this perspective, newer, more commercially oriented approaches are needed. Academic institutions, including but not limited to research universities, have responded by adding industrial affiliate programs, building research parks, establishing patenting offices, and forming liaisons with venture capital firms. Yet the effectiveness of these newer mechanisms also has been questioned.[49]

To redress the claimed inadequacy of technology transfer, recommendations for change typically focus on organizational structure and institutional policies. Establishing nondepartmental units to promote interdisciplinary research[50] and developing contractual mechanisms to identify and resolve conflicts of interest and to protect academic freedom[51] are common recommendations to improve the effectiveness of technology transfer. The assumption here is that administrative structures and contractual devices ensure the overlap of academic and corporate interests, and assist academic leaders in developing successful strategies for technology transfer.[52]

I believe attention has been concentrated too heavily on the structure and administration of technology transfer. Instead, more attention to the likely acceptance of and participation by faculty, who are the crucial resource in higher education's participation in technology transfer, and to academic cultures, created and reinforced by faculty and administrators alike, is warranted. In particular, I believe that academic institutions—faculty and administrators—should encourage faculty to participate in activities that promote the *public* good rather than simply encouraging *private* gain. These activities might include individual faculty consulting arrangements to promote technology transfer as an alternative to cumbersome, expensive technology transfer entities (e.g., research parks). Also relevant is faculty participation in continuing education, and in reforming curricula to meet changing societal needs.

## PARTICIPATING INSTITUTIONS

The high-technology research arrangements between industry and higher education have contributed to another misconception, namely that prestigious research universities are the only academic institutions which contribute to the economy. Research universities, by definition, receive the majority of federal funds for research.[53] They house the majority of research alliances with industry and most of the National Science Foundation's Engineering Research Centers.[54] However, the national focus of research by faculty in these institutions makes them potentially ill suited for regional and local economic initiatives.[55] Other types of 4-year colleges, especially comprehensive institutions which offer master's degree programs, can and do play substantial roles in regional economic development, primarily through education and training and through technical assistance to local companies.[56]

Also overlooked are the substantial ties between industry and community colleges, and the economic contributions made by these institutions through personnel development and training.[57] Community colleges are especially important to local and regional economies. Typical relationships with industry include seeking advice from industrial leaders to assist in reforming curricula, offering employee training programs, working with local economic development offices, and retraining workers.[58]

## SUMMARY

The research-oriented reward structure in many 4-year institutions and the emphasis on research alliances between elite universities and major corporations combine to paint a misleading picture of the contributions of higher education to the economy, one which can prove harmful. I close this section with two examples of strategies that have affected local and regional economies adversely, one based on a study of a regional comprehensive institution and the other based on a study of state economic development policies. The regional comprehensive institution, located in the upper Midwest, was founded as a teachers' college. Its mission was to serve the population in the southwestern portion of the state. Six years ago, a newly appointed president decided to enhance institutional prestige (and state funding) by increasing the value of research in the faculty reward structure and deemphasizing service and teaching. Doctoral programs were added and resources reallocated in line with the new policies. As a consequence, the College of Education was reduced from 65 faculty to 29, effectively removing the capacity for in-service teacher training. By reducing the capacity to enhance the quality of practicing teachers and by removing a local source of information and support from the regional teaching community, the new policies could accentuate regional economic difficulties which result from inadequate preparation of students in local secondary schools. This institution serves as an example of moving away from meeting societal needs, instead responding to internally motivated norms that emphasize research and prestige.

In a state in the mid-Atlantic region, the legislature enacted programs based on the premise that the development of new doctoral programs in high technology fields and university involvement in technology transfer through research parks were crucial to attract new industry to the state. The high technology industries being courted did not need access to doctoral programs; Ph.D.'s could be recruited nationwide. Instead, these industries needed access to continuing professional education and to a source of well-trained technicians. The high technology industries eventually located in another state which had stronger educational capacity in continuing education.[59] This example shows that external constituencies also can contribute to the pursuit of research and prestige by directing the allocation of funds and the creation of doctoral programs.

I believe the heart of the matter lies in understanding that *good teaching enhances the economy in a variety of ways,* and that *enhancing teaching requires clarifying institutional missions, developing enlightened leadership strategies, understanding (and confronting) faculty motivation, and reforming the faculty reward structure.* If research and scholarship have replaced teaching, curricular reform, and service to the extent suggested by many authors,[60] then programs of corrective action must inevitably fail without changes to the incentives for faculty behavior. In an era when faculty at land grant institutions are virtually indistinguishable from their counterparts in private research universities,[61] and when comprehensive and doctoral-granting institutions seek to emulate their research brethren, refocusing faculty incentive systems may be the most crucial act of all.

## NOTES

1. Public Policy Center, SRI International, *The Higher Education–Economic Development Connection: Emerging Roles for Public Colleges and Universities* (Washington, D.C.: American Association of State Colleges and Universities, 1986).
2. R. L. Geiger, "Milking the Sacred Cow: Research and the Quest for Useful Knowledge in the American University since 1920," *Science, Technology and Human Values*, 13 (1988): 332–48; National Science Foundation, *University–Industry Research Relationships: Myths, Realities, and Potentials* (Washington, D.C.: National Science Foundation, 1982); L. Peters and H. Fusfeld, "Current U.S. University/Industry Research Connections," in *University–Industry Research Relationships: Selected Studies* (Washington, D.C.: National Science Foundation, 1983), 1–162.
3. R. L. Geiger, "The Ambiguous Link: Private Industry and University Research," in *The Economics of Higher Education*, ed. W. E. Becker and D. R. Lewis (Boston: Kluwer, 1992), 266.
4. J. S. Fairweather, "Education: The Forgotten Element in Industry–University Relationships," *Review of Higher Education*, 14 (1990): 33–43.
5. Association of American Universities, *Trends in Technology Transfer at Universities* (Washington, D.C.: Association of American Universities, 1986).
6. R. E. Anderson, "The Advantages and Risks of Entrepreneurship," *Academe*, 76 (1990): 11.
7. Geiger, "The Ambiguous Link."
8. J. S. Fairweather, *Entrepreneurship and Higher Education: Lessons for Colleges, Universities, and Industry*, ASHE-ERIC Higher Education Research Report No. 6 (Washington, D.C.: Association for the Study of Higher Education, 1988).
9. D. Gray, T. Gidley, and N. Koester, "Outcomes of Participation in Industry–University Cooperative Research Centers," paper presented at the IUCDC Evaluator's Meeting, Arlington, Va., 1988.
10. Geiger, "The Ambiguous Link"; G. W. Matkin, *Technology Transfer and the University* (New York: ACE/Macmillan, 1990), 252; S. Slaughter, *The Higher Learning and High Technology: Dynamics of Higher Education Policy Formation* (Albany, N.Y.: State University of New York Press, 1990); R. Stankiewicz, *Academics and Entrepreneurs: Developing University–Industry Relations* (London: Frances Pinter, 1986).
11. D. R. Powers, M. F. Powers, F. Betz, and C. B. Aslanian, *Higher Education in Partnership with Industry: Opportunities for Training, Research, and Economic Development* (San Francisco: Jossey–Bass, 1988).

12. D. Blumenthal, S. Epstein, and J. Maxwell, "Commercializing University Research: Lessons from the Experience of the Wisconsin Alumni Research Fund," *New England Journal of Medicine*, 314 (1986): 1621–6.

13. For a thorough discussion of the contributions of higher education to the economy, see L. L. Leslie and P. T. Brinkman, *The Economic Value of Higher Education* (New York: ACE/MacMillan, 1988).

14. D. Alpert, "Performance and Paralysis: The Organizational Context of the American Research University," *Journal of Higher Education*, 56 (1985): 241–81; B.R. Clark, *The Higher Education System* (Berkeley, Calif.: University of California Press, 1983).

15. Public Policy Center, *The Higher Education–Economic Development Connection*.

16. J. S. Fairweather, "Higher Education and the Economy: From Social Good to Economic Development to ...," paper presented at the Annual Meeting of the Western Interstate Commission on Higher Education, Seattle, Wash., 1991.

17. National Research Council, *Engineering Education and Practice in the United States: Foundations of our Techno–economic Future* (Washington, D.C.: National Academy Press, 1985).

18. H. Brooks, "Seeking Equity and Efficiency: Public and Private Roles," in *Public–private Partnership: New Opportunities for Meeting Social Needs*, ed. H. Brooks, L. Liebman, and C. Schelling (Cambridge, Mass.: Ballinger, 1984), 3–30; National Research Council, *Engineering Education and Practice in the United States: Continuing Education of Engineers* (Washington, D.C.: National Academy Press, 1985), 51.

19. Business–Higher Education Forum, *Corporate and Campus Cooperation: An Action Agenda* (Washington, D.C.: Business–Higher Education Forum, 1984), 11–19; L. G. Johnson, *The High–Technology Connection: Academic/Industrial Cooperation for Economic Growth*, ASHE–ERIC Higher Education Research Report No. 6 (Washington, D.C.: Association for the Study of Higher Education, 1984), 25–37.

20. J. Stark, M. Lowther, and B. Hagerty, "Faculty Roles and Role Preferences in Ten Fields of Professional Study," *Research in Higher Education*, 25 (1986), 69.

21. K. Rockhill, *Academic Excellence and Public Service* (New Brunswick, N.J.: Transaction Books, 1983), 225.

22. C. Houle, *Continuing Learning in the Professions* (San Francisco: Jossey-Bass, 1980), 167–99.

23. N. P. Eurich, *Corporate Classrooms: The Learning Business* (Princeton, N.J.: Carnegie Foundation for the Advancement of Teaching, 1985).

24. T. Chmura, J. Fairweather, and J. Melville, *From Bystander to Leader: Challenging Higher Education to Join in Building Baltimore's Economic Future* (Menlo Park, Calif.: SRI International, 1988).

25. Chmura, Fairweather, and Melville, *From Bystander to Leader*.

26. For example, J. S. Fairweather and D. M. Shaver, "A Troubled Future? Participation in Postsecondary Education for Youth with Disabilities," *Journal of Higher Education*, 61 (1990): 332–48.

27. Public Policy Center, *The Higher Education–Economic Development Connection*.

28. K. M. Albert, W. B. Hull, and D. M. Sprague, *The Dynamic West: A Region in Transition* (Denver: The Council of State Governments, 1989).

29. J. S. Fairweather and M. P. Hancock, *Quality and Recruitment Desirability of Selected Programs in Engineering, Computer Science, and Business* (Menlo Park, Calif.: SRI International, 1987).
30. See Chapter 5 for a discussion of change in engineering curricula.
31. Fairweather, "Education," 36.
32. Peters and Fusfeld, "Current U.S. University/Industry Research Connections," 37.
33. Peters and Fusfeld, "Current U.S. University/Industry Research Connections," 20.
34. National Science Foundation, *National Patterns of R&D Resources: 1989* (Washinton, D.C.: National Science Foundation, 1989).
35. National Science Board, *Science and Engineering Indicators, 1987* (Washington, D.C.: National Science Board, 1987).
36. D. Blumenthal, M. Gluck, K. Louis, M. Stoto, and D. Wise, "University–Industry Research Relationships in Biotechnology: Implications for the University," *Science*, 232 (1986), 1361; M. Kenney, *Biotechnology: The University–Industrial Complex* (New Haven, Conn.: Yale University Press, 1986).
37. Business–Higher Education Forum, *Corporate and Campus Cooperation*, 11–19; Johnson, *The High–Technology Connection*, 54–68.
38. L. G. Tornatzky and M. Fleisher, *The Process of Technological Innovation* (Lexington, Mass.: Lexington Books, 1990).
39. I. Feller, "Political and Administrative Aspects of State High Technology Programs," *Policy Studies Review*, 3 (1984): 460–6; C. S. Lenth, *State Priorities in Higher Education: 1990* (Denver: State Higher Education Executive Officers and the Education Commission of the States, 1990).
40. Geiger, "Milking the Sacred Cow."
41. Johnson, *The High–Technology Connection*, 54–68.
42. Tornatzky and Fleisher, *The Process of Technological Innovation*.
43. J. W. Bartlett and J. V. Siena, "Research and Development Limited Partnerships as a Device to Exploit University Owned Technology," *Journal of College and University Law*, 10 (1983–84): 434–54; Geiger, "The Ambiguous Link."
44. Fairweather, "Education," 37–8.
45. Matkin, *Technology Transfer and the University*, 252.
46. Chmura, Fairweather, and Melville, *From Bystander to Leader*.
47. Government–University–Industry Research Roundtable, *New Alliances and Partnerships in American Science and Engineering* (Washington, D.C.: National Academy Press, 1986).
48. Tornatzky and Fleisher, *The Process of Technological Innovation*; E. A. Lynton and S. E. Elman, *New Priorities for the University* (San Francisco: Jossey–Bass, 1987); Office of Science and Technology Policy, *A Renewed Partnership: Report of the White House Science Council Panel on the Health of U.S. Colleges and Universities* (Washington, D.C.: Office of Science and Technology Policy, 1986).
49. Geiger, "The Ambiguous Link."
50. R. L. Geiger, "Organized Research Units—Their Role in the Development of University Research," *Journal of Higher Education*, 61 (1990): 1–19.

51.  D. Bok, *Beyond the Ivory Tower* (Cambridge, Mass.: Harvard University Press, 1982); D. S. Tatel and R. Guthrie, "The Legal Ins and Outs of University–Industry Collaboration," *Educational Record*, 64 (1983): 19–25.

52.  M. J. Dooris and J. S. Fairweather, "Structure and Culture in Faculty Work: Implications for Technology Transfer," *Review of Higher Education*, 17 (1994): 161–78.

53.  Carnegie Foundation for the Advancement of Teaching, *A Classification of Institutions of Higher Education* (Princeton, N.J.: Carnegie Foundation for the Advancement of Teaching, 1987).

54.  J. A. Haddad, "New Factors in the Relationship between Engineering Education and Research," in *The New Engineering Research Centers: Purposes, Goals, and Expectations* (Washington, D.C.: National Academy Press, 1986), 129–36; Peters and Fusfeld, "Current U.S. University/Industry Research Connections."

55.  I. Feller, "University-Industry Research and Development Relationships," paper prepared for the Woodlands Center for Growth Studies Conference, Houston, Tex., 1988.

56.  L. B. Logan and J. O. Stampen, "Smoke Stack Meets Ivory Tower: Collaborations with Local Industry," *Educational Record*, 66 (1985): 26–9; Public Policy Center, *The Higher Education–Economic Development Connection*.

57.  D. Parnell and R. Yarrington, *Proven Partners: Business, Labor, and Community Colleges* (Washington, D.C.: American Association of Community and Junior Colleges, 1982).

58.  Fairweather, *Entrepreneurship and Higher Education*, 29–30.

59.  M. Kane and J. S. Fairweather, *Issues in the Preparation of Special Education Teachers* (Washington, D.C.: Pelavin Associates, 1988).

60.  For example, H. R. Bowen and J. H. Schuster, *American Professors: A National Resource Imperiled* (New York: Oxford University Press, 1986).

61.  G. E. Schuh, "Revitalizing Land Grant Universities: It's Time to Regain Relevance," *Choices* (1986): 6–10.

# ▶ 8

## Traditional Knowledge and Technology Transfer

Faculty consulting and the investment by industry in academic research are two traditional forms that colleges and universities use to involve faculty in knowledge and technology transfer. Although these are widely accepted practices, are they effective either in promoting technology transfer or in enhancing the value of public service within faculty work life? In this chapter, I examine the potential effectiveness of these traditional mechanisms of involving faculty in knowledge and technology transfer and study their consistency with research- and prestige-oriented norms versus more innovative concepts of faculty roles.

I use survey data on faculty consulting and on industrial investment in faculty research to answer three policy questions:

- How useful are consulting and industrially- funded research in technology transfer?
- Does involvement with industry adversely affect traditional academic functions?
- Are current faculty reward structures consistent with technology transfer?

## TECHNOLOGY TRANSFER AND FACULTY REWARDS

Geiger classifies university involvements in technology transfer as either gnostic (i.e., traditional) or commercial.[1] The former are activities which fit mainstream academic practice and the old-fashioned linear model of technology transfer, such as publishing and consulting. The latter encourage more active participation in venture capital arrangements, patenting, and so on. In Table 8.1, I start by dividing technology transfer activities into traditional and commercial types. Next, using literature and empirical evidence already cited, I first evaluate each activity according to *perceived institutional benefits*. These include *financial gain, political benefits,* and *enhanced prestige*. Financial gain and political benefits are outcomes consistent with resource dependence,[2] and enhanced prestige is derived from the role of status in institutional drift.[3] Each activity is then assessed according to *perceived value in the faculty reward structure* (high, moderate, low).

## Perceived Institutional Benefits

Academic institutions pursue technology transfer to meet obligations to society. Yet in an era of contracting resources, 4-year colleges and universities pursue commercial forms of technology transfer with the expectation of financial gain. Some institutions also make money from continuing educa-

**TABLE 8.1**  Technology Transfer Mechanisms, by Resource Dependence and Status

| | Perceived Institutional Benefits | | | Perceived Value in Faculty Reward Structure |
|---|---|---|---|---|
| | Financial Gain | Political Benefits | Enhanced Prestige | |
| *Traditional* | | | | |
| Teaching | No | No | No | Moderate |
| Continuing Education | Yes | No | No | Low |
| Publishing | No | No | Yes | High |
| Research Grants | Yes | No | Yes | High |
| Conferences | No | No | Unknown | Moderate |
| Consulting | No | Yes | Yes | Moderate |
| Personnel Exchange | No | No | No | Low |
| Other Public Service | No | No | No | Low |
| *Commercial* | | | | |
| Research Parks | Yes | Yes | No | Low |
| Industrial Affiliates | Yes | Yes | No | Low |
| Incubators | Yes | Yes | No | Low |
| Patenting | Yes | Yes | No | Unknown |
| R&D Partnerships | Yes | Yes | No | Low |
| For-Profit Mechanism | Yes | Yes | No | Low |

tion programs, and research grants are an important additional source of revenue (especially in light of increased competition for federal research
monies). In addition, commercially oriented endeavors are viewed as sources
of political benefit, particularly as a demonstration of responsiveness to societal needs. The presumption is that "political capital" can be used to generate
additional resources in state budget processes or can assist private institutions in obtaining federal research monies.

Historically, financial and political gain are not necessarily related to
institutional prestige, however. Ratings of the quality of academic programs
typically rest on measures of faculty research productivity, including
research dollars generated and publications; percentage of faculty holding
the Ph.D.; student test scores; and acceptance rates.[4] In this context, publishing and research grants, two traditional vehicles for technology transfer, are
measures which colleges and universities use to assess their change in status
and prestige.

## Perceived Value in Faculty Reward Structure

Traditional approaches to technology transfer may be consistent with academic tradition, but many have low value in faculty reward structures. Publishing and research have high payoffs for faculty promotion and tenure.
Teaching, presenting papers at conferences, and consulting also count to
some extent. Continuing education, personnel exchanges with industry, and
other forms of public service often have limited value.[5] Similarly, none of the
more commercial forms of technology transfer to date have demonstrable
value in faculty rewards with the possible exception of patenting.

The value attached to research and publishing make it difficult for
administrative strategies to alter faculty behavior in favor of many of the
newer forms of technology transfer: "Developing specific policies may send
a signal [to encourage entrepreneurship], but the organization is basically
very dependent on behavioral expectations that are reinforced [from]
below."[6] Creating administrative devices such as organized research units
may provide a buffer between faculty and industry, thus preserving some
integrity of academic missions, but this strategy does not fundamentally alter
the incentives to which faculty respond.[7] The forms of technology transfer
accepted and supported by academic leaders historically have been the ones
most likely to enhance prestige through the research reputations of individual faculty rather than to meet emerging societal needs. Indeed, faculty
devoting a high percentage of their time to less mainstream knowledge and
technology transfer activities, such as working with new companies and even
participating in personnel exchanges with industry, may be at risk in promotion and tenure decisions. In the remainder of this chapter, I examine the two
most commonly accepted forms of faculty involvement in technology trans-

fer, consulting and carrying out research supported by industry. I examine whether administrators can trust these traditional forms of faculty involvement in technology transfer to meet increased demands for the involvement of higher education in the economy.

## CONSULTING

Although today the multiyear, multimillion dollar research agreements between industry and elite universities may receive the most attention, faculty entrepreneurial activity has a long history through individual consulting.[8] Faculty whose research is supported by industry also can be seen as participants in technology transfer, whether directly through working with industry or indirectly through generating useful knowledge and training future members of the workforce.[9] Bird and Allen, and Boyer and Lewis argued that faculty consulting is a form of entrepreneurship because it reduces communication barriers with industry, promotes technology transfer, and can lead directly to product development.[10] Bird and Allen are careful to distinguish consulting activity from traditional academic research: "the principal investigator mentality (characterized by collegial behavior and control over the research agenda) vastly differs from the entrepreneurial mentality."[11]

Unlike research funded by industry, consulting often is thought of as a public service activity. In particular, consulting is justified because "it strengthens the university's presence in, and service commitment to, the broader community."[12] Yet precisely because of its designation as "service," in most fields consulting is not highly valued;[13] service tends to be an afterthought in a reward structure which emphasizes research and teaching.[14]

The primary cost to academic institutions of allowing faculty to consult is the potential for conflict of interest, particularly through avoiding regular duties while pursuing consulting activities.[15] Such concerns typically are addressed through formal university policies which place specific limits on consulting activities.[16] Most academic leaders believe the benefits of consulting outweigh the risks. Consulting benefits the individual through supplemental income and through keeping abreast of the discipline.[17] Institutions benefit from faculty consulting because the supplemental income may make faculty less likely to change positions and because consulting can enhance institutional prestige.[18] According to Boyer and Lewis, additional societal benefits accrue from consulting through technical assistance to help solve social and economic problems.[19]

The existing research on faculty consulting is too piecemeal to draw conclusions about the effectiveness of consulting in technology transfer.[20] To redress this shortcoming, I used the 1987–88 NSOPF data. For NSOPF, consulting included any paid work for legal or medical services or for psychological counseling, outside consulting, and professional performances or exhibitions.[21] In this section, I examine the distribution of the percentage of faculty with any consulting during Fall term 1987, the average percent of time spent on consulting, and the percent of total income derived from consulting.[22]

## Type of Institution

Almost 33 percent of faculty in 4-year institutions spent some time on consulting during Fall term 1987 (Table 8.2). Faculty in other 4-year institutions—predominantly engineering and medical schools—and in research universities were the most likely to spend at least some time consulting, followed by their peers in doctoral-granting and comprehensive universities. Faculty in liberal arts colleges were least likely to have spent at least some time consulting during Fall term 1987.[23] These findings are consistent with studies based on the 1975 survey by the Carnegie Foundation for the Advancement of Teaching, which showed that about 37 percent of all faculty participate in consulting.[24]

Faculty in other 4-year institutions spent about 10 percent of their total work week on outside consulting. Faculty in research universities spent about 6 percent of their working time on consulting. Their colleagues in other institutions spent less than 4 percent of their time on consulting.[25] These

**TABLE 8.2   Consulting Activity, by Type of Institution**

|                | Percent with any Consulting | Average Percent of Time, Consulting | Percent of Total Income from Consulting |
| -------------- | --------------------------- | ----------------------------------- | --------------------------------------- |
| All 4-year     | 32.6%                       | 4.8%                                | 4.6%                                    |
| SE             | .70                         | .17                                 | .16                                     |
| Research       | 37.8                        | 6.1                                 | 5.3                                     |
| SE             | 1.26                        | .35                                 | .29                                     |
| Doctoral       | 31.1                        | 3.4                                 | 4.7                                     |
| SE             | 1.65                        | .25                                 | .38                                     |
| Comprehensive  | 28.4                        | 3.6                                 | 3.5                                     |
| SE             | 1.11                        | .21                                 | .23                                     |
| Liberal Arts   | 17.8                        | 1.6                                 | 2.9                                     |
| SE             | 1.87                        | .23                                 | .46                                     |
| Other 4-year   | 46.2                        | 10.4                                | 9.1                                     |
| SE             | 4.18                        | 1.44                                | 1.46                                    |

Source: NSOPF 1988

results are consistent with previous research which found that faculty in more prestigious institutions spent the most time consulting.[26]

Consulting income does not make up a substantial portion of the total incomes of most faculty. For faculty in 4-year institutions, consulting income makes up less than 5 percent of their total compensation. This ranges from about 9 percent for faculty in other 4-year institutions to 3 percent or so for faculty in liberal arts colleges.[27] These data indicate much smaller percentages of total income derived from consulting than earlier work by Bowen and by Ladd, which indicated a contribution of 19 percent and 15 percent, respectively, of consulting to total faculty income.[28]

## Program Area

In 1987–88, faculty in the health sciences spent the most time consulting (about 13 percent). Faculty in agriculture/home economics, education, the humanities, the natural sciences, the social sciences, and other fields spent less than average amounts of time on consulting (Table 8.3).[29] Less varied is the percentage of total income derived from consulting. Faculty in agricul-

**TABLE 8.3   Consulting Activity, by Program Area: 4-Year Institutions**

| Program Area | Percent of Time Consulting | Percent of Total Income from Consulting |
|---|---|---|
| Agriculture/Home Economics | 1.6% | 2.5% |
| SE | .33 | .42 |
| Business | 4.8 | 7.0 |
| SE | .65 | .91 |
| Education | 3.6 | 3.8 |
| SE | .38 | .46 |
| Engineering | 4.1 | 5.9 |
| SE | .57 | .80 |
| Fine Arts | 4.4 | 4.8 |
| SE | .53 | .49 |
| Health Sciences | 13.3 | 6.6 |
| SE | 1.23 | .87 |
| Humanities | 1.4 | 1.4 |
| SE | .14 | .12 |
| Natural Sciences | 2.2 | 3.6 |
| SE | .24 | .44 |
| Social Sciences | 2.9 | 4.1 |
| SE | .24 | .35 |
| Other Fields | 3.0 | 4.3 |
| SE | .36 | .56 |

Source: NSOPF 1988

ture/home economics, the humanities, and the natural sciences derived less than average amounts of income from consulting (between 1 and 3½ percent); faculty in business had above-average percentages of total income from consulting (7 percent).[30]

These results partially contradict previous work summarized by Boyer and Lewis.[31] In research based on the Carnegie Foundation for the Advancement of Teaching, Ladd and Lipset, and the National Science Foundation, Boyer and Lewis found that faculty in the sciences and engineering spend the most time consulting, faculty in the humanities the least. The NSOPF data indicate that faculty in the *health* sciences spend the most time consulting, but faculty in the *natural* sciences spend *less* than average percentages of their work week consulting. Faculty in engineering spend only an average amount of their time consulting. Consistent with previous work, the NSOPF data reveal that faculty in the humanities spend the least time consulting.

## Academic Rank

Unlike the 1970s,[32] in 1987–88 faculty time spent on consulting did not vary significantly by academic rank (Table 8.4). However, in 4-year institutions associate professors earned a higher percentage of their total income from consulting than did assistant professors.[33]

## Correlates of Consulting Activity

As shown in Table 8.5, percent of time spent on consulting is positively correlated with basic salary for faculty in 4-year institutions ($r = .24$). Percent of time spent on consulting is negatively correlated with percent of time spent on teaching ($r = -.33$). The positive relationship with basic salary is consistent

**TABLE 8.4   Consulting Activity, by Academic Rank**

| Rank | Percent of Time Consulting | Percent of Total Income from Consulting |
| --- | --- | --- |
| Professor | 4.7% | 5.4% |
| SE | .24 | .27 |
| Associate | 4.7 | 4.7 |
| SE | .30 | .29 |
| Assistant | 5.1 | 3.5 |
| SE | .40 | .28 |

Source: NSOPF 1988

with previous work by Boyer and Lewis.[34] The negative relationship between consulting and time spent on teaching contradicts previous work indicating that faculty who consult teach as much as their colleagues who do not consult.[35] This may reflect a growing trend toward increased emphasis on research at the cost of time spent on teaching. (The remainder of Table 8.5 is discussed later.)

## Profile: The Top Consultant

To examine the relationships between consulting and personal demographics, workload, and productivity in more detail, I present the profile of individuals who are in the top 10 percent of faculty who spend time consulting (more than 14 percent of their time consulting, for faculty in 4-year schools). No single demographic characteristic distinguishes top consultants across types of institution (Table 8.6). Male faculty are statistically more likely to be

**TABLE 8.5   Correlates of Consulting and Receiving Funds from Industry**

| Variable | Percent of Time, Consulting | Received Research Funds from Industry |
|---|---|---|
| *Income* | | |
| Basic Income from Institution | .24 | .07 |
| *Teaching* | | |
| Percent of Time, Teaching | −.33 | −.12 |
| Student Contact Hours | .04 | .00 |
| Hours in Class/Week | .07 | −.03 |
| Taught Only Undergraduate Students | −.06 | .04 |
| Taught Only Graduate Students | .12 | .06 |
| *Research* | | |
| Percent of Time, Research | −.09 | .12 |
| Publications (career) | .09 | .09 |
| Principal Investigator | .07 | .35 |
| *Other* | | |
| Percent of Time, Administration | −.07 | .00 |
| Percent of Time, Service | −.02 | −.01 |

Source: NSOPF 1988

top consultants in research universities but not in other institutions. Doc-toral-granting institutions are the only location where minority faculty are less likely than nonminorities to be top consultants. Being younger is charac-teristic of top consultants only for other 4-year institutions.

In all institutions, top consultants spend less time teaching than their col-leagues. They do not, however, generate fewer student contact hours. At research universities, top consultants actually spend more hours in the class-room per week than their peers, but this relationship was not statistically sig-nificant at other types of institutions. In research, doctoral-granting, and comprehensive universities, top consultants spend less time on research than their colleagues. In only one type of institution—other 4-year—are top con-sultants more likely to have been a principal investigator on a funded research project. Although top consultants have slightly higher numbers of publications, in no case are the differences significant. Faculty in research and doctoral-granting institutions who consult the most spend less time on administration. Top consultants in other 4-year institutions spend less time on service. Finally, in 1987–88 top consultants received significantly higher base salaries than their less consulting-oriented colleagues in research, com-prehensive, and other 4-year universities, but not in doctoral-granting uni-versities.

Looking at percent of time spent on teaching, faculty who consult spend less time teaching than their colleagues. Using student contact hours and hours spent in class per week, however, top consultants demonstrate about the same involvement in teaching as their colleagues.

Contrary to previous work, the NSOPF data show that top consultants spend less time on research in graduate-oriented institutions than their col-leagues. The NSOPF data give no indication that faculty who spend the most time consulting publish more than other faculty, which also contradicts pre-vious research.[36] These findings suggest that time spent on any activity must come at the cost of time spent on another, even if the activities, such as research, publishing, and consulting, are related. The NSOPF data also par-tially confirm previous work that indicated that top consultants receive higher salaries,[37] although this pattern does not hold true for all types of insti-tutions.

## *Discussion*

The distribution of consulting activities has important consequences for tech-nology transfer. Consistent with broadly defined institutional missions, Boyer and Lewis found that faculty in research universities were more likely to spend their consulting time with federal agencies and national associa-tions.[38] Faculty in less prestigious, regional 4 year institutions spent more time consulting with local governments and industries. The latter types of

**TABLE 8.6   Profile of Tenure-Track, Full-time Faculty Who Spend the Most Time Consulting, by Type of Institution[a]**

| | Research Universities | | Doctoral Universities | |
|---|---|---|---|---|
| | Top 10% of Time Spent Consulting (Mean) | Other Faculty (Mean) | Top 10% of Time Spent Consulting (Mean) | Other Faculty (Mean) |
| *Demographics* | | | | |
| Minority | 12.0% | 10.2% | 1.2% | 7.8%*** |
| Male | 90.0% | 81.4%** | 83.9% | 77.0% |
| Age | 47.7 | 47.5 | 48.9 | 47.7 |
| Years at Current Institution | 11.5 | 12.6 | 13.0 | 11.7 |
| Highest Degree– Doctorate | 91.6% | 92.4% | 82.2% | 84.7% |
| *Income* | | | | |
| Basic Salary from Institution | $60,204 | $48,096 | $40,728 | $38,272 |
| *Teaching* | | | | |
| Percent of Time, Teaching | 29.4% | 44.6%*** | 45.1% | 54.5%*** |
| Hours in Class/Week | 11.7 | 7.1** | 9.5 | 8.8 |
| Student Contact Hours | 479.0 | 301.7 | 332.7 | 300.9 |
| Taught only Undergraduates | 4.5% | 12.3%*** | 6.6% | 9.4% |
| Taught only Graduates | 23.4% | 19.6% | 3.3% | 6.8% |
| *Research* | | | | |
| Percent of Time, Research | 21.3% | 33.0%*** | 16.5% | 24.3%*** |
| Publications (career) | 42.8 | 37.8 | 26.7 | 23.1 |
| Principal Investigator | 41.6% | 39.9% | 22.9% | 22.3% |
| *Administration and Service* | | | | |
| Percent of Time, Administration | 10.9% | 15.1%*** | 9.3% | 13.7%*** |
| Percent of Time, Service | 1.6% | 1.6% | 3.3% | 2.1% |

Source: NSOPF 1988
[a]Liberal arts college category had too few cases for reliable estimates.
*** $p < .001$; ** $p < .01$; * $p < .05$.

| Comprehensive Universities | | Other 4-Year Institutions | |
|---|---|---|---|
| **Top 10% of Time Spent Consulting (Mean)** | **Other Faculty (Mean)** | **Top 10% of Time Spent Consulting (Mean)** | **Other Faculty (Mean)** |
| 10.7% | 11.8% | 11.5% | 11.3% |
| 79.3% | 74.7% | 96.1% | 87.3% |
| 47.7 | 48.2 | 45.5 | 50.1* |
| 11.9 | 12.9 | 11.6 | 11.7 |
| 77.4% | 72.1% | 95.7% | 86.0% |
| $40,712 | $36,449* | $76,392 | $49,820*** |
| 44.7% | 65.7%*** | 19.4% | 46.8%*** |
| 11.1 | 11.0 | 11.4 | 9.0 |
| 324.2 | 318.3 | 450.5 | 510.8 |
| 2.7% | 6.2%* | 0% | 4.8%* |
| 8.4% | 2.8%* | 38.5% | 31.1% |
| 10.0% | 12.9%* | 27.3% | 27.5% |
| 14.3 | 11.2 | 52.2 | 42.8 |
| 10.8% | 10.7% | 62.0% | 24.9%*** |
| 11.1% | 13.6% | 13.3% | 16.1% |
| 2.8% | 2.4% | 0.4% | 1.6%** |

relationships—assisting local industry and government—appear especially crucial to economic development.[39] Yet faculty in the more regionally-oriented institutions spend the least time on consulting.

In the modern economy, particularly important to industry are academic contributions in engineering, computer science, medicine, agriculture, chemistry, and biotechnology.[40] The NSOPF data are not promising in this regard. Only faculty in the health sciences spend a substantial portion of their time consulting. Faculty in engineering spend only an average amount of time consulting, and their peers in agriculture and the natural sciences spend less than average percentages of time on this activity.

As lifelong learning and training in languages and cultural differences increasingly become the foundations of the new economy, greater participation by humanities faculty in knowledge and technology transfer is needed. Again, the NSOPF data are not encouraging: humanities faculty seldom consult. Moreover, their role is not considered crucial in traditional concepts of technology transfer, especially when the focus is on product development rather than on training individuals to cope with changing economic conditions.

In sum, the relatively small percentage of time accorded to consulting and the concentration of consulting in a handful of disciplines suggest that it cannot be the main mechanism for achieving technology transfer. Consistent with Bowen and Schuster's[41] argument that heavy faculty workloads mean that an increase of time spent on one activity must come at the expense of time spent on another, the NSOPF evidence suggests that colleges and universities cannot increase faculty participation in consulting without incurring costs to teaching and academic research. Furthermore, encouraging faculty consulting directly confronts a faculty reward structure which denigrates public service.[42]

## INDUSTRY FUNDING AND ACADEMIC RESEARCH

The costs and benefits of industrial funding of academic research have not been established empirically. Instead, rhetoric and posturing rule. Academic and industrial leaders have touted industrial funding of faculty research as an effective vehicle for enhancing technology transfer.[43] Tornatzky and Fleisher, however, found little evidence that industrial funding of academic research enhances technology transfer or economic development *writ large*.[44] Instead, they claim that colleges and universities simply use funds from industry to continue supporting academic research and to reinforce entrenched disciplinary values.

Taking a position in opposition to Tornatzky and Fleisher, some individuals have criticized industrial funding of academic research precisely because it may affect traditional academic norms. Critics have raised questions about the effect of industrial funding on academic freedom and about neglecting other duties to pursue client-driven research.[45] The data are sketchy. One case study showed intrusion by industry in conducting research.[46] However, a large survey of biotechnology departments found that faculty who received funding from industry were the most productive, obtaining the most federal research dollars as well and publishing the most. These faculty achieved lofty research and scholarly goals without diminishing their role in teaching.[47]

The question remains whether funding from industry has the potential to generate large-scale transfer of technology from academe. Also unanswered on a national basis is the potential conflict of industrially-funded research with traditional functions, such as teaching. In this section, I use the 1987–88 NSOPF data to study these questions. Measures used include whether or not the faculty member *received research funds from industry*, the amount of *research funds from industrial sources*, and the *percentage of research funds received from industry out of all research monies*.

## Receiving Research Funds from Industry

Less than 4 percent of all faculty in 4-year institutions received research funding support from industry during 1987–88 (Table 8.7). Faculty in research and

**TABLE 8.7    Percent of Tenure-track, Full-Time Faculty Receiving Research Funds from Industry, by Type of Institution**

| Type of Institution | Received Research from Industry |
| --- | --- |
| All 4-year | 3.8% |
| SE | .29 |
| Research | 6.6 |
| SE | .64 |
| Doctoral | 4.7 |
| SE | .76 |
| Comprehensive | 1.2 |
| SE | .27 |
| Liberal Arts | * |
| SE | * |
| Other 4-year | * |
| SE | * |

Source: NSOPF 1988
* = Too few cases with funding from industry for reliable estimate.

**TABLE 8.8    Percent of Tenure-track, Full-time Faculty in 4-Year Institutions Receiving Research Funds from Industry, by Program Area**

| Program Area | Received Research Money from Industry |
|---|---|
| Agriculture/Home Economics | 8.9% |
| SE | 2.03 |
| Business | 1.3 |
| SE | .82 |
| Education | 0.9 |
| SE | .46 |
| Engineering | 11.1 |
| SE | 2.41 |
| Fine Arts | 1.4 |
| SE | .65 |
| Health Sciences | 6.6 |
| SE | 1.49 |
| Humanities | 0.9 |
| SE | .27 |
| Natural Sciences | 6.5 |
| SE | 1.06 |
| Social Sciences | 1.9 |
| SE | .49 |
| Other Fields | 2.2 |
| SE | .81 |

Source: NSOPF 1988

doctoral-granting institutions were about equally likely to have received research funds from industry, whereas their peers in comprehensive colleges and universities were less likely to work with industrial sponsors.[48]

Research funding from industry varies by academic discipline (Table 8.8). Faculty in agriculture/home economics, engineering, health sciences, and the natural sciences were more likely to have received support from industry in 1987–88. Faculty in business, education, fine arts, the humanities, and the social sciences were less likely to have received research monies from industry.[49]

Receiving research support from industry does not vary by academic rank. Although a slightly higher percentage of full professors received industrial support for research, the difference is not significant (Table 8.9).

As shown in Table 8.5, the only significant correlate of receiving research funds from industry is being a principal investigator. None of the other measures of faculty activity and workload are related to receiving research funds from industry.

## Profile: Researchers Receiving Monies from Industry

The demographic characteristics of faculty who receive research funds from industry vary by type of institution (Table 8.10). Faculty in research universities are more likely to be male and to hold the doctorate. Faculty in comprehensive institutions are younger and have spent fewer years at their institution.

At research and doctoral-granting institutions, faculty supported by industry spend less time on teaching than their colleagues; faculty in comprehensive institutions with such funding spend less time in class per week. In doctoral-granting and comprehensive universities, faculty with research funding from industry spend more time on research than their compatriots. In research and doctoral-granting institutions, faculty supported by industry publish more than their colleagues. The salaries of faculty who receive research support from industry are equivalent to salaries of their faculty colleagues who do not have such funding.

## Research Funding for Principal Investigators

Limiting the analysis to faculty who were principal investigators (or co-principal investigators) on an externally- funded research project during 1987–88, I examine the average research dollars from federal and industrial sources,[50] and the percentage of research monies received from industry (Table 8.11). I also examine these results by program area (Table 8.12).

Principal investigators receiving research funds from industry have fewer federal funds than do principal investigators receiving funds from other sources, both overall and by type of institution (with the exception of doctoral-granting universities).[51] In comprehensive colleges, principal investigators supported by industry received about the same total research funding as principal investigators without industrial funding. Principal

**TABLE 8.9   Percent of Tenure-Track, Full-Time Faculty Receiving Research Funds from Industry, by Academic Rank (all 4-year institutions)**

| Rank | Received Research Money from Industry |
|------|:---:|
| Professor | 4.5% |
| SE | .47 |
| Associate | 3.4 |
| SE | .49 |
| Assistant | 3.4 |
| SE | .56 |

Source: NSOPF 1988

**TABLE 8.10**    Profile of Tenure-Track, Full-Time Faculty Who Receive Research Funds from Industry, by Type of Institution[a]

| | Research Universities | | Doctoral Universities | | Comprehensive Universities | |
|---|---|---|---|---|---|---|
| | Received Research $ from Industry (Mean) | Other Faculty (Mean) | Received Research $ from Industry (Mean) | Other Faculty (Mean) | Received Research $ from Industry (Mean) | Other Faculty (Mean) |
| *Demographics* | | | | | | |
| Minority | 6.8% | 10.7% | 3.8% | 7.4% | 5.1% | 11.8% |
| Male | 94.8% | 81.6%*** | 80.6% | 77.4% | 78.9% | 75.1% |
| Age | 47.5 | 47.5 | 49.0 | 47.8 | 41.7 | 48.2** |
| Years at Current Institution | 12.3 | 12.4 | 10.9 | 11.9 | 8.8 | 12.8* |
| Highest Degree– Doctorate | 97.1% | 91.9%* | 92.0% | 84.1% | 79.2% | 72.5% |
| *Income* | | | | | | |
| Basic Salary from Institution | $53,098 | $49,414 | $44,621 | $38,177 | $39,391 | $36,789 |
| *Teaching* | | | | | | |
| Percent of Time, Teaching | 37.2% | 43.0%* | 40.0% | 54.3%*** | 59.2% | 63.8% |
| Hours in Class/ Week | 7.6 | 7.7 | 7.9 | 8.9 | 9.1 | 11.1* |
| Student Contact Hours | 270.9 | 326.4 | 322.0 | 302.7 | 355.4 | 318.4 |
| Taught only Undergraduates | 13.7% | 11.1% | 19.2% | 8.6% | 11.7% | 5.8% |
| Taught only Graduates | 25.5% | 19.7% | 15.6% | 6.0% | 7.0% | 3.2% |
| *Research* | | | | | | |
| Percent of Time, Research | 35.2% | 31.1% | 42.3% | 22.7%*** | 21.9% | 12.5%** |
| Publications (career) | 52.7 | 37.4* | 46.5 | 22.3* | 11.8 | 11.4 |
| *Administration and Service* | | | | | | |
| Percent of Time, Administration | 15.3% | 14.5% | 12.3% | 13.4% | 10.7% | 13.4% |
| Percent of Time, Service | 2.0% | 1.5% | 1.0% | 2.3%* | 2.1% | 2.4% |

Source: NSOPF 1988
[a] Too few faculty in liberal arts colleges and other 4-year institutions for reliable estimates.
*** = p < .001; ** = p < .01; * = p < .05.

**TABLE 8.11    Funding Sources for Principal Investigators, by Type of Institution**[a]

| Type of Institution/ Funding Source | Average Research Dollars | | | Percent of Research $ from Industry |
| --- | --- | --- | --- | --- |
| | Federal | Industry | Total[b] | |
| *All 4-year* | | | | |
| Received Research $ from Industry | $13,336 | $61,356 | $85,261 | 72.0% |
| SE | 2,609 | 20,518 | 21,025 | 3.05 |
| Other PIs | 47,793 | 0 | 67,273 | NA |
| SE | 3,770 | 0 | 4,749 | NA |
| *Research Universities* | | | | |
| Received Research $ from Industry | 11,352 | 73,781 | 96,784 | 76.2% |
| SE | 3,026 | 32,083 | 32,496 | 3.66 |
| Other PIs | 45,851 | 0 | 68,364 | NA |
| SE | 4,189 | 0 | 6,431 | NA |
| *Doctoral Universities* | | | | |
| Received Research $ from Industry | 24,299 | 60,353 | 98,836 | 61.1% |
| SE | 7,745 | 23,161 | 27,231 | 7.17 |
| Other PIs | 22,276 | 0 | 39,457 | NA |
| SE | 4,216 | 0 | 5,058 | NA |
| *Comprehensive Universities* | | | | |
| Received Research $ from Industry | 6,347 | 19,279 | 30,146 | 64.0% |
| SE | 5,395 | 5,580 | 9,998 | 7.30 |
| Other PIs | 27,915 | 0 | 38,014 | NA |
| SE | 4,202 | 0 | 4,513 | NA |

Source: NSOPF 1988
NA= Not Applicable
[a] Too few faculty in liberal arts colleges and other 4-year institutions who were funded by industry for reliable estimates.
[b] Includes additional research funds from associations, state governments, and foundations.

investigators in doctoral-granting institutions and research universities who received industrial funds had higher total research funding than their peers without such funds, although in the latter case the difference was not statistically significant.[52] For principal investigators who received research money from industry, the percentage of total research funds derived from industrial sources ranged from 61 percent for faculty in doctoral-granting universities to 76 percent for those in research universities.

Five program areas had sufficient respondents supported by industry to make meaningful estimates: agriculture/home economics, engineering, health sciences, the natural sciences, and the social sciences. Except for faculty in engineering, faculty who received research support from industry had fewer federal research dollars than their colleagues.[53] For faculty in the natural and social sciences, receiving research support from industry was unrelated to total research funds. Faculty in engineering, natural sciences, and social sciences who received research support from industry had more total research funds than their colleagues, although in the latter two program areas the differences were not statistically significant. Faculty in agriculture and in the health sciences had fewer total research dollars than their colleagues who did not receive funds from industry.[54] The percentage of total research funds accounted for by industrial sources ranged from 58 percent for faculty in engineering to 88 percent for those in the natural sciences.

## Discussion

Blumenthal, Gluck, and colleagues conducted the major study to date about the effect of receiving research funds from industry on faculty behavior.[55] In a study limited to biotechnology faculty, Blumenthal and colleagues found that receiving research funds from industry was an indicator of productivity: biotechnology faculty who received research funds from industry also had the most federal research dollars, published more, and did as much teaching as their colleagues who did not have similar research support. The NSOPF data show the dangers of assuming that biotechnology faculty are representative of their peers in other fields and of assuming that faculty behavior does not vary by type of institution. The correlational analysis indicates that faculty productivity and workload across institutions are unrelated to having research money from industry. Within type of institution, faculty receiving research money from industry either spend less of their time on teaching or spend fewer hours in the classroom. Within type of institution, faculty receiving funds from industry did publish more than their colleagues who did not have similar research support.

Looking only at principal investigators,[56] faculty who receive research funds from industry were far more dependent on these sources than implied by Blumenthal and colleagues. Engineering faculty who receive support

**TABLE 8.12** Funding Sources for Principal Investigators in 4-year Institutions, by Program Area[a]

| Program Area | Average Research Dollars | | | Percent of Research $ from Industry |
|---|---|---|---|---|
| | Federal | Industry | Total[b] | |
| *Agriculture/Home Economics* | | | | |
| Received Research $ from Industry | $ 3,362 | $15,565 | $21,992 | 70.8% |
| SE | 1,205 | 5,405 | 6,135 | 7.49 |
| Other PIs | 31,540 | 0 | 49,209 | NA |
| SE | 11,188 | 0 | 12,355 | NA |
| *Engineering* | | | | |
| Received Research $ from Industry | 18,008 | 65,056 | 112,610 | 57.8% |
| SE | 5,742 | 16,278 | 24,635 | 7.54 |
| Other PIs | 13,447 | 0 | 36,201 | NA |
| SE | 3,551 | 0 | 8,094 | NA |
| *Health Sciences* | | | | |
| Received Research $ from Industry | 19,071 | 34,606 | 56,551 | 61.2% |
| SE | 8,184 | 9,721 | 13,062 | 7.33 |
| Other PIs | 56,589 | 0 | 97,516 | NA |
| SE | 10,533 | 0 | 18,921 | NA |
| *Natural Sciences* | | | | |
| Received Research $ from Industry | 11,111 | 114,489 | 130,543 | 87.7% |
| SE | 4,242 | 73,882 | 73,848 | 5.59 |
| Other PIs | 36,412 | 0 | 43,113 | NA |
| SE | 4,180 | 0 | 4,243 | NA |
| *Social Sciences* | | | | |
| Received Research $ from Industry | 1,332 | 89,919 | 119,872 | 75.0% |
| SE | 4,831 | 42,013 | 48,889 | 9.70 |
| Other PIs | 35,505 | 0 | 50,948 | NA |
| SE | 6,977 | 0 | 8,378 | NA |

Source: NSOPF 1988
NA = Not Applicable
[a] Too few cases in business, education, fine arts, humanities, and other fields for reliable estimates.
[b] Includes additional research funds from associations, state governments, and foundations.

from industry, some of whom are in biotechnology, fit the Blumenthal profile, receiving more total research funds than their colleagues. However, faculty in agriculture/home economics and health sciences, some of whom are also in biotechnology, do not fit this pattern, having either the same or less total research funding than their colleagues. This dependency on research support from industry indicates a far greater potential for conflict of interest and for incursions into choice of research topic than implied by Blumenthal and colleagues.

## POLICY QUESTIONS

### How useful are consulting and industrially funded research in technology transfer?

Geiger has argued that technology transfer activities which are consistent with traditional teaching and research functions are more likely to gain acceptance by academics.[57] These traditional mechanisms, which include publishing, consulting, carrying out research funded by industry, and continuing professional education, fit into the broad categories of *consulting*, *research*, and *service*. Although acceptable to academe, in the past these traditional approaches have not resulted in consistently effective transfer of technology.[58]

The NSOPF data reveal that faculty spend a very small proportion of their time on public or community service. Even though about one-third of all faculty spend some time consulting, the average time spent is only about 5 percent of the total work week. Furthermore, when faculty consult they seldom perform technology transfer services.[59] Faculty in two of the major fields which industry relies on for technology transfer—agriculture and the natural sciences—actually spend below-average time on consulting and, in the case of the latter, on public service as well. Faculty in regional 4-year colleges and universities, which might have the greatest potential utility for enhancing local and regional economies, spend the least time consulting.

Faculty who receive research funding from industry are heavily reliant on this funding source, but less than 4 percent of all faculty participate in industrially funded research. Although this percentage is substantially higher in agriculture (8.9 percent), engineering (11.1 percent), the health sciences (6.6 percent), and the natural sciences (6.5 percent), the participation of faculty in these fields who carry out research funded by industry is still quite small.

These data suggest that consulting, service, and research funding by industry affect a relatively small number of faculty. Faculty who do consult and practice public service spend only a small percentage of their time on these tasks. The traditional mechanisms for involving faculty in technology transfer may be consistent with academic mores, but they seem unlikely to provide dependable vehicles for institutional strategies for technology transfer.

### Does involvement by industry adversely affect traditional academic functions?

The majority of funds contributed by industry to academic institutions focus on applied research and graduate education.[60] For this reason, some critics claim that industry–university partnerships may detract from undergraduate education and from other traditional faculty activities:

> The type of activities carried out by faculty working in business-university partnerships are potentially harmful to instructional quality. The almost exclusive focus on research in business-university liaisons reinforces the tendency of faculty to devote more of their workload to research at the expense of instruction. This is especially critical in several science and engineering disciplines where student/faculty ratios are already much too high.[61]

Although Blumenthal, Gluck, and colleagues'research on biotechnology faculty found no evidence of decreased time spent on teaching,[62] the NSOPF data show that faculty in all disciplines who receive research funding from industry spend less time on teaching and more on research. Faculty in agriculture and the health sciences, which are important to technology transfer, already spend less-than-average percentages of their time on teaching, and participation in research funded by industry may exacerbate this trend. Consulting, another form of technology transfer, is also negatively related to time spent on teaching at 4-year universities. The potential adverse effect on teaching from forming research partnerships with industry is real.

Yet the trend away from teaching and toward research is hardly a function of industrially supported research support. Nor are industrial sponsors responsible for the low status of public service or continuing education:

> Economic development activities are much more likely to be added to the already long and growing list of desirable public-service activities to which academe pays lip service but which everyone on the inside knows occupies a distant third place in the hierarchy of institutional values.[63]

### Is the faculty reward structure consistent with technology transfer?

Some critics have argued that effective technology transfer requires drastic changes in the faculty reward structure.[64] The apparent limited utility of consulting, service, and research funded by industry as mechanisms for technology transfer supports this position. It appears that most colleges and universities view (and reward) consulting and research funded by industry less in terms of their value in technology transfer and more in terms of their usefulness in enhancing faculty (and institutional) revenue and prestige.

## NOTES

1. R. L. Geiger, "The Ambiguous Link: Private Industry and University Research," in *The Economics of Higher Education*, ed. W. E. Becker and D. R. Lewis (Boston: Kluwer, 1992), 265–98.
2. For example, J. Pfeffer and G. R. Salancik, *The External Control of Organizations* (New York: Harper and Row, 1978).
3. For example, M. A. Trow, "The Analysis of Status," in *Perspectives in Higher Education: Eight Disciplinary and Comparative Views*, ed. B. Clark (Berkeley, Calif.: University of California Press, 1984), 132–64.
4. C. F. Conrad and R. T. Blackburn, "Program Quality in Higher Education: A Review and Critique of the Literature," in *Higher Education: Handbook of Theory and Research, Volume I*, ed. J. C. Smart (New York: Agathon, 1985), 283–308; J. S. Fairweather and D. F. Brown, "Dimensions of Academic Program Quality," *Review of Higher Education*, 14 (1991): 155–76; D. S. Webster, *Academic Quality Rankings of American Colleges and Universities* (Springfield, Ill.: Charles C. Thomas, 1986).
5. P. Crosson, *Public Service in Higher Education: Practices and Priorities*, ASHE-ERIC Higher Education Research Report No. 7 (Washington, D.C.: Association for the Study of Higher Education, 1983).
6. K. S. Louis, D. Blumenthal, M. Gluck, and M. Stoto, "Entrepreneurs in Academe: An Explanation of Behaviors among Life Scientists," *Administrative Science Quarterly*, 34 (1989): 129.
7. M. J. Dooris and J. S. Fairweather, "Structure and Culture in Faculty Work: Implications for Technology Transfer," *Review of Higher Education*, 17 (1994): 161–78; R. S. Friedman and R. C. Friedman, "Organized Research Units in Academe Revisited," in *Managing High Technology: An Interdisciplinary Perspective*, ed. B. W. Mar, W. T. Newell, and B. O. Saxberg (New York: Elsevier, 1985): 75–91.
8. J. S. Fairweather, *Entrepreneurship and Higher Education: Lessons for Colleges, Universities, and Industry*, ASHE-ERIC Higher Education Research Report No. 6 (Washington, D.C.: Association for the Study of Higher Education, 1988).
9. Fairweather, *Entrepreneurship and Higher Education*, 27.
10. B. J. Bird and D. N. Allen, "Faculty Entrepreneurship in Research University Environments," *Journal of Higher Education*, 60 (1989): 583–96; C. M. Boyer and D. R. Lewis, "Maintaining Faculty Vitality through Outside Professional Consulting," in *Faculty Vitality and Institutional Productivity*, ed. S. M. Clark and D. R. Lewis (New York: Teachers College Press, 1985), 183.
11. Bird and Allen, "Faculty Entrepreneurship," 593.
12. Boyer and Lewis, "Maintaining Faculty Vitality," 182.

13. A. E. Austin and Z. F. Gamson, *Academic Workplace: New Demands, Heightened Tensions*, ASHE-ERIC Higher Education Research Report No. 10 (Washington, D.C.: Association for the Study of Higher Education, 1983), 20.

14. Crosson, *Public Service in Higher Education*; S. E. Elman and S. M. Smock, *Professional Service and Faculty Rewards* (Washington, D.C.: National Association of State Universities and Land-Grant Colleges, 1985).

15. R. Aggarwal, "Faculty Members as Consultants: A Policy Perspective," *Journal of the College and University Personnel Association*, 32 (1981): 17–20.

16. K. E. Dillon and K. L. Bane, "Consulting and Conflict of Interest: A Compendium of Policies of Almost One Hundred Major Colleges and Universities," *Educational Record*, 61 (1980): 52–72.

17. C. M. Boyer and D. R. Lewis, *And on the Seventh Day: Faculty Consulting and Supplemental Income*, ASHE-ERIC Higher Education Research Report No. 3 (Washington, D.C.: Association for the Study of Higher Education, 1985), 181.

18. S. W. Golomb, "Faculty Consulting: Should it be Curtailed?" *National Forum: Phi Kappa Phi Journal*, 69 (1979): 34–7.

19. Boyer and Lewis, *And on the Seventh Day*, 183.

20. Boyer and Lewis, *And on the Seventh Day*.

21. S. H. Russell, J. S. Fairweather, R. S. Cox, C. Williamson, J. Boismier, and H. Javitz, *Faculty in Higher Education Institutions* (Washington, D.C.: U.S. Department of Education, 1990).

22. Total income included basic salary, other institutional income (i.e., supplements not included in basic salary, such as summer teaching), consulting income, and other outside income (e.g., self-owned business, royalties, pay from another academic institution).

23. $t(\text{res}/\text{doc}) = 3.22^{**}$; $t(\text{comp}/\text{lib}) = 4.87^{***}$ [where $^{***} = p < .001$; $^{**} = p < .01$; $^* = p < .05$].

24. J. D. Marver and C. V. Patton, "The Correlates of Consultation: American Academics in the Real World," *Higher Education*, 5 (1976): 319–35.

25. $t(\text{res}/\text{doc}) = 6.21^{***}$; $t(\text{comp}/\text{lib}) = 6.43^{***}$; $t(\text{other}/\text{res}) = 2.93^{**}$.

26. Boyer and Lewis, "Maintaining Faculty Vitality," 191.

27. $t(\text{doc}/\text{comp}) = 2.82^{**}$; $t(\text{other}/\text{res}) = 2.57^*$.

28. H. R. Bowen, *Academic Compensation: Are Faculty and Staff in American Higher Education Adequately Paid?* (New York: TIAA-CREF, 1978); E. C. Ladd, Jr., "The Work Experience of American College Professors: Some Data and an Argument," *Current Issues in Higher Education* (Washington, D.C.: American Association of Higher Education, 1979).

29. $t(\text{agriculture}) = -9.16^{***}$; $t(\text{education}) = -3.14^*$; $t(\text{health sciences}) = 7.32^{***}$; $t(\text{humanities}) = -17.33^{***}$; $t(\text{nat sci}) = -9.67^{***}$; $t(\text{soc sci}) = -7.44^{***}$; $t(\text{other}) = -4.88^{**}$.

30. $t(\text{business}) = 2.71^*$; $t(\text{humanities}) = -18.01^{***}$; $t(\text{agriculture}) = -4.87^{**}$; $t(\text{nat sci}) = -2.59^*$.

31. Boyer and Lewis, *And on the Seventh Day*.

32. Bowen, *Academic Compensation*; Boyer and Lewis, *And on the Seventh Day*.

33. $t(\text{assoc}/\text{asst}) = 3.00^{**}$.

34. Boyer and Lewis, *And on the Seventh Day*.

35. Marver and Patton, "The Correlates of Consultation."
36. Boyer and Lewis, "Maintaining Faculty Vitality"; Marver and Patton, "The Correlates of Consultation."
37. Boyer and Lewis, *And on the Seventh Day*.
38. Boyer and Lewis, *And on the Seventh Day*, 21–2.
39. L. B. Logan and J. O. Stampen, "Smoke Stack Meets Ivory Tower: Collaborations with Local Industry," *Educational Record*, 66 (1985): 26–9; Public Policy Center, SRI International, *The Higher Education–Economic Development Connection: Emerging Roles for Public Colleges and Universities* (Washington, D.C.: American Association of State Colleges and Universities, 1986).
40. E. I. Holmstrom and J. Petrovich, *Engineering Programs in Emerging Areas, 1983–84*, Higher Education Panel Report No. 64 (Washington, D.C.: American Council on Education, 1985).
41. H. R. Bowen and J. H. Schuster, *American Professors: A National Resource Imperiled* (New York: Oxford University Press, 1986).
42. Crosson, *Public Service in Higher Education*.
43. Fairweather, *Entrepreneurship and Higher Education*.
44. L. G. Tornatzky and M. Fleisher, *The Process of Technological Innovation* (Lexington, Mass.: Lexington Books, 1990).
45. M. Kenney, *Biotechnology: The University-Industrial Complex* (New Haven, Conn.: Yale University Press, 1986); R. Nelson, "Institutions Supporting Technical Advance in Industry," *American Economic Review*, 76 (1986): 186–90; L. Wofsy, "Biotechnology and the University," *Journal of Higher Education*, 57 (1986): 477–92.
46. M. N. Richter, "Industrial Funding of Faculty Research," *Humanity and Society*, 9 (1985): 459–85.
47. D. Blumenthal, M. Gluck, K. Louis, M. Stoto, and D. Wise, "University-Industry Research Relationships in Biotechnology: Implications for the University," *Science*, 232 (1986): 1621–6.
48. $t(\text{doc}/\text{comp}) = 4.35^{***}$.
49. $t(\text{agriculture}) = 2.60^*$; $t(\text{business}) = -2.99^*$; $t(\text{education}) = -5.73^{**}$; $t(\text{engineering}) = 3.13^*$; $t(\text{fine arts}) = -3.60^{**}$; $t(\text{humanities}) = -8.36^{***}$; $t(\text{nat sci}) = 2.80^*$; $t(\text{soc sci}) = -3.89^{**}$.
50. Total external research funding comprises monies from federal, state, and local governments; associations; foundations; and industry.
51. $t(\text{all 4-year}) = 7.52^{***}$; $t(\text{res}) = 6.68^{***}$; $t(\text{comp}) = 3.15^{**}$.
52. $t(\text{doc}) = 2.14^*$.
53. $t(\text{agriculture}) = 2.50^*$; $t(\text{health sciences}) = 2.81^{**}$; $t(\text{nat sci}) = 4.25^{***}$; $t(\text{soc sci}) = 4.03^{***}$.
54. $t(\text{agriculture}) = -1.97^*$; $t(\text{engineering}) = 2.95^{**}$; $t(\text{health sciences}) = -2.12^*$.
55. The Blumenthal, Gluck et al. survey was replicated for agricultural biotechnology faculty in land grant universities by J. Curry and M. Kenney, "Land-grant University-Industry Relationships in Biotechnology: A Comparison with Non-Land-grant Research Universities," *Rural Sociology*, 55 (1990): 44–57. The replication, using the original survey instrument, confirmed the Blumenthal and colleagues' findings.
56. One reason for the differences in findings between these data and Blumenthal, Gluck, and colleagues is that the latter may have included in their analyses fac-

ulty who did not have any research funds. This approach distorts the mean comparisons between faculty having research funds from industry (who by definition have received research funding) with those who have not (some of whom do not have any research monies). By limiting the analysis to faculty who received some research funding during 1987–88, I have a truer estimate of the relationship between having funding from industry and total research funding.

57. Geiger, "The Ambiguous Link."
58. E. C. Johnson and L. G. Tornatzky, "Academia and Industrial Innovation," in *Business and Higher Education: Toward New Alliances,* ed. G. G. Gold (San Francisco: Jossey-Bass, 1981), 47–63.
59. Bird and Allen, "Faculty Entrepreneurship."
60. Fairweather, *Entrepreneurship and Higher Education.*
61. J. S. Fairweather, "Academic Research and Instruction: The Industrial Connection," *Journal of Higher Education,* 60 (1989): 401.
62. Blumenthal, Gluck, Louis, Stoto, and Wise, "University-Industry Research Relationships in Biotechnology."
63. P. Crosson, "Encouraging Faculty Involvement in University Economic Development Programs," in *Issues in Higher Education and Economic Development* (Washington, D.C.: American Association of State Colleges and Universities, 1986), 119.
64. For example, R. S. Hambrick, Jr., and G. S. Swanson, "The Mobilization of Expertise: The Problems of Managing Applied Research in a University," in *Linking Science and Technology to Public Policy: The Role of Universities,* ed. A. I. Baaklini (Albany, N.Y.: New York State Assembly and State University of New York at Albany, 1979), 115–42.

# ► 9

## Three Case Studies:

### Leadership, Policy, and Structure

**THOMAS J. CHMURA**        **JAMES S. FAIRWEATHER**
*UNIVERSITY OF MASSACHUSETTS*

In previous chapters, we have seen the positive influence of administratively-controlled incentives on faculty research behavior, particularly through compensation and workload assignments. We also have shown that administrative incentives combine with faculty socialization to create and maintain norms that emphasize research and publishing. In this chapter, using the theme of responding to changes in the economy, we examine another aspect of administration—leadership—and its influence on faculty culture and, indirectly, on faculty behavior. The ability of academic leaders to transform faculty cultures rests on three principal tenets: (a) administrative policy affects faculty norms, (b) faculty behavior can be altered by creating alternative organizational structures, and (c) transformational and/or symbolic leadership can move academic institutions toward new norms for faculty behavior. Three recent case studies of administrative action and faculty behavior provide the data for this analysis. The first, based on Matkin's study of four research universities, is an analysis of the effectiveness of institutional patent policy in increasing the amount of time and effort faculty expend on technology transfer activities.[1] The second is a study of the relative importance of organizational structure and traditional disciplinary norms in biotechnology faculty research and technology transfer behavior.[2] The final study, unique in its application, describes the role of institutions of higher education in the Baltimore regional economy and the success or failure of leadership to make institutions more responsive to local economic needs.[3]

## POLICY, STRUCTURE, AND CULTURE

### Policy

Matkin argues that administrative policies can affect faculty participation in technology transfer. The primary contemporary policies to encourage (or discourage) faculty involvement in technology transfer include incentives (or disincentives) for faculty control of intellectual property rights, faculty participation in financial rewards derived from their inventions, explicit but not prohibitive statements about conflict of interest and conflict of duties, liberal definitions of allowable use of university facilities, and flexible arrangements for the use of proprietary information.[4]

Matkin and Geiger present historical evidence in support of the usefulness of administrative policy in promoting (or limiting) faculty participation in technology transfer.[5] Examining the evolution of research policy at the Massachusetts Institute of Technology (M.I.T.), Matkin found that in the 1930s President Compton created a policy to restore the academic reputation of the institute by promoting traditional faculty research behavior and reducing consulting with industry. Matkin claims that this policy was successful in altering faculty research behavior toward different norms:

> With these [policy] changes, Compton worked on a transformation of M.I.T., restoring it to prominence and ending its philosophical detour from the accepted standards of the academic world. Compton's use of policies on faculty consulting and research sponsorship illustrates the administrative potential for policy formulation and implementation in universities.[6]

Another example of the influence of administrative policy cited by Matkin and by Leslie concerns the use of policies to encourage faculty research activity at Stanford University.[7] Leslie claims that the senior administrators at Stanford made it a conscious policy to promote faculty involvement in classified research—sponsored by both the federal government and industry—as a means of enhancing institutional prestige. According to Matkin, "it is a strategy that still exerts a strong influence on Stanford's organizational structure, its academic culture, and its response to the changes brought about by technology transfer."[8]

### Organizational Structure

Organized research units (ORUs) long have been seen as a mechanism to respond to changing societal needs while maintaining traditional academic norms.[9] These mechanisms, which include research institutes and centers, business incubators, and consortia, among many others, have become popular for attempting to stimulate faculty involvement in technology transfer.[10] The large majority of consortia between academe and industry were created since 1979, growing by a factor of five during the 1980s.[11] According to Dooris and Fairweather,

> In theory, ORUs appear responsive to societal and economic pressures that place a premium upon multidisciplinary cooperation and application-oriented research. They seem to be a mechanism for attracting funding—particularly from industry—and for promoting interdisciplinary cooperation, while providing a buffer against direct involvement in commercialization. Ideally, ORUs would provide a sufficiently "academic" environment to protect faculty choice and academic freedom while infusing sufficient interest in multidisciplinary work and technology transfer to benefit both society and universities. The proliferation of ORUs signals a belief that these units can achieve institutional goals while defusing problems such as conflicts of interest or a de-emphasis of teaching.[12]

The belief by academic administrators that alternative structures can affect faculty behavior is grounded broadly in organizational theory. Many important works in organizational theory support the influence of structure on individual behavior.[13] Indeed, in a review of the theoretical literature Veen found that "structure is one of the most essential concepts in the organization literature."[14]

The relationship between structure and behavior in academic settings, however, is less well understood. Key concepts in structure, including formalization, centralization, and technological complexity, do not translate well into the academic setting. According to some researchers, culture and academic values, not structure, are the determinants of faculty behavior. Discipline, rank, tenure status, type of institution, and the like are more important to faculty than their organizational location.[15] From this perspective, structural solutions may not alter faculty behavior substantially.

### Transformational and Symbolic Leadership

Many theories of leadership exist. These include theories based on individual traits, power and influence, behavior, contingencies, cognitive abilities, and culture and symbolism.[16] Only two of these—theories of power and influence and theories of cultural and symbolic leadership—address the ability of leaders to transform norms and cultures. Transformative leadership is based on the use of power by leaders to engage participants "in such a way as to raise them to new levels of morality and motivation."[17] The emphasis of transformational leaders is on reforming existing norms and cultures through articulation of vision. Transformational leaders exude charisma and focus on agendas beyond the immediate concerns of participants.[18] Bensimon and colleagues define five steps which leaders can take to transform institutional cultures:

> (1) create readiness for change by focusing attention on the unsatisfactory aspects of the organization; (2) overcome resistance by using nonthreatening approaches to introduce change; (3) articulate a vision by combining rational reason and symbolic imagery; (4) generate commitment; (5) institutionalize commitment.[19]

Although transformative leadership contains parts of a symbolic approach to cultural change, other forms of leadership tackle cultural change more directly. From this perspective, leaders elucidate a new "saga" for the institution, develop new symbols to reinforce the new vision, and establish new forms and targets for reinforcing altered norms.[20]

## The Questions

Do institutional policies toward technology transfer affect faculty behavior? Do alternative structures for research alter faculty behavior? Are particular leadership styles more effective than others in reforming institutional norms? To answer the first policy question, Matkin's case studies of patenting and technology transfer are studied.[21] Work by Dooris and Fairweather is examined to study the usefulness of structures in modifying faculty behavior.[22] Finally, a case study of the Baltimore region provides an in-depth study of the utility (or lack of it) of leadership in reforming institutional missions and norms.[23]

## Institutional Policy

Matkin studied the effectiveness of technology transfer policies at four research universities: Massachusetts Institute of Technology (M.I.T.), Pennsylvania State University, Stanford University, and the University of California—Berkeley. He defined technology transfer in research universities as "the transfer of the results of basic and applied research to the design, development, and commercialization of new or improved products, services, or processes."[24] Matkin's intent was to examine the influence of various policy alternatives on faculty contributions to technology transfer, particularly through inventions, patenting, and licensing.

Matkin categorized the four research universities along a continuum of low to high encouragement for faculty to participate in technology transfer. At the low end was the University of California—Berkeley. According to Matkin, Berkeley seems to have a culture which disdains technology transfer as a university function. Faculty are expected to assign all intellectual property rights to the university. Of the four institutions studied, Berkeley has the most restrictive policy toward sponsors, allowing them rights to first refusal but not protecting their investment in any other way. In sum, the University of California—Berkeley patent policies "seem to be governed by concern for avoiding the appearance of conflict of interest or violation of public trust" rather than promoting technology transfer.[25]

Rated higher on a scale to promote faculty involvement in technology transfer is Penn State University. Penn State actively encourages participation in economic development through the Ben Franklin Partnership. Penn State currently is establishing a research park. The university also has a long tradition of creating and maintaining interdisciplinary research programs, some of which focus substantial efforts on technology transfer. Unlike Berkeley, Penn State apportions the rights from invention or patent partly to the school and partly to the faculty member. Penn State is the second most liberal of the four schools in allocating rights to sponsors. The overall approach at Penn State is to develop policies and create structures to encourage faculty involvement in technology transfer, but not to address faculty involvement directly through traditional faculty rewards, such as salary or promotion and tenure.[26]

Next highest in encouraging technology transfer is M.I.T. It has an entrepreneurial culture, best evidenced by the plethora of alternative structures for research and technology transfer. Like Penn State, M.I.T. apportions royalties from inventions partly to the school and partly to the inventor. M.I.T. also has a liberal policy permitting industrial sponsors to share in the revenues from technology transfer.[27]

The most aggressive institution in promoting faculty involvement in technology transfer is Stanford University. Even the academic departments encourage faculty entrepreneurship at Stanford. Unlike the other institutions, Stanford assigns all rights from inventions to the inventor. Stanford does not have a formula for assigning rights to sponsors. Instead, each relationship is negotiated separately by the Office of Technology Licensing.[28]

According to Matkin's hypothesis, faculty involvement in promoting technology transfer, in this case through inventions, patents, and licenses, should follow the policies stated above: the fewest patents and licenses should go to Berkeley faculty, followed by Penn State, M.I.T., and Stanford. Instead, Matkin found in 1986–87 that Berkeley faculty produced the *most* inventions, followed by faculty at M.I.T., Stanford, and Penn State. Patent applications and patents issued followed the identical pattern.[29] Faculty *attitudes*, on the other hand, were more consistent with Matkin's hypothesis. Faculty at Stanford rated the contribution to the university of technology transfer highest, followed by faculty at M.I.T., Penn State, and Berkeley.[30]

These findings indicate that institutional policy may affect (or may reflect) faculty attitudes about technology transfer; however, policies appear only modestly related to faculty behavior. Over time, perhaps these attitudes will result in a cultural change which promotes technology transfer. For now, the effectiveness of institutional policy to encourage more active faculty participation in technology transfer is ambiguous at best.

Matkin's view of leadership, in which senior administrators set goals and create relevant incentives, appears inadequate for an academic setting. Instead, participative decision making between administrators and faculty, in which administrators create the tone and develop some incentives and faculty help develop goals and identify activities to achieve them, seems more likely to succeed. Administrative action certainly is relevant to the situations reported at M.I.T., Penn State, Stanford, and Berkeley; without statements and policies endorsed by presidents and provosts it is unlikely that faculty acting alone will create change from the bottom up. Indeed, it appears that senior administrators have achieved some change in faculty attitudes by creating specific policies and incentives. But department chairs, faculty leaders, and individual faculty members interpret these messages and act according to a variety of influences, only one of which is a policy statement about technology transfer. Values and beliefs, workload, and rewards all can serve as counterbalances to administrative policies.

## Structure versus Culture

In 1990 and 1991, Dooris and Fairweather studied biotechnology faculty behavior in three research universities. The research focused on four areas of faculty behavior: teaching, advising, research, and scholarship. The universities studied varied by source of control (public or private), enrollment (6,500 to 38,000), size of external funding for biotechnology research ($700,000 to $4.2 million annually), professed institutional interest in technology transfer (judged moderate to very high), and type of ORU. The latter ranged from a biotechnology program within a traditional academic department, to a biotechnology center with weak departmental affiliation, to an independent biotechnology institute. In each case, the ORU was meant to stimulate additional research funding (primarily from industry) and to encourage faculty participation in technology transfer. A mix of faculty of differing ranks and disciplines was studied. The latter included biology, biochemistry, botany, chemical engineering, chemistry, microbiology, plant pathology, poultry and avian science, and veterinary pharmacology. Faculty from both the ORUs and from traditional departments in these disciplines were interviewed. The study focused on the behavioral differences between faculty located solely in traditional programs or departments (called *departmental faculty*) and those affiliated with quasi-independent ORUs but who had tenure-track faculty appointments (called *ORU faculty*).[31]

Departmental faculty published more frequently in refereed journals than did ORU faculty. About two-thirds of departmental faculty published at least three articles per year; less than one-half of the ORU faculty published as often. Teaching and advising loads, on the other hand, did not vary substantially by organizational location. Biotechnology faculty members in both departments and ORUs taught on average about two courses per year. Doctoral dissertation advising was slightly higher for faculty in departments than in ORUs.

Were faculty in ORUs more successful in generating research funds (especially from industry) than their peers in departments? Dooris and Fairweather found little difference in level or type of funding source between faculty in ORUs and departments. For example, when departmental faculty were compared with their counterparts in ORUs, the percentage receiving funding from industry in the three institutions was 9 percent versus 5 percent in one institution, 13 percent versus 9 percent in another, and equal percentages in the third. In two out of three schools a slightly higher percentage of departmental faculty received funding from industry. Little evidence was found to indicate that forming an ORU increases the percentage of research funds garnered from industry.[32]

Were ORUs successful in changing the orientation of faculty from identification with departmental norms to a technology-transfer orientation espoused by ORUs? Using support from industry as the criterion, the answer is negative. Despite each ORU's having a stated policy of enhancing research partnerships with industry, the percentage of research funding from industry ranged from only 5 to 15 percent. The federal government was the largest funding source for research in the three ORUs just as it was for traditional academic departments.

When the results were studied by faculty characteristics, such as discipline, rank, and tenure status, the results were more marked. Unlike the differences between ORUs and departments, funding levels from industry varied dramatically by discipline regardless of organizational location. Faculty in chemistry and chemical engineering were far more likely to obtain funds from industrial sources than were faculty in other disciplines. For example, faculty in chemistry and chemical engineering averaged about $200,000 in funds from industry per year; their colleagues in biology averaged about $50,000. In addition, teaching and advising loads also varied substantially by academic discipline.

Rank and tenure status were also better predictors of differences in faculty behavior than was organizational affiliation. Not surprisingly, senior faculty had more publications than junior faculty. They also taught fewer courses per year. Dooris and Fairweather summarized these results as follows:

> ...what matters most to professors in research universities are the values and norms of their academic discipline, and their standing in the larger profession...The effect of new mechanisms for organizing faculty research depends on how well they match existing structures—such as departments—and how they mesh with the values and norms of faculty...The patterns of our research suggest that, for faculty in biotechnology, ORUs are unlikely to lead to changes in faculty self-identification or to enhance technology transfer beyond what can be achieved through traditional academic departments. Academic administrators should thus not assume that the creation of ORUs will lead inevitably to enhanced technology transfer and interdisciplinary research; traditional disciplinary norms still influence faculty whatever their organizational location.[33]

## LEADERSHIP AND INSTITUTIONAL CHANGE: THE BALTIMORE STORY

In 1988, the Greater Baltimore Committee commissioned a report to establish the economic needs for the Baltimore region, assess the capacity of local colleges and universities to meet them, and make recommendations for changes in institutional direction to meet economic needs.[34] In this section, we first review the status of the Baltimore region circa 1988. This review starts with a description of the colleges and universities and their roles, an assessment of current and future economic needs, and recommendations for systemic changes in higher education to meet those needs. We follow the 1988 review with a 1993 status report on five institutions to determine the role (or lack of it) of institutional leadership in changing academic institutions to meet emerging economic needs.

### 1988 Status

In 1988, the Baltimore region was served by twelve 4-year institutions and seven community colleges. The 4-year institutions included two research universities (Johns Hopkins University, University of Maryland—College Park), one doctoral-granting institution (University of Maryland—Baltimore County), a specialized medical/professional institution (University of Maryland at Baltimore), six comprehensive or master's-level schools (College of Notre Dame of Maryland, Coppin State College, Loyola College of Maryland, Morgan State University, Towson State University, University of Baltimore), one liberal arts college (Goucher College), and a 2-year institution which offered some bachelor's degrees (Villa Julie College). The community colleges consisted of the Community College of Baltimore and six colleges in the region: Catonsville, Dundalk, Essex, Harford, Howard, and Ann Arundel.

Based on interviews with more than 100 leaders from higher education, industry, and state and federal governments, and an analysis of economic trends, Chmura, Fairweather, and Melville identified future economic needs and opportunities for the Baltimore region and compared the policies and practices of academic institutions in the region to assist in meeting these economic needs. The contributions to the regional economy by academic institutions included:

- The highest level of federal research and development investment in the nation,
- A substantial core of programs in strategic technologies, especially in biotechnology,
- Diversity and quality in liberal arts programs across a variety of institutions,
- A major capacity for continuing education in engineering,
- A growing number of continuing education programs in business, particularly at private schools,
- Emerging programs in important fields, including business (at Loyola) and science and engineering (at the University of Maryland—Baltimore County),
- Increasing institutional interest in forming liaisons with industry, and
- Clear progress in improving the quality of many of the academic institutions in the region.[35]

Yet overall the authors concluded that the region was "surprisingly deficient in many of the basic requirements for today's advanced industrial and service economy".[36] The weaknesses included inadequate provision of technical education, lack of support for continuing education by public institutions in the region, missing programs in engineering education, weak linkages between higher education and industry, and a poor record of capturing economic benefits from the research carried out by academic institutions.

### Technical Education and Training
In 1988, many industries in Baltimore had turned to more sophisticated technical operations, automating assembly lines, adding computer-based operations, and developing new technologies. Unlike doctorates, which can be imported, most of the trained technicians for these industries had to come

from local schools. Interviews with personnel from a cross-section of more than 50 regional firms indicated a growing shortage of a highly technically trained workforce needed for firms to remain competitive. With one exception, the regional community colleges and some of the comprehensive institutions provided excellent technical programs, but the scale was insufficient to meet demand. The Community College of Baltimore was the exception, being poorly linked with local industry, badly managed, and failing to meet a variety of local needs besides those from industry. The result?

> Employers in the city of Baltimore have no local public technical education resource to turn to as their competitors do in other cities. In the San Francisco Bay Area, for example, a group of hotels have worked with San Francisco City College to establish a cooperative training program in hotel management, while a group of telecommunications companies have developed a training consortium with the College of San Mateo. Such consortia appear to be absent in both Baltimore City and the region...these problems are particularly serious for small and mid-size companies in the region. Whereas the major firms have the capacity and resources to launch internal programs or use costly vendors, the smaller firms cannot and have to survive somehow with this serious competitive disadvantage.[37]

### Continuing Education

Continuing education, like technical education, is not a glamorous activity. It compares poorly with the prestige of forming alliances with major industries, developing new genetic solutions to medical problems, and building rockets for aerospace industries. Yet continuing education is the lifeblood of any regional economy. In a field such as electrical engineering, the college-degree program material becomes outdated long before the engineer retires. The only solution to keeping current is some form of continuing or lifelong education, available locally. In 1988, the Baltimore County community colleges and public comprehensive universities offered strong programs in continuing education, many involved directly with local industry. On the whole, however, these programs were underfunded and insufficient in size to meet demand.

Private institutions also offered many programs. Loyola offered the only executive education program (for leaders from industry). Goucher and Notre Dame delivered programs to help women seeking new careers. Johns Hopkins through its Applied Physics Laboratory (APL) and its downtown center offered substantial programs in many fields. Yet these programs had the disadvantage of being expensive, having to generate sufficient revenues for the private schools to maintain them.

The large gap in continuing education came on the public side. Despite having the largest continuing education program in the world, the University College of the University of Maryland at College Park had little presence in Baltimore in 1988. Public comprehensive colleges and universities had sufficient traditional programs for part-time students taking traditional programs, but offered little in the way of advanced technical training.

### Engineering and Science

In 1988, most state and academic leaders conceded that Baltimore was underserved in the field of engineering. Regional academic institutions produced only 200 bachelors and fewer than 200 graduate-degree recipients annually.[38] In addition, colleges and universities in the region did not offer a sufficient number of programs in many emerging fields, such as manufacturing science and materials science. Johns Hopkins had a small engineering school whose focus, consistent with the mission of a research university, was to conduct research and train new faculty rather than to form linkages with local industry. The University of Maryland—College Park provided substantial programs in many fields, but was not directly linked with the Baltimore region on a sufficient scale. Recognizing these deficiencies, the State Board for Higher Education created divided programs at the University of Maryland—Baltimore County (UMBC) and Morgan State University. UMBC offered undergraduate programs in mechanical and chemical engineering and graduate programs in several major engineering fields. The engineering programs were administered by the College of Engineering in College Park. Morgan State was restricted to offering undergraduate degrees in other engineering programs, including electrical engineering. The university attracted a strong group of students in its first years (average SAT scores about 400 points higher than the institutional average). Morgan State faculty chose to focus on engineering applications, a gap not filled by the more research-oriented schools in the region.

In 1988, the question remained whether this divided set of programs attached to two universities, one managed at a distance by a research university, could expand to meet the needs of the local populace and industry. We review their progress in the next section.

### Weak Research Linkages with Industry

Academic institutions in the Baltimore region collectively receive more research and development funds from the federal government than their peers in any other region in the nation. In 1988, Johns Hopkins University ranked first in federal research and development funds, the University of Maryland—College Park ranked 34th, and the University of Maryland at Baltimore (UMAB) ranked 76th (National Science Foundation, 1989). These three institutions offer significant programs in many fields critical to regional economic health, including public health, biotechnology, biomedical science, and computer science.

Despite this substantial research and development base, Chmura, Fairweather, and Melville found little evidence of collaboration between academic institutions with industry except on an ad hoc basis. In 1988, the State of Maryland sought to stimulate relationships with industry, especially those designed to promote technology transfer, by investing $5 million in a Biotechnology Institute. Relatedly, the Maryland Industrial Partnership Program provided $1 million annually in matching funds to promote technology transfer. Unfortunately, although each program had a strong presence in the Baltimore region and was highly regarded by regional firms, the investment was insufficient to make a major contribution to the regional and state economies.[39]

### Capturing Economic Benefits

Despite the substantial research base in the Baltimore region, the economic benefits derived from the research investment were relatively small:

> There is a strikingly weak record of patents, commercialization, and new company spin-offs from the region's massive research base. Although Maryland is one of the principal sources of venture capital in the nation, there are few links between academic entrepreneurs and the venture capital community. More generally, Maryland institutions seem to be lacking in the kind of entrepreneurial culture that characterizes the institutions which have generated the most direct economic activity from their research base.[40]

In 1988, both Johns Hopkins (though the DOME Corporation) and UMBC (through a new research park) were trying to promote better technology transfer from their faculty research base. Yet in 1988 it was clear colleges and universities in the region "still lack the kind of institutional culture, supportive policies, and mechanisms necessary to facilitate their involvement in entrepreneurial activities. Thus, the region's potential to capitalize on its massive research base is still very much in question."[41]

## 1993 Status

The 1988 report generated substantial debate in the Baltimore region about how academic institutions could and should respond to an agenda for change. Leaders from state and local governments, higher education, and industry met to decide how and to what extent colleges and universities might better serve the region. Five years after the report, we examined efforts in five colleges and universities: an engineering school at a young public doctoral-granting university, an engineering school in a historically black university, an innovative research institute in the public university system, the medical school at a prestigious private research university, and an inner-city community college. In particular, we are concerned with the roles of leadership, structure, and incentives in changing (or failing to change) the challenges identified in the 1988 report.

### *University of Maryland, Baltimore County, (UMBC)*

Established in 1966, UMBC struggled during the first 20 years of its existence to define its mission within the greater Baltimore region. Originally intended as a regional doctoral-level university with a comprehensive array of degree programs, UMBC was caught between dependence on the flagship campus at College Park and responding on its own to regional social and economic needs. In 1986, a dynamic new president filled the gap in institutional mission by explicitly tying the university to the economic future of Baltimore City and County. In many ways, the president led the call for academic institutions to take into account the emerging knowledge-based economy in shifting their missions and activities. He led efforts with the state legislature to make faculty participation in technology transfer easier, such as by pushing for changes in state conflict-of-interest laws to enable faculty to participate in start-up companies.

On campus, the president actively participated in planning, budgeting, and personnel decisions to move UMBC in this new direction. New resources were spent on programs which responded to regional economic needs. As one example, the president sought the advice of local industry about the specific fields of engineering that the new college of engineering should emphasize. Rather than simply replicating traditional programs in mechanical and chemical engineering, UMBC emphasized bioprocessing, robotics, and photonics. In the sciences, biotechnology fields were given high priority for funding.

In addition to obtaining funds and ensuring the direction of their expenditure, the president made sure that the faculty recruited for these new engineering and science programs understood and agreed with the emerging mission of the institution. He achieved this goal by staffing search committees with both faculty and scientists from industry, and by asking all candidates about their desire to work with industry as part of their academic responsibilities. In making these efforts, the president targeted fields which had potential benefits for the regional economy, such as engineering and bioscience; he did not alter the decision-making process in the liberal arts.

As one consequence, UMBC secured substantial support for sponsored research from local industry. The first business incubator in the Baltimore region was developed at UMBC, focusing on biotechnology. The president and his administration made plans for a research park.

Several years later, the strategy is working. Entering student SAT scores have reached near equivalence with the flagship institution in College Park. UMBC is recognized nationally for its program to attract women and minorities into the sciences and engineering. In addition, UMBC's research program has grown tenfold. The bioprocessing program is strongly positioned to help local industry move from research and development to manufacturing. The biotechnology incubator has exceeded expectations, adding a second building to house new companies. Westinghouse recently decided to house its corporate robotics research center adjacent to UMBC.

In 1992, another president took charge at UMBC. The new president has continued and extended activities in line with making UMBC responsive to regional economic needs. University officials and faculty visit local companies frequently, expanding access to research facilities for faculty and students alike. UMBC is expanding its engineering capacity, seeking independence from College Park. In spite of budget difficulties, the strategic priorities for science and engineering have been maintained. These actions suggest that the effort to make UMBC distinctive by emphasizing its relationship with the regional community and the effort to recruit faculty in engineering and the sciences who agree with this mission have succeeded.

### Morgan State University

Morgan State is the urban university for Baltimore City.[42] We focus here on the School of Engineering, less than a decade old. Like UMBC's president, the dean of engineering, with support from his president, moved away from a traditional engineering school model and toward responding to local needs. At Morgan State, these were defined as providing outreach programs to encourage inner-city youth to take mathematics and science courses, building applied programs in engineering, and sticking with an undergraduate emphasis rather than trying to convince the state to allow Morgan to add doctoral programs in engineering.

The dean hired faculty who believed in these missions, and pushed for a reward structure which valued teaching and service as highly as research. The faculty have responded to this leadership. Morgan State currently has a nationally recognized outreach program in Baltimore City, one which involves instructional faculty as well as professional staff. Successful linkages with specific high schools have enabled Morgan State to develop a pipeline for new minority engineers; enrollment already has exceeded expectations. Faculty at Morgan State are among the very few in the nation to attempt a radical restructuring of the engineering curriculum, one aimed at making phenomena rather than content the centerpiece. This approach enables the engineering programs to emphasize design and hands-on experiences, and to involve faculty from other disciplines. For example, faculty in history teach engineering students about the history of technology.

In its first years of offering engineering programs, Morgan State has achieved sufficient recognition to be sought as a member of one of the National Science Foundation's engineering coalitions. This effort aided faculty at Morgan State to expand the opportunities available to its students, and to form linkages with faculty in other institutions who share a commitment to design and to promoting access for minority students. Most impressively, the faculty in engineering and their dean have continued to emphasize responding to local needs as their primary function rather than evolving toward the research university model.

### Maryland Biotechnology Institute (MBI)

Established in 1985, the Maryland Biotechnology Institute is a multicampus institute unique within the University of Maryland system. Alone among state higher education institutions, MBI was founded by the legislature specifically to serve the economic development needs of Maryland. MBI was founded to make Maryland a leader in biotechnology; the institution was placed outside the traditional academic campus and departmental structure to make this goal achievable.

Although MBI has made some progress toward achieving its stated mission, it has not become the radically different type of organization the legislature intended. Most of the research funds received by MBI are from the federal government, not from industry. MBI lacks close and synergistic ties with industry. Only recently has the institute created an external advisory board with modest involvement from industry (three members from biotechnology industries). Faculty appear to pursue their own research agendas, mostly in basic research, not agendas shaped in conjunction with industry. Despite the specified goal of technology transfer, MBI does not have a technology transfer office. As a consequence, although the technology transfer record is somewhat better than those of traditional departments in the University of Maryland system, the demonstrable contributions to state and regional economic development have been modest.

The assumption that different institutional structures can shape the behavior of recruited faculty appears incorrect. Traditional norms for promotion and tenure were adopted rather than creating new criteria more in line with the mission of the institute. Although faculty with strong scientific backgrounds have been attracted to MBI, their emphasis has been on traditional disciplinary research behavior, not applied research and technology transfer. The failure of structure alone, particularly without realigning reward criteria, is consistent with findings by Dooris and Fairweather[43] and with the NSOPF data on faculty pay.

Reacting to external criticism, MBI administrators are now developing alternative reward criteria for faculty. These criteria place greater weight on technology transfer. Some MBI research centers are adding business incubators; others are making specialized equipment available for use by industrial scientists. Time will tell whether these changes lead MBI away from the traditional research university model and toward the institute originally envisioned by the legislature.

### Johns Hopkins University School of Medicine

Johns Hopkins is the most prestigious academic institution in the Baltimore region. Johns Hopkins is a major research university, the leading recipient of federal research dollars. Among its many strengths, none is more highly regarded than its medical school, regularly rated among the top schools nationwide.

Johns Hopkins is the key scientific asset to economic development in the Baltimore region. The university has the greatest potential among schools in the region to contribute to technology transfer, commercialization, and new company formation. Yet Johns Hopkins has not had a strong record of patenting, commercialization, and new company spin-offs, especially given the size of its research base.[44]

Prior to 1991, Johns Hopkins School of Medicine also had limited involvement in regional economic development. Relations with industry were minimal, and linkages with the biotechnology industry in particular were surprisingly minimal. The previously described DOME Corporation, which was jointly administered by Johns Hopkins University and the School of Medicine, is an example of the lack of success in promoting faculty involvement in technology transfer.

Substantive change in the School of Medicine began in 1991 with the appointment of a new dean. While mindful of the need to preserve academic excellence, the dean articulated a new mission for the school, one which added social responsibility to education, research, and patient care. Social responsibility included improving relations with the African American neighborhoods in East Baltimore and participation in regional economic development.

The motivation for adding social responsibility as an institutional goal was partly philanthropic and partly survival-oriented. The dean believed that Johns Hopkins should be more responsive to local needs. However, he also understood that the availability of federal research funds was declining and that the institution must add additional sources of revenue to continue its research and service missions.

Through speeches, memoranda, private meetings, and participation in meetings with local community leaders and with venture capitalists, the dean encouraged medical school faculty to play a stronger role in their community. Policies were changed to permit faculty to hold equity in corporations which sponsored their research, but disclosure processes were added to regulate conflict of interest. New and more balanced formulas for sharing financial rewards for technology transfer activities provided incentives for faculty participation.

The medical school upgraded the technology transfer office. Johns Hopkins built new centers to increase liaisons with industry. These included a drug and device development center for preclinical and clinical evaluations of medical products, and centers to help move medical technology into the marketplace. The university-sponsored venture capital fund, which had failed to attract sufficient interest from industry, was restructured and merged with a private fund to create a privately managed entity. For the first time, the School of Medicine cosponsored technology seminars with industry.

The changes initiated by the new dean were not limited to commercialization or profit making. He also made unprecedented changes in the ways in which the local community participated in medical research grants. In one case, he made sure that leaders in the African American community received a substantial part of a large research grant to ensure that the rewards of the research were shared equally between the School of Medicine and the community.

The results are marked. Faculty applications for patents and licenses have increased. Two new companies have been formed using medical technology developed at Johns Hopkins, and a leading venture fund made a public commitment to form ten or more companies with Johns Hopkins over the next five years.

By adding a commitment to social responsibility, and by incorporating both economic development and benefits to the local community into the goal, the dean at Johns Hopkins School of Medicine has moved the faculty and the institution toward greater participation in the local community. The dean has succeeded, at least in part, in achieving a balance between preserving the unique values and strengths of a world-class research institution and meeting the needs of the locality and region.

### Baltimore City Community College (BCCC)

The 1988 report was sharply critical of Baltimore City's only community college. The report recommended either radically reforming the college or abandoning the school and starting over. Frequently cited criticisms of the then-named Community College of Baltimore were weak leadership, excessive bureaucracy, inadequate resources, weak faculty, poor academic quality, and lack of relationships with industry.

Responding to these criticisms, in 1990 the state legislature approved legislation enabling the state to take over the college, assuming responsibility for its governance and financing. Renaming the institution Baltimore City Community College (BCCC), a new board of trustees with strong private sector participation was set up and a new president appointed. The existing faculty union was abolished and tenure ended, replaced by a system of multiyear faculty contracts. The board and president established an evaluation process for faculty, which led to terminations and closures in some programs and to promotions and enhancements in others.

The college administration opted for a new mission, one which called for strong linkages with local industry and an aggressive role in regional economic development. The president met with all of the constituencies, internal and external, to set expectations for faculty to establish the faculty role as one which transcended college boundaries. To reinforce this vision, community involvement was added to hiring and promotion criteria. Centers for business and continuing education were established to promote nontraditional programming. A Life Sciences Institute was added to train technicians needed by local industry.

Have these efforts succeeded? In 1990, BCCC had a poor image, declining enrollment, and few ties with industry. By 1993, BCCC was seen by the local community and industry as an asset. One sign of this change is the increase in enrollment. Up 30 percent in one year, BCCC now has the fastest growing enrollment in the state. BCCC also has negotiated several training contracts with local industry. The Life Sciences Institute is becoming a focal point for education and training initiatives in the region, including special programs linking inner-city high schools with postsecondary institutions.

In many respects, BCCC is now doing no more than the successful community colleges in Baltimore County. The source of change, however, was not a "model of the effective community college" but a response to the economic and training needs of Baltimore City, particularly for minority youth. For BCCC, leadership as symbolized by new policies and rewards resulted in a closer connection between the college and its constituencies.

## IMPLICATIONS FOR ADMINISTRATORS AND FACULTY

Leadership is a necessary but not sufficient ingredient in changing academic cultures. The complex interplay between administrators and faculty, and between institutional and disciplinary norms, mediates the potential impact of direct action by senior administrators. Yet without support from top leadership, and in some cases without specific directions from the central administration or at least from deans, long lasting change is impossible; even short-term change is unlikely. The training, socialization, and incentives for faculty to behave in ways accepted by their academic peers is so strong that it is unlikely that a groundswell for new norms or new directions will come solely from the faculty. Even when change is initiated by individual faculty, senior administrative support is required for institutionalization to take hold.

Effective leadership requires understanding the links between presidents and provosts, on the one hand, and deans and department chairs on the other. Deans and department chairs interpret messages from central administration, modifying their content to fit their own needs and preferences. Even when a president or provost is committed to reforming institutional norms, he or she cannot count on the message being conveyed to faculty in its original form. This organizational structure requires more direct feedback between faculty and senior administrators, and direct communication between provosts and department chairs.

Symbolism is a principal ingredient of transformational leadership. Symbolism embodied in *action* is far more convincing to faculty than symbolism embedded in *rhetoric*. Senior administrators, deans, and department chairs who issue statement after statement in support of technology transfer, teaching, or public service can find their message outweighed by a single highly visible promotion and tenure decision that contradicts these statements.[45] The rhetoric at MBI, for example, suggested a commitment to new forms of research and technology transfer and a new vision of the faculty role. The administrative (and faculty) decisions, however, whether through hiring or through the promotion and tenure process, indicated a commitment to more traditional prestige-oriented norms.

Vision, ability to hire new faculty, identifying and gaining the support of key administrators and faculty—all are important to effective academic leadership. Even in concert, however, these abilities and capacities are insufficient. UMBC succeeded in transforming itself within a specific mission, a unique niche in the Baltimore region. MBI, which had similar advantages (although not the existing capacity), emulated the research university model, at least early in its history, and did not develop a unique niche. MBI can recover and develop a niche at least in part because it has the capacity to hire new faculty; a high percentage of new hires means that departments can be transformed relatively quickly. Although hiring criteria are important levers in attempts to reform institutional norms, they are less effective when the total number of new hires is modest and the percentage of new hires within specific departments or colleges is small.

The importance of institutional distinctiveness; appropriateness of mission relative to the needs of constituencies; and hiring, socializing, and rewarding faculty in a manner consistent with these institutional norms is illuminated by the Morgan State experience. Successful implementation of a teaching-oriented program with special emphasis on local economic needs (primarily addressed through educating students) was based on a combination of active leadership and vision by the dean of engineering, hiring faculty committed to teaching and to responding to local and regional needs, promoting faculty who devoted their time to teaching and service, gaining support from the central administration, and forming liaisons with well-established programs (e.g., the University of Maryland—College Park).

The Johns Hopkins University School of Medicine story shows the potential utility of liaisons with external constituencies as a means to promote internal change. This approach, similar to the one used by deans and department chairs when they prompt their faculty to try something new because faculty members in a respected peer institution are trying it, points to the potential usefulness of looking beyond immediate boundaries, whether within a department or even an institution, in forming coalitions to promote transformation.

Finally, the Baltimore case studies, the Dooris and Fairweather research, and the Matkin book demonstrate the limitations of structural solutions to promoting cultural change. Surely structures do help; ORUs likely increase the research capacity of colleges and universities and coherent patent and licensing policies make it possible for faculty to assess the pros and cons of participating in one form of technology transfer. But structure and policies alone play a very modest role in reformulating faculty roles and rewards. College or university presidents who assume that merely creating a new structure—whether devoted to technology transfer, teaching, or any endeavor which runs counter to dominant disciplinary norms—results in institutional reform will be disappointed.

## NOTES

1. G. W. Matkin, *Technology Transfer and the University* (New York: ACE/Macmillan, 1990).
2. M. J. Dooris and J. S. Fairweather, "Structure and Culture in Faculty Work: Implications for Technology Transfer," *Review of Higher Education*, 17 (1994): 161–78.
3. T. Chmura, J. Fairweather, and J. Melville, *From Bystander to Leader: Challenging Higher Education to Join in Building Baltimore's Economic Future* (Menlo Park, Calif.: SRI International, 1988). Follow-up data for the Baltimore study were gathered by T. Chmura in 1993.
4. Matkin, *Technology Transfer and the University*, 48–53.
5. R. L. Geiger, *To Advance Knowledge: The Growth of American Research Universities, 1900–1940* (New York: Oxford University Press, 1986), 182; Matkin, *Technology Transfer and the University*, 26–7.
6. Matkin, *Technology Transfer and the University*, 27.
7. S. W. Leslie, "Playing the Education Game to Win: The Military and Interdisciplinary Research at Stanford," *Historical Studies in the Physical and Biological Sciences*, 18 (1987): 55–88; Matkin, *Technology Transfer and the University*.
8. Matkin, *Technology Transfer and the University*, 38.
9. R. S. Friedman and R. C. Friedman, "Organized Research Units in Academe Revisited," in *Managing High Technology: An Interdisciplinary Perspective*, ed. B. W. Mar, W. T. Newell, and B. O. Saxberg (New York: Elsevier, 1985), 75–91.

10. L. Peters and H. Fusfeld, "Current U.S. University/Industry Research Connections," in *University-Industry Research Relationships: Selected Studies* (Washington, D.C.: National Science Foundation, 1983), 1–162.

11. J. S. Fairweather, *Entrepreneurship and Higher Education: Lessons for Colleges, Universities, and Industry*, ASHE-ERIC Higher Education Research Report No. 6 (Washington, D.C.: Association for the Study of Higher Education, 1988).

12. Dooris and Fairweather, "Structure and Culture in Faculty Work," 162.

13. For example, P. R. Lawrence and J. W. Lorsch, *Organization and Environment: Managing Differentiation and Integration* (Boston: Harvard University Press, 1967).

14. P. Veen, "Characteristics of Organizations," in *Handbook of Work and Organizational Psychology*, ed. P. J. D. Drenth, H. Thierry, P. J. Williams, and C. J. de Wolff (New York: John Wiley & Sons, 1984), 677–712.

15. P. M. Blau, *The Organization of Academic Work* (New York: John Wiley & Sons, 1973).

16. E. M. Bensimon, A. Neumann, and R. Birnbaum, *Making Sense of Administrative Leadership: The "L" Word in Higher Education*, ASHE-ERIC Higher Education Research Report No. 1 (Washington, D.C.: Association for the Study of Higher Education, 1989).

17. Bensimon, Neumann, and Birnbaum, *Making Sense of Administrative Leadership*, 10.

18. B. M. Bass, *Leadership and Performance Beyond Expectation* (New York: Free Press, 1985).

19. Bensimon, Neumann, and Birnbaum, *Making Sense of Administrative Leadership*, 42.

20. B. R. Clark, "The Organizational Saga in Higher Education," *Administrative Science Quarterly*, 17 (1972): 178–84.

21. Matkin, *Technology Transfer and the University*.

22. Dooris and Fairweather, "Structure and Culture in Faculty Work."

23. Chmura, Fairweather, and Melville, *From Bystander to Leader*.

24. Matkin, *Technology Transfer and the University*, 5.

25. Matkin, *Technology Transfer and the University*, 2–3, 44, 84, 97.

26. Matkin, *Technology Transfer and the University*, 45–6, 84, 92–3.

27. Matkin, *Technology Transfer and the University*, 13, 84, 92–3.

28. Matkin, *Technology Transfer and the University*, 47, 84, 92–3.

29. Matkin, *Technology Transfer and the University*, 120–30.

30. Matkin, *Technology Transfer and the University*, 282–3.

31. Dooris and Fairweather, "Structure and Culture in Faculty Work."

32. Dooris and Fairweather, "Structure and Culture in Faculty Work."

33. Dooris and Fairweather, "Structure and Culture in Faculty Work," 175.

34. Chmura, Fairweather, and Melville, *From Bystander to Leader*.

35. Chmura, Fairweather, and Melville, *From Bystander to Leader*, 34.

36. Chmura, Fairweather, and Melville, *From Bystander to Leader*, 33.

37. Chmura, Fairweather, and Melville, *From Bystander to Leader*, 36–7.

38. Chmura, Fairweather, and Melville, *From Bystander to Leader*, 39.

39. Chmura, Fairweather, and Melville, *From Bystander to Leader*, 48.

40. Chmura, Fairweather, and Melville, *From Bystander to Leader*, 49.

41. Chmura, Fairweather, and Melville, *From Bystander to Leader*, 49.

42.   Data on Morgan State were gathered by S. B. Millar and J. S. Fairweather, *NSF Coalition: Report on the Second Year of Activities: 1991–92* (University Park, Penn.: Center for the Study of Higher Education, Penn State University, 1992).

43.   Dooris and Fairweather, "Structure and Culture in Faculty Work."

44.   Chmura, Fairweather, and Melville, *From Bystander to Leader.*

45.   Millar and Fairweather, *NSF Coalition.*

# ▶ 10

## Reform from Without:

### Lessons for State and Federal Policymakers

The emphasis on research characteristic today of many academic institutions has served the United States well. American colleges and universities, particularly their graduate programs and research productivity, are highly regarded worldwide. Yet the fit between a research-based postsecondary model derived from needs emerging from World War II, especially the evolution of research to meet criteria relevant mainly to the internal academic world, and contemporary societal needs no longer seems adequate. Research is a necessary part of the American system of postsecondary education and a vital part for meeting the challenges of the future, but it is not sufficient to meet the growing number of education and training needs required to meet the challenges of the global economy. I am concerned for the consequences of viewing the subtle, long-term evolution toward accepting research as the primary basis for prestige across types of institutions as a public relations problem rather than as a growing discrepancy between academic values and public needs—concerned that this will lead to the dismantling of one of the great achievements of American society, its collection of colleges and universities. As Bok has said:

> Notwithstanding the improvements that may have taken place in the quality of undergraduate education in this country, the public has finally come to believe quite strongly that our institutions—particularly our leading universities—are not making the education of students a top priority... With the passage of time, the public is

beginning to catch on to our shortcomings. They may not have it quite right—they are often wrong about the facts—but they are often right about our priorities, and they do not like what they see.[1]

In the next two chapters, I examine key factors in helping first state and federal policymakers and then faculty and administrators make choices in meeting complex, competing agendas. In this chapter, I discuss the applicability of the historical response to meeting emerging societal needs, namely creating new types of institutions. Next, I examine the meaning and consequences of societal responsibility for higher education, followed by the importance of developing consensus among various external constituencies in pushing for change in academe. I conclude with lessons for state and federal policymakers. In Chapter 11, I focus on policies and actions by academic administrators. I discuss the implications of change for faculty rewards and academic culture. I conclude with recommendations for changes in administrative action, followed by a description of the professoriate designed to enhance the effectiveness of academe in society and to restore public trust.

## THE HISTORICAL HOPE: NEW TYPES OF INSTITUTIONS

As institutions mature in an arena where mimicry of elites is often the norm, we can expect growing homogeneity in faculty rewards across types of institutions and disciplines. The research on compensation supports this hypothesis. The driving force in many 4-year institutions is to achieve higher status by emphasizing research and scholarship. One consequence is that other goals can be left behind. When sufficient numbers of institutions pursue the same goal by the same means, other goals are shortchanged.

The goal conflict inherent in this transition is evident in the story of a department chair in special education at a research university in the south. Hired when the college of education was devoted more to in-service and teacher training, the department chair spent substantial effort in working with community groups for individuals with disabilities. As the college and university became more research oriented, he published more but continued to work with community service groups. The consequence? The department chair has two letters framed in his office, one from several state groups thanking him for service to people with disabilities, the other from the dean saying that he spent too much time working on matters peripheral to the mission of the college.[2]

This story does not demonstrate inappropriate expectations for a college of education in transition toward a research-oriented model. Nor does this episode show that research per se is an inappropriate outcome; many youth with disabilities and their families have been helped by research carried out in colleges and universities. Instead, this experience exhibits the trade-offs or conflicts inherent in any shift in mission or in an institution where a single activity becomes dominant in faculty rewards—increased emphasis on one activity means less on another.

The pursuit of prestige and emphasis on research and scholarship are not inherently bad. Indeed, these foci are the natural result of pursuing a national agenda established during World War II and after Sputnik to emphasize research in the sciences and engineering.[3] The research accomplishments achieved during this era cannot be denied. What has changed is the flexibility to meet goals that are deemphasized as academic institutions pursue the same research-oriented model. In the past, the policy of the states or the federal government to meet emerging needs in which participation by colleges and universities was deemed essential was to establish new types of institutions. Land grant colleges were established to meet the growing needs of agriculture and mining industries. Community colleges were built to provide access to postsecondary education for students who could not afford to attend otherwise. Although it can be argued that land grant institutions are no longer distinguishable from their prestigious private counterparts,[4] especially in faculty behavior and reward structures, they met the needs for which they were created, and moved onward and upward as the original missions diminished in importance (i.e., in changing from an agrarian to an industrial society).

Without evidence of a substantial change in focus, academic leaders can no longer expect substantial growth in investment for traditional forms of higher education. It is unlikely that state governments or private agencies will create additional colleges and universities to meet traditional missions, such as a modern-day land grant university or an undergraduate college, given the propensity of colleges and universities to evolve toward a research-oriented model. When administrators and faculty seem more motivated by prestige and faculty research productivity than by other missions, including teaching and technology transfer, then investment in other forms of postsecondary education may make more sense. As one example, while the public investment in traditional higher education has slowed, the private investment in alternative forms of postsecondary education, such as corporate colleges and industrial research-and-development consortia, has grown.[5] The meaning of these trends for teaching and training, which historically have been the domain of colleges and universities, is unclear. More obvious is the need to establish and reinforce distinct models for academic institutions, each of which has a different basis for prestige.

Each college or university cannot be all things to all people. Scarce resources demand that difficult choices be made between various desirable activities. The key is to make certain that not all institutions come up with the same answer—research and scholarship—and that the changes in direction are tied with some specific response to societal needs. These choices must be translated into specific departmental and faculty rewards, and into recruiting and hiring decisions, if implementation is to have any meaning.

## SOCIETAL RESPONSIBILITY: MEANING AND CONSEQUENCES

"Academic institutions exist to serve society." Such a simple phrase, yet what complex meaning. Responsiveness to societal needs can mean preservation of traditional functions, such as teaching, and at the same time adding new tasks, such as enhancing literacy and continuing professional education. "Societal needs" hardly connotes a simple, straightforward set of goals or an agenda immune to changes over time. Confronted with conflicting, changing needs and unclear priorities, many academic leaders, not surprisingly, follow internally directed criteria, which they at least understand.

Although Bok and many others have questioned the motivation of academic leaders who pursue prestige through research and scholarship at the expense of other fundamental activities, particularly undergraduate instruction and public service, the lack of a national agenda, agreed upon by a majority of constituencies, makes it difficult to push academic institutions from the outside to change direction.[6] An emphasis on technology transfer demands primacy for applied research and service at selected research universities; undergraduate education and continuing professional education require different priorities. The list of societal demands increases, the relative priority of goals lies unstated, and the responsible party for meeting each need remains ambiguous.

As reflected in the recent large state budget cuts, the consequence of a backlash against higher education institutions which seem unresponsive to societal needs is hardly whimsical. Certainly, better public relations, particularly about the nature of faculty work and workloads, is needed to promote more rational dialogue about the achievements and shortcomings of higher education. But public relations campaigns alone do not resolve how to respond to competing societal needs and agendas, nor do they automatically restore public trust.[7]

In the spirit of using budget crises to achieve positive change, and to make clear where important tasks are being shortchanged because of fiscal inadequacies, I examine the effectiveness of various traditional and emerging academic roles. Research and scholarship are given high priority in many 4-year institutions and this emphasis has paid off. American higher education, particularly graduate education, is highly respected throughout the world. Undergraduate education, both in teaching and curricular development, are more problematic across academic institutions as a whole. The inattention to undergraduate education, according to Bok,[8] can be seen in faculty rewards which emphasize research and publishing, administrative emphasis on graduate and research programs, and the failure to encourage use of teaching techniques which improve learning. Curricula seem out of control, character-ized in complex universities by too many graduate courses with few enroll-ments, too many undergraduate classes with large enrollments, and course duplication.[9]

Public service plays a limited role in faculty time allocation and rewards at all types of 4-year institutions, including those with a professed service mission. Placing greater emphasis on traditional service activities, whether technology transfer through faculty consulting or improving the professions through continuing education, may be useful in meeting service goals. Newer forms of service, including joint ventures with industry, incubators, industrial extension, and aggressive pursuit of patents, fall within both the research and service domains, although their appropriateness for academic institutions and the effectiveness of colleges and universities in achieving in these commercially oriented endeavors is largely unproved. The small num-ber of demonstrable successes so far have been in the field of agriculture and in a small number of elite research institutions which have integrated quality education, research productivity, and links with industry.

Crucial to identifying and choosing between activities to enhance and activities to delete or deemphasize is how *as a system* to integrate traditional missions, such as teaching, with new needs, such as technology transfer. For many institutions, this will require making trade-offs between, say, research and teaching. For others, it will require assessing the trade-offs between research and technology transfer. Regardless, a systemic view of roles and responsibilities is needed. As a society and as a collective of academic insti-tutions, we need to examine which activities academe as a whole should address. Next, we must determine which roles are best suited for higher edu-cation systems within specific states, which are best met by a particular type of institution, which are best suited to a particular institution in a given set-ting, and which disciplines are in the best position to meet particular societal needs. The emerging homogeneity of some types of faculty rewards across types of 4-year institutions and disciplines suggests that as a society we need to find alternative forms of prestige to enable institutions and disciplines to pursue distinct activities and receive rewards for them. To date, a single insti-tutional model, the research university, based on needs expressed 50 years ago, serves as the model to which colleges and universities aspire.

Nowhere is the combination of pursuit of a single research-oriented model and goal conflict more evident than in the professional schools. Col-leges and schools of education, as one example, have become more oriented toward the social sciences and toward mainstream faculty rewards than toward service of the profession.[10] This approach has succeeded in making schools of education accepted within academe; it has not resulted in improved student performance in elementary and secondary schools. Engi-neering is another example: adopting the natural sciences as the norm for professional behavior has increased internal prestige while making service to the profession and to American industry of secondary concern.[11] As a consequence, design has been all but eliminated from many engineering curricula.[12] In both cases, reformers have tried to restore a balance between service to the profession and academic values, transcending the concept of a trade school while simultaneously responding to societal needs. The predominance of the research-oriented model, however, makes such attempts difficult to start and their institutionalization unlikely.

## EXTERNAL PRESSURE AND A NEW CONSENSUS

Although academic institutions are widely perceived to be motivated solely by internal aims,[13] particularly the pursuit of prestige and status, I have argued that internal norms are only part of the picture. History is replete with examples of academic institutions responding to changes in society.[14] Most recently, following World War II, a clear mandate for increased access and for research led institutions to alter their size and functions radically. The shaping of consensus about national priorities for higher education "served to bring our universities into an active, ongoing alliance with government, with business and foundations, with the whole American people in pursuit of goals that everybody agreed were important."[15] Sheridan believes that a "sustained national leverage" is needed to restore teaching to a higher-priority function in academe.[16] She calls for a new national consensus about the importance of teaching as expressed through legislation, funding priorities, and dialogue with academic leaders. Such a consensus requires state and federal governments, the nonprofit sector, industry, community groups, elementary/secondary education, and postsecondary institutions to work together to establish priorities for the multitude of potential missions for colleges and universities. One lesson from the ENGINEER coalition is that support from a prestigious national organization, the NSF, can assist colleges and universities to push the importance of teaching and curricular reform. Institutionalization of change, however, requires fundamental reform in the academic culture and in faculty rewards.

A consensus about the role of academic institutions in the economy is also needed. For most institutions, the greatest long-term economic benefits to society will result from educating the youth of the nation, retraining workers, and providing continuing professional education. Keeping curricula in scientific and technical fields current is also fundamental to keeping the nation competitive in the world economy. Ironically, most of these tasks are consistent with a renewed emphasis on teaching. These human capital functions may be far less glamorous than high-technology research-and-development agreements, but the latter apply to only a handful of schools and faculty; *all* institutions have a stake in education and training. Again, external pressure brought by a union of concerned parties—state and federal (and local) governments, industry, nonprofit associations, parents—is an important ingredient in changing academic institutions.

Faculty and administrators who encourage and pursue a prestige-oriented model that may exacerbate a mismatch with many emerging societal needs are at risk if they believe themselves immune from external events. Recent drastic budget cuts in several states are ample indication of the importance of external support for academic pursuits. As global competition replaces the Cold War as a major external force, the rationale given by both colleges and universities and funding agencies for large investments in research, particularly research devoted to technology with defense applications, seems increasingly outmoded. Developing one or more alternatives to the research and prestige norms is not simply a matter of courage, battling upstream against conventional norms; it is a matter of survival.

## LESSONS FOR STATE AND FEDERAL POLICYMAKERS

Recent congressional action and proposed state legislation indicates the seriousness attached by the public to the apparent lack of attention paid by colleges and universities to undergraduate education. Some states have proposed adopting mandatory standards for hours spent in the classroom to ensure that faculty pay more attention to teaching and learning.[17] These external expressions of values are useful in making academic leaders aware of emerging societal needs and of needs which are perceived as neglected. Legislation is not useful, however, in reforming faculty cultures or reward structures; faculty may spend less time doing research and publishing under proposed legislative schemes, but that alone does not reduce the *value* of these activities in faculty rewards. Moreover, increased hours spent in the classroom do not guarantee more effective teaching and learning.

Legislation to force changes in faculty workloads also does not address the conflicting values placed by various external constituencies on academic activities. For example, legislation and federal and state policy also encourage colleges and universities to participate in applied research, technology transfer, and economic development. Legislation alone does not make a coherent national agenda, nor does it establish relative criteria by which academic institutions can judge their performance.

To assist academic institutions in improving the quality of undergraduate instruction and public service, state and federal policymakers first must understand that their role is primarily indirect. Regardless of regulation or legislative action, teaching and learning (and research and public service) take place in classrooms, libraries, laboratories, computer facilities, and professors' offices, not in state or federal capitols. Students learn by working with their peers, talking with and receiving feedback from faculty, and through various out-of-class experiences. However much a legislator or policymaker desires to enhance the value of teaching or public service, the policymaking role can only be indirect.

The second fact of life for policymakers is that state and federal governments have more than one educational policy goal. Although improving undergraduate education and increasing affordability are important, so are increased economic development, technology transfer, and even basic research. Conflicting messages about state and federal educational priorities simply make it easier for administrators and faculty to follow internally directed norms.

The combination of complex legislative goals and the local nature of teaching, research, and service (that is, academic functions typically involve professors and students and take place on or near campus) makes legislative attempts to micromanage academic affairs problematic. The complexity of any single academic institution, much less a system of institutions, and the competing interests at the state and federal policy levels mean that attempts to specify faculty workloads, time spent on instruction, and so forth can have disastrous consequences. No piece of regulation or legislation can take account of the various local needs of institutions, the variety of disciplines and course sizes, and so on. A more effective approach is for federal and (especially) state policymakers to make clear the relative priorities of academic activities (perhaps by type of institution) and to provide incentives for achieving a redirection of focus in line with these priorities.

The first step in this direction is to replace the tired old research-oriented national agenda, which dates to World War II and Sputnik, with a more relevant vision for the next century. Whether in the form of presidential address, governor's state-of-the-state address, or other highly visible and prestigious vehicles, a redirection of the national interest in higher education must be presented in a coherent form. Without replacing the existing research-oriented mandate with a new one, piecemeal change will be the rule, not the exception.

Communication mechanisms to get the word out exist but currently are underutilized. Nonprofit organizations such as the Western Interstate Commission for Higher Education, the Education Commission of the States, the Southern Regional Education Board, and even the regional accreditation associations can form a link between policymakers and academic leaders. Currently, this interconnection is tenuous and not relied on as a regular network for informing academic institutions about legislative intent (or for informing policymakers about the needs of academic institutions).

Broad mandates are not enough. They must be supplemented by action. One example of a successful effort to reform academic cultures through incentives in line with a commitment to improving teaching is the National

Science Foundation's (NSF) broad-based efforts to enhance the undergraduate student experience. By providing significant funds for teaching activities, this high-prestige organization is succeeding in enhancing the value of instruction in faculty rewards because its name is being lent to instructional activities.[18] Indeed, it is the availability of large funds for research by agencies such as the NSF that has also contributed substantially to the creation of a research-oriented culture in academe.

The NSF experience suggests that targeted funds may act as incentives for change. Rather than specifying specific instructional practices, the NSF provides funds on the basis of likelihood of improving the student learning experience. State and federal policymakers might use the same incentive-oriented practice, specifying and setting aside funds specifically for teaching and/or service but without mandating specific practices.

Relatedly, capital expenditures typically are based on replacing or restoring facilities, not on enhancing particular functions. Why not tie a certain portion of capital expenditures to instruction-related buildings, such as classrooms, laboratories, and libraries?

California provides an example of a state-wide system-level approach to codify commitment to teaching by distinguishing between types of institutions and their purposes. California has specified that the California State University system be devoted primarily to teaching and has mandated a minimum teaching load for faculty in this sector. The University of California system, on the other hand, offers doctoral degrees and has a greater focus on research. Yet the system-level approach has not been without problems. Despite the concern about teaching, the California legislature has recently drastically hurt the instructional capacity of California State Universities with severe budget cuts. The cuts have made it difficult even to offer enough courses for students to graduate. Even though the University of California has been criticized for a lack of commitment to undergraduate education (including by an internal report, the Pfister Report), the university system is far less dependent on state monies and less influenced by state decrees. Certainly, leaders in the California State University system would find it difficult to enhance the value of teaching in their institutions with the existing budget cuts.

Finally, direct state or federal intervention in faculty workloads and work assignments seems unlikely to generate the type of reform envisioned by policymakers. The variety of local faculty situations and the difference in institutional types and missions precludes developing a useful uniform workload statement. Yet state legislators, in particular, can express their concern about student learning by stating that students attending public colleges and universities should expect to be taught by full-time, tenure-track professors for at least part of their undergraduate experience.

In summary, the role of state and federal policymakers is not to run academic institutions but to provide a coherent policy framework which can guide administrative decision making. More than ever, academic administrators attempting to restore the instructional and service missions require a coherent message from external policymakers about the importance of these neglected missions.

## NOTES

1. D. Bok, "Reclaiming the Public Trust," *Change*, 24 (1992): 15, 18.
2. M. Kane and J. Fairweather, *Issues in the Preparation of Special Education Teachers* (Washington, D.C.: Pelavin Associates, 1988).
3. R. L. Geiger, *To Advance Knowledge: The Growth of American Research Universities, 1900–1940* (New York: Oxford University Press, 1986).
4. G. E. Schuh, "Revitalizing Land Grant Universities: It's Time to Regain Relevance," *Choices* (1986): 6–10.
5. N. P. Eurich, *Corporate Classrooms: The Learning Business* (Princeton, N.J.: Carnegie Foundation for the Advancement of Teaching, 1985).
6. Bok, "Reclaiming the Public Trust," 16.
7. G. C. Winston, "Hostility, Maximization, and Public Trust," *Change*, 24 (1992): 20–7.
8. Bok, "Reclaiming the Public Trust."
9. M. Lazerson and U. Wagener, "Rethinking How Colleges Operate," *Chronicle of Higher Education*, 39 (1992): A44.
10. G. J. Clifford and J. W. Guthrie, *Ed School: A Brief for Professional Education* (Chicago: University of Chicago Press, 1988).
11. J. A. Haddad, "New Factors in the Relationship between Engineering Education and Research," in *The New Engineering Research Centers: Purposes, Goals, and Expectations* (Washington, D.C.: National Academy Press, 1986), 129–36.
12. S. B. Millar and J. S. Fairweather, *NSF Coalition: Report on the Second Year of Activities: 1991–92* (University Park, Penn.: Center for the Study of Higher Education, Penn State University, 1992).
13. For example, R. E. Anderson, "The Advantages and Risks of Entrepreneurship," *Academe*, 76 (1990): 9–14.
14. J. Ben-David, *Trends in American Higher Education* (Chicago: University of Chicago Press, 1972).
15. Bok, "Reclaiming the Public Trust," 18.
16. H. W. Sheridan, "Ichabod Crane Dies Hard: Renewing Professional Commitments to Teaching," in *How Administrators Can Improve Teaching*, ed. P. Seldin (San Francisco: Jossey-Bass, 1990), 169.
17. R. L. Jacobsen, "Colleges Face New Pressure to Increase Faculty Productivity," *Chronicle of Higher Education*, 38 (April 15, 1992): 1.
18. Millar and Fairweather, *NSF Coalition*.

# ► 11

## Reform from Within:
### Lessons for Academic Administrators

Contrary to claims made by many critics,[1] faculty inactivity or lack of productivity is not at the heart of the growing disparity between academic norms and societal needs. Instead, the key issues are how faculty spend their time and an increasingly uniform set of behavioral expectations based on research productivity for faculty in all types of 4-year institutions. The creation and maintenance of a faculty culture relies on both socialization and rewards. Faculty cultures are also reinforced by administrative behavior. I discuss socialization, rewards, leadership, and administrative behavior in this section.

## THE FACULTY CULTURE

### Faculty Socialization

The NSOPF data show that faculty beliefs about the importance of research in assessing faculty performance are powerful predictors of behavior. The influence of faculty beliefs on behavior, including faculty governance and personnel decisions as well as teaching and research, places boundaries on administrative influence. The variety of expectations about research, teaching, and service which faculty bring with them to an academic position are developed initially in graduate school. Whether during experience as a research assistant or a teaching assistant, graduate students are clearly shown the importance of research over teaching and service. Few institutions provide training for teaching assistants. The emphasis of research assistants is less on preparing for a well-rounded faculty position and more on helping their mentors achieve high status in their professional communities. Indeed, the doctoral-degree experience emphasizes subject matter expertise and research design, not pedagogical preparation.

Redressing the imbalance in faculty behavior toward research and away from teaching and service must start with reforming the graduate-school experience. Whether adding courses in pedagogy or including training for teaching assistants, the doctoral experience must expose students to a broader array of activities than is currently available in most institutions. Graduate research assistants should learn that the implications of research, including technology transfer, are as important as the rewards derived from publishing research results. To be effective, graduate students must also see that faculty are *rewarded* for activities other than publishing and research, including teaching and service. When good teachers, faculty who spend time on public service, and staff who assist in technology transfer are not rewarded, the implicit message for graduate students is that research and publishing are all that count, and that they should be prepared to spend their time accordingly when they enter an academic position.

Prior to  entering the profession, new faculty also receive strong signals about expected behavior during the hiring process.[2] In tight labor markets, teaching-oriented institutions have been able to attract a higher percentage of Ph.D. graduates from research and doctoral-granting universities, which over time may lead to an institutional culture less devoted to teaching. Hiring criteria are especially important in comprehensive and liberal arts colleges, where survey data show that faculty socialization is a major factor in faculty research behavior. In these institutions, when the criteria for hiring new professors emphasize research above all else, the result is more research, less teaching and service.[3] In all institutions, potential hires should be asked to demonstrate their teaching ability. This experience should not be superficial—say a one-hour lecture given only to faculty—but should be an exercise sufficient to establish the teaching ability of new recruits. When technology transfer of a specific type is the goal, evidence of ability is also useful. Above all, mere evidence of ability to publish in refereed journals does not warrant belief in the capacity of new faculty to perform in other areas.

The message given during the hiring process about the importance of teaching and public service should be reinforced early in the new professor's experience. Making assessment and improvement of teaching, for example, an expected part of the job, and making instructional development a useful and easily available resource, rather than an office whose materials are filed in the wastebasket, lets new faculty know that administrators and their faculty peers take teaching seriously. Without immediate reinforcement, new faculty question the seriousness of administrative support.

Finally, faculty must confront their contribution to the continuation of a prestige-oriented model. As participants in promotion and tenure decisions, faculty need not rely solely on administrative direction to assert the value of teaching in faculty work lives. How discouraging for new faculty to find that their newly tenured colleagues who have survived the publish-or-perish gauntlet simply vote to continue the emphasis on research and publishing when they become eligible to vote on promotion and tenure committees. Taking a stand in favor of teaching excellence in the personnel review process is a contribution faculty members can make to reforming the prestige-oriented academic culture.

## Redefining Research and Public Service

Faculty and administrators must confront the teacher/scholar ideology dominant in academe, and assess decisions about faculty rewards and behavior in light of the trade-offs and conflicts between various activities. We can no longer expect that investment in research per se benefits teaching, continuing professional education, technology transfer, or other forms of public service. Indeed, the entire configuration of faculty research activities needs reexamining. How much research is needed and of what types? How much of faculty research is directed toward professional development and rewards instead of societal needs? An honest assessment of faculty research behavior *and its larger social impact* may point out ways in which faculty can redirect their efforts toward other tasks without significantly harming the research mission.

Redefining research first requires expanding the acceptable form of research productivity beyond refereed articles and books. Applied research with demonstrable benefit to a region or locality but which is not published in traditional outlets, testimony to a state or federal legislature, and the like should become acceptable forms of research dissemination, especially when consistent with institutional missions. Regional institutions, in particular, should treat regionally responsive knowledge and technology transfer activities as highly in their tenure, promotion, and pay considerations as nationally directed refereed publications. Faculty will not pursue these alternative forms of research and dissemination if they are punished in the promotion and tenure process for doing so.

Redefining research also means shifting toward measures of impact and away from volume. Donald Kennedy attempted such an approach while president of Stanford University, asking faculty to present their most important works when coming up for promotion rather than submitting the entire volume of their work. Shifting toward impact, however, requires a more labor-intensive faculty evaluation process; simply counting the number of articles published is easier. Without making the effort to change, the emphasis on research volume restricts efforts to enhance teaching or public service because it inevitably reduces the amount of time faculty can devote to other tasks.

Research has another value quite apart from its contribution to promotion, tenure, and pay, and the social good it produces. For faculty with heavy teaching loads, research offers the opportunity for professional advancement and renewal whether or not publication results. This process of renewal helps keep faculty teaching fresh; it should be valued for its professional development benefits rather than for its research impact.

Redefining public service is also in order. An expanded view would incorporate the contributions to the economy of teaching, continuing education, basic and applied research, and direct forms of technology transfer. In this arena, public relations are important; many colleges and universities and their faculty do not receive credit for the contributions they already make to the economy.

Especially important is understanding and conveying that good teaching enhances economic impact in a variety of ways. Having students learn to work in teams and to engage actively in solving problems makes for a more highly skilled workforce. Businesses which do not have to invest scarce resources in educating employees in how to work together and how to think critically can be more productive and innovative. Ironically, active and collaborative learning experiences have the further advantage of promoting enhanced learning outcomes, which is the ultimate goal of refocusing faculty work on teaching.

When new forms of technology transfer are needed, which is especially true for research universities and for high-technology disciplines in the sciences and engineering, then administrators and faculty need to add these new tasks to the consideration of trade-offs for faculty time. These additional tasks, such as direct involvement with industry, can be achieved in several ways. First, as described later, not all faculty need to follow the same behavioral model. Some can devote their efforts to technology transfer for a period of time while others add research and teaching activities. Alternatively, new tasks can be added by examining the effort already devoted to research and redirecting the energy consumed by the singular pursuit of research volume. Finally, public service as a concept must be reinforced in faculty rewards. Rather than thinking about service as a marginal activity accounting for an average of two percent of a faculty member's time, service should receive the attention it deserves in a modern economy that requires faster and faster transferral of knowledge from colleges and universities to the outside world.

## *Faculty Rewards*

Direct faculty rewards, whether through promotion and tenure or compensation, also strongly influence faculty behavior. The move toward a research-based model for faculty rewards across types of institutions and disciplines is as much a function of rewards as of socialization. The NSOPF data show that professed differences in institutional missions are not matched by differences in faculty pay. Instead, pay in all types of 4-year schools contributes to early faculty socialization by paying assistant professors who spend their time on research and publishing considerably more than their counterparts who devote their time to teaching and service.

The problem is twofold. First, all rewards—promotion, tenure, pay—are based to some extent on research productivity. The emphasis of each type of reward on a single primary behavior strongly reinforces norms in favor of research fostered during graduate school. Levin argues that the various forms of reward should emphasize different behaviors.[4] Leaders in colleges and universities who desire more evenly distributed rewards might, for example, pay their top teachers high salaries while keeping promotion and tenure tied more closely to research productivity.

The second factor in using rewards to reinforce research productivity is the ambiguity of the promotion and tenure process. The ambiguity promotes a "ratcheting effect," in which assistant professors must choose higher and higher standards for research performance to make certain they achieve enough publications for tenure.[5] Department chairs, deans, and provosts might be better served by making expectations for research productivity clear, especially the difference between quality of research and volume. Unless the ambiguity of research volume is addressed, the time faculty devote to research will inevitably rise.

## Redefining Faculty Productivity

Johnathan Cole, provost at Columbia University, claims that no single campus has the resources to address an infinite variety of fields of inquiry. Crucial to enhancing institutional effectiveness, including instructional excellence, is making choices between areas of inquiry, with the goal of reducing the expanse of institutional pursuits while enhancing quality: "If… universities can no longer cover all areas of knowledge, then each university will have to determine those areas in which it has comparative advantages in developing and maintaining true distinction."[6] Concomitant with the need to make choices between potential fields of study is the need to enhance teaching without destroying the research mission: "The real puzzle is how to reshape a reward system, which has been created by the competition for quality and prestige in research and which has upset the balance between teaching and research, so that the scales are rebalanced and research is unimpaired."[7]

Determining the quality and desirability of different fields of inquiry and defining the commitment to service and teaching require an academic institution to assess its strengths and weaknesses. This assessment should be used to clarify institutional commitment to teaching, research, and public service. Such a clarification is the first step in redefining faculty roles and in creating relevant measures of faculty productivity.

When a college or university requires faculty to demonstrate in detail the success of their research agendas while requiring only minimal documentation of teaching effectiveness and commitment to public service, by default the measures of faculty productivity reinforce prestige-oriented norms. Redefining teaching productivity should start with distinguishing between measures of time devoted to teaching and instructional effectiveness. Accurate measures of hours spent in the classroom and total time devoted to instructional activities should be added to student assessments of instructional effectiveness in faculty records. More detailed information about instructional effectiveness, including teaching portfolios, peer review of syllabi and instructional performance, and the like would increase the seriousness with which faculty treat teaching activities.

Criteria for assessing faculty teaching effectiveness should be based on research about effective pedagogy. By adding such indicators to faculty dossiers, and by attaching resource allocation decisions to these assessments, academic leaders can demonstrate a commitment to teaching: "[The current environment demonstrates] the absence of institutional interest in understanding the basis for a productive advanced learning experience, and an unwillingness of many research universities to commit the resources necessary to improve teaching performance."[8]

Similarly, academic leaders can help redress the imbalance between teaching and research by stressing the quality of faculty research over volume and by examining the focus of research relative to institutional mission. If public service is an important function, faculty should be required to demonstrate their participation and effectiveness in meaningful ways. In an urban comprehensive college with a professed mission of increasing access for minority youth, working with local schools to encourage minority youth to enroll in college should be treated more seriously than giving a speech or serving on a committee. The more clarity given to the definition of and importance assigned to various measures of faculty productivity, especially undervalued functions such as teaching and public service, the more likely reform is to succeed.

## LEADERSHIP AND STRUCTURAL SOLUTIONS

### *Reformed Administration*

Are academic administrators to blame for the perceived imbalance between teaching, research, and service, and for the claimed mismatch between emerging societal needs and current academic values? This question, implicit in many recent criticisms of academe, portrays the chief focus of academic administrators as the pursuit of prestige and status: "What presidents and deans are held accountable for is improving the prestige of their institutions, and the prestige of their institutions comes from the research reputation of their faculties."[9] Added weight is given to this perspective by the recent overhead fiascos at some institutions and by the interest in making profit from commercially oriented ventures: "We need to pay less attention to what's legal and a good deal more attention to the appropriateness of what we do. We need, more often, to decide that some activities—especially when they are well-funded—simply aren't appropriate to our purposes."[10]

Yet if academic leaders are to blame for the current state of distrust, surely they must also receive credit for meeting the research directives implicit in the post–World War II national agenda and for enhancing the prestige of American higher education internationally through the value placed on research and graduate education. Credit is also due for the high economic value of higher education to society, both for individuals and for society as a whole.[11] These achievements are not trivial; they are the cornerstone of much of the economic growth and social well-being of the nation.

These contrasting views—leaders as villains and leaders as saviors—reflect the unfair distribution of blame and credit allocated to administrators for the perceived accomplishments and inadequacies of their institutions.[12] Confronted with ambiguous messages from state and federal governments, and from the public about the relative importance of undergraduate education, on the one hand, and research and technology transfer, on the other, many top administrators have continued to pursue a research-and-graduate-training model which has been shown effective in enhancing institutional prestige.

What criticisms of administrators are fair and what can they do to improve the responsiveness of academe to societal needs? Academic leaders can and should be more aggressive in leading a public discourse about emerging societal needs and about the trade-offs involved in changing the direction of academic endeavors. Although some schools have attempted to reshape faculty values about the relative importance of teaching and service, more often the call for change has come from the outside, such as in Boyer's call for new definitions of scholarship.[13] Developing alternative models to achieve prestige, one based on criteria other than refereed publications, and to encourage acceptance of these alternatives inside and outside of academe is especially important.

Perhaps even more important is to recognize that the evolution toward a research-oriented reward structure can lead over time to the loss of institutional identity; colleges and universities can become interchangeable places for faculty to hang their disciplinary hats.[14] Alpert's claim that the institutional focus on meeting societal needs conflicts with the inwardly directed focus in the disciplines on research and publishing (and on acceptable forms of these behaviors) rings hollow when data on compensation show that the institutional focus is *in concert with* that of the disciplines.[15] In this context, academic leaders need to *restore* the conflict between meeting societal and internally motivated, disciplinary-oriented values.

Administrators are not justified in decrying the lack of faculty involvement in continuing professional education or in solving community problems while they pay faculty who spend more time on service and teaching less than those who publish and conduct research. The formation of organized research units to promote interdisciplinary research, of cluster colleges to foster interdisciplinary education, and even of joint industry ventures to foster technology transfer tends to happen on the periphery of core academic activities, placed there intentionally to avoid confrontation with departments. While this approach may appear to allow administrators to "have their cake and eat it too" by preserving traditional functions while pursuing new ones, in effect it simply reinforces to most faculty the lack of legitimacy and importance of interdisciplinary work, of attempts to enhance undergraduate education, and of technology transfer.

Finally, administrators must recognize that the administrator-as-representative model of leadership, in which a provost, dean, or department chair sees her or his role as one of representing colleagues rather than leading them in a new direction, is consistent with democratic values and maintaining traditional faculty norms but ineffective in pushing for changes needed by the society the university was established to serve. When deans feel powerless to enhance the value of teaching in faculty rewards because faculty committees have the initial vote in promotion and tenure, they ignore their influence in determining faculty pay, another reward, and in the symbolic importance of their position in affecting faculty committees.[16] The key to enhancing undergraduate education, creating more effective and realistic forms of knowledge and technology transfer, serving underrepresented groups, and even preserving research and scholarship ultimately lies in changing faculty cultures. Although faculty involvement is obviously crucial, institutions cannot hope to evolve without more directive and supportive leadership.

## *Effective Management*

The purported answer to enhancing the performance of academic institutions is better management.[17] Management is essential to improve the efficiency of institutional operations, to justify the expenditures of public (and private) monies, to ensure the appropriate use of overhead expenditures, and to enhance efficiency.[18] Management is seen by state legislators as the key to enforcing standards for faculty workloads and productivity. Finally, management is cited as a tool for choosing between competing agendas. In this context, strategic planning is a mechanism to make fair choices between competing needs by involving affected parties in a democratic process.

Without question, better management is essential to making effective use of resources. Yet management alone is not sufficient to make choices between competing agendas. Strategic planning, for example, often hides the actual choices being made. Consider the all-too-typical scenario in which a provost asks department heads to demonstrate the productivity of their faculty to assist in making difficult choices about which departments should be continued and which should be eliminated. The process is intended as a democratic endeavor to choose between difficult alternatives. Whether encouraged by the provost or in response to academic norms, the department heads collect a little data about teaching loads, perhaps one or two items from student evaluations of teaching, and several measures of research productivity. The latter are seen, correctly, as the key to prestige and are the most likely to be heavily weighted in decisions when administrators pursue the enhancement of status. What does *not* enter this decision process is whether the relative values of teaching, research, and service are appropriate to meet needs other than enhanced prestige.

## Structural Solutions

Even the most ardent faculty supporters of change in undergraduate education or public service eventually must pay a professional price for long-term participation in curricular innovation, technology transfer, or other less prestigious activities. In this context, structural options are important to give administrators, faculty, students, and parents a way to improve undergraduate learning. One such mechanism, the cluster or experimental college, has been tried, often quite successfully, in the 1960s and 1970s.[19] The concept, embodied by colleges such as the Residential College at the University of Michigan, creates a "living/learning" environment by placing students into a small subset within a larger college or university. This approach, and others like it, creates an "undergraduate experience radically at odds with a vision of the college as either a vocational training facility or an anteroom to the graduate schools."[20]

Most cluster colleges founded in the 1960s and 1970s failed, not because of ineffective student outcomes but because of disciplinary conflicts.[21] Interdisciplinary colleges whose faculty joined the new units because of an interest in undergraduate education did not fit the traditional disciplinary, research-oriented faculty model. Even though student outcomes often were improved in the cluster-college approach,[22] the inability to institutionalize change because of the consequences for faculty, many of whom did not achieve tenure or were not accepted in traditional departments, was the rule, not the exception.[23] To respond adequately to societal needs, whether in teaching or research, academic institutions eventually must address the need for interdisciplinary work whose status is accepted in traditional departments. Peripheral organizations, such as experimental colleges or even organized research units, do not threaten or even necessarily impact departmental values and activities.[24] Rather, cluster colleges or similar approaches must become a mainstream form for undergraduate education. Perhaps differential rewards for faculty are needed, or adoption of student-oriented outcomes added to departmental definitions of program quality.

Beyond structure lies the larger academic goal, changing the emphasis from course content as an expression of faculty research interests and pro forma collection of credits toward reforming the student intellectual and social experience.[25] At the least, some overlap between student experiences and faculty research interests is needed to improve undergraduate learning. By starting with desirable student experiences as the focus, it is possible to design appropriate structures and change curricula to achieve these experiences.

## Creating and Maintaining Distinctiveness

Clark has shown that distinctiveness benefits colleges and universities by attracting students, faculty, and funds.[26] The pursuit of prestige through faculty research productivity, however, can minimize distinctiveness and promote the status of existing elites. Why should parents send their children to institutions which attempt to mimic elites when they can send them directly to the elites? The answer has been that elite institutions have insufficient space for all, and that other schools which follow the dominant norms can provide a similar experience for students who cannot afford to attend an elite institution or who cannot meet entrance requirements. Yet why not offer an alternative model for higher education, one which emphasizes the quality of the educational experience, or exposure to alternative forms of research activity, or participation in community service? Academic leaders need to clarify differences between institutions and their missions, and to redefine distinctiveness in a manner more in line with societal needs.

Enhancing distinctiveness requires reform in faculty rewards and in faculty careers. One mechanism to create distinctiveness is to add external criteria to the assessment of faculty and institutional performance. Research productivity, for example, might be judged both by its acceptance among academic peers and by its value to society. The benefits of technology transfer should go beyond those accruing to the institution.

Another factor is to recognize the effects of time allocation and workload on faculty behavior, and the contribution which administrators make through work assignments to an emphasis on publishing and research productivity as the dominant research-driven model. Teaching loads, types of classes, and administrative assignments influence how faculty spend their time; modification of these assignments can lead to changes in faculty behavior.

Finally, policies which encourage uniform faculty behavior during the career reinforce existing norms and detract from distinctiveness. Rewards currently emphasize publishing and research *throughout the career*. Why not encourage faculty to spend their time differently as they progress through their careers? This policy might lead to a greater devotion to teaching, technology transfer, or other activities at different times during the career.

## THE FACULTY PROFESSION REVISITED

Neither legislation to impose standard teaching workloads nor the current faculty reward systems confront the main barrier to reform, namely the individual nature of faculty rewards based on a limited definition of performance. The focus of higher education on the individual faculty member, on specialized programs within discipline-oriented departments, and on a single dominant model—the research university—has ensured perpetuation of the current emphasis on research and scholarship. Faculty within an institution, a department, or a program are required to follow the same behavioral pattern as other faculty to receive promotion, tenure, and high pay.

Missing in this approach to faculty rewards is any concept of group responsibility or of the importance to quality assessment of student-related outcome measures. *Faculty* are judged individually on their achievements; *departments* or other *units* are judged not by a measure of larger good but by the sum of the performance by individual faculty. The primacy of research and publishing in faculty rewards, even at nonresearch universities, indicates that the performance of groups is judged by limited criteria. It is possible for a department or other unit to be judged of high quality because the faculty adhere individually to high standards for publishing. Yet the same department might have a low graduation rate, poor advising standards, and limited student satisfaction. Research and publishing are not inherently related to low performance on teaching-related indicators or to poor student performance, but they are not necessarily indicative of positive student learning outcomes either.[27]

Some concept of group is required to free faculty from pursuing identical behaviors. Incorporating student outcomes not just for individual faculty evaluations but for the group as well is crucial to meeting a wider variety of societal needs. In this vision, a mixture of faculty, some spending more time on teaching, others on research and service, is more likely to achieve a wider array of goals than a faculty in which each member within a unit is judged on the same limited criteria. Adopting group-centered values, or at least enhancing their relevance in faculty evaluations, requires recognizing the value of the role an individual plays in the group. Consider a hypothetical department with ten faculty. The group must meet both individual performance criteria and group-centered outcomes. The faculty decide to meet the group obligations (e.g., advising, teaching, student satisfaction, graduation rates) by having faculty best-suited to advising and teaching spend more time on these roles, while faculty more capable at research spend a higher proportion of their time on that activity. I am not arguing that some faculty in a group should neglect the wider array of faculty activities; faculty who spend more time teaching should also publish, and faculty who spend more time on research should also teach. I am advocating a new reward system for faculty, one which encourages teaching and service as well as research and scholarship, includes group as well as individual achievement, and recognizes that faculty are not the only constituency that counts in academic institutions.

Unless faculty and administrators develop and implement acceptable standards for assessing student performance, determining faculty effectiveness in activities other than research, and evaluating the fit between institutional outcomes and societal needs, then legislatures, federal agencies, and even nonprofit entities may impose such standards. I believe it much preferable for academic leaders to develop solutions to these problems from within. If academic administrators and their faculty fail to respond, complaints about outside intervention and its threat to academic freedom will fall on deaf ears.

## NOTES

1. For example, M. Anderson, *Imposters in the Temple* (New York: Simon and Schuster, 1992).
2. M. A. Faia, "Teaching and Research: Rapport or Mésalliance," *Research in Higher Education*, 4 (1976): 242.
3. D. E. Finnegan, "Academic Career Lines: A Case Study of Faculty in Two Comprehensive Universities," unpublished doctoral dissertation (University Park, Penn.: Penn State University, 1992).
4. H. M. Levin, "Raising Productivity in Higher Education," *Journal of Higher Education*, 62 (1991): 241–62.
5. R. Zemsky, W. F. Massy, and P. Oedel, "On Reversing the Ratchet," *Change*, 25 (1993): 56–62.
6. J. R. Cole, "Balancing Acts: Dilemmas of Choice Facing Research Universities," *Daedalus*, 122 (1993): 10.
7. Cole, "Balancing Act," 24–5.
8. Cole, "Balancing Act," 27.
9. D. Bok, "Reclaiming the Public Trust," *Change*, 24 (1992): 16.
10. G. C. Winston, "Hostility, Maximization, and the Public Trust," *Change*, 24 (1992): 27.
11. L. L. Leslie and P. T. Brinkman, *The Economic Value of Higher Education* (New York: ACE/Macmillan, 1988).

12. E. M. Bensimon, A. Neumann, and R. Birnbaum, *Making Sense of Administrative Leadership: The "L" Word in Higher Education*, ASHE-ERIC Higher Education Research Report No. 1 (Washington, D.C.: Association for the Study of Higher Education, 1989).
13. E. L. Boyer, *Scholarship Reconsidered: Priorities of the Professoriate* (Princeton, N.J.: Carnegie Foundation for the Advancement of Teaching, 1990).
14. J. P. Bieber, J. H. Lawrence, and R. T. Blackburn, "Through the Years—Faculty and their Changing Institution," *Change*, 24 (1992), 35.
15. D. Alpert, "Performance and Paralysis: The Organizational Context of the American Research University," *Journal of Higher Education*, 56 (1985): 241–81.
16. S. B. Millar and J. S. Fairweather, *NSF Coalition: Report on the Second Year of Activities: 1991–92* (University Park, Penn.: Center for the Study of Higher Education, Penn State University, 1992).
17. For example, G. Keller, *Academic Strategy* (Baltimore: Johns Hopkins University Press, 1983).
18. Winston, "Hostility, Maximization, and the Public Trust," 27.
19. J. G. Gaff and Associates, *The Cluster College* (San Francisco: Jossey-Bass, 1970); G. Grant and D. Riesman, *The Perpetual Dream: Reform and Experiment in the American College* (Chicago: University of Chicago Press, 1978).
20. Grant and Riesman, *The Perpetual Dream*, 355.
21. Grant and Riesman, *The Perpetual Dream*, 368.
22. E. T. Pascarella and P. T. Terenzini, *How College Affects Students* (San Francisco: Jossey-Bass, 1991).
23. Grant and Riesman, *The Perpetual Dream*, 370.
24. M. J. Dooris and J. S. Fairweather, "Structure and Culture in Faculty Work: Implications for Technology Transfer," *Review of Higher Education*, 17 (1994): 161–78.
25. Pascarella and Terenzini, *How College Affects Students*.
26. B. R. Clark, *The Distinctive College: Antioch, Reed and Swarthmore* (Chicago: Aldine, 1970).
27. K. A. Feldman, "Research Productivity and Scholarly Accomplishment of College Teachers as Related to Their Instructional Effectiveness," *Research in Higher Education*, 26 (1987): 227–98.

# References

Aggarwal, R. 1981. Faculty members as consultants: A policy perspective. *Journal of the College and University Personnel Association* 32:17–20.

Albert, K. M., W. B. Hull, and D. M. Sprague. 1989. *The dynamic west: A region in transition*. Denver: The Council of State Governments.

Alfred, R. L., and J. Weissman. 1987. *Higher education and the public trust: Improving stature in colleges and universities*. ASHE-ERIC Higher Education Research Report No. 6. Washington, D.C.: Association for the Study of Higher Education.

Allison, P., and J. A. Stewart. 1974. Productivity differences among scientists: Evidence for accumulative advantage. *American Sociological Review* 39:596–606.

Alpert, D. 1985. Performance and paralysis: The organizational context of the American research university. *Journal of Higher Education* 56:241–81.

American Association of University Professors. 1989. The annual report on the economic status of the profession, 1988–89. *Academe* 75.

Anderson, M. 1992. *Imposters in the temple*. New York: Simon and Schuster.

Anderson, R. E. 1990. The advantages and risks of entrepreneurship. *Academe* 76:9–14.

Angelo, T. A. (ed). 1991. *Classroom research: Early lessons from success*. San Francisco: Jossey-Bass.

Angelo, T. A., and K. P. Cross. 1993. *Classroom assessment techniques: Handbook for college teachers*. 2nd ed. San Francisco: Jossey-Bass.

Ashby, E. 1974. *Adapting universities to a technological society*. San Francisco: Jossey-Bass.

Association of American Colleges. 1985. *Integrity of the college curriculum: A report to the academic community*. Washington, D.C.: Association of American Colleges.

Association of American Universities. 1986. *Trends in technology transfer at universities*. Washington, D.C.: Association of American Universities.

Austin, A. E. 1992. Supporting junior faculty through a teaching fellows program. In *Developing new and junior faculty*, ed. M. D. Sorcinelli and A. E. Austin, 73–86. New Directions for Teaching and Learning No. 50. San Francisco: Jossey-Bass.

Austin, A. E., and Z. F. Gamson. 1983. *Academic workplace: New demands, heightened tensions*. ASHE-ERIC Higher Education Research Report No. 10. Washington, D.C.: Association for the Study of Higher Education.

Bach, M., and R. Thornton. 1983. Academic-industrial partnerships in biomedical research: Inevitability and desirability. *Educational Record* 64:26–32.

Baldridge, J. V., D. Curtis, G. Ecker, and G. Riley. 1978. *Policy making and effective leadership*. San Francisco: Jossey-Bass.

Baldwin, R. G., and R. T. Blackburn. 1981. The academic career as a developmental process: Implications for higher education. *Journal of Higher Education* 52:598–614.

Bardo, J. W., J. T. Jones, M. Bowden, E. Traynham, and J. Perry. 1990. Economic development and AASCU institutions: An examination of roles and critical questions for state policy makers. In *Defining the missions of AASCU institutions*, ed. J. W. Bardo, 105–17. Washington, D.C.: American Association of State Colleges and Universities.

Bartlett, J. W., and J. V. Siena. 1983–84. Research and development limited partnerships as a device to exploit university-owned technology. *Journal of College and University Law* 10:435–54.

Bass, B. M. 1985. *Leadership and performance beyond expectation.* New York: Free Press.

Battenburg, J. R. 1980. Forging links between industry and the academic world. *Journal of the Society of Research Administrators* 12:5–12.

Baumol, W. T., and W. G. Bowen. 1966. *Performing arts: The economic dilemma.* New York: Twentieth Century Fund.

Bayer, A. E. 1973. Teaching faculty in academe: 1972–1973. *ACE Research Reports* 8:1–68.

Bell, D. 1973. *The coming of the post-industrial society: A venture in social forecasting.* New York: Basic Books.

Ben-David, J. 1972. *Trends in American higher education.* Chicago: University of Chicago Press.

Bensimon, E. M., A. Neumann, and R. Birnbaum. 1989. *Making sense of administrative leadership: The "L" word in higher education.* ASHE-ERIC Higher Education Research Report No. 1. Washington, D.C.: Association for the Study of Higher Education.

Bess, J. L. 1978. Anticipatory socialization of graduate students. *Research in Higher Education* 8:289–317.

Bieber, J. P., J. H. Lawrence, and R. T. Blackburn. 1992. Through the years—Faculty and their changing institution. *Change* 24:28–35.

Bird, B. J., and D. N. Allen. 1989. Faculty entrepreneurship in research university environments. *Journal of Higher Education* 60:583–96.

Birnbaum, R. 1988. *How colleges work: The cybernetics of academic organization and leadership.* San Francisco: Jossey-Bass.

Blau, P. M. 1973. *The organization of academic work.* New York: John Wiley & Sons.

Blumenstyk, G. 1992. States re-evaluate industrial collaborations built around research grants to universities. *Chronicle of Higher Education* 38(25):1, 24–5.

Blumenthal, D., S. Epstein, and J. Maxwell. 1986. Commercializing university research: Lessons from the experience of the Wisconsin Alumni Research Fund. *New England Journal of Medicine* 314:1621–6.

Blumenthal, D., M. Gluck, K. Louis, M. Stoto, and D. Wise. 1986. University-industry research relationships in biotechnology: Implications for the university. *Science* 232(4756):1361–6.

Boice, R. 1992. *The new faculty member.* San Francisco: Jossey-Bass.

Bok, D. 1982. *Beyond the ivory tower.* Cambridge, Mass.: Harvard University Press.

———. 1992. Reclaiming the public trust. *Change* 24:12–19.

Botkin, J., D. Dimancescu, and R. Strata. 1982. *Global stakes: The future of high technology in America.* Cambridge, Mass.: Ballinger.

Bowen, H. R. 1977. *Investment in learning: The individual and social value of American higher education.* San Francisco: Jossey-Bass.

———. 1978. *Academic compensation: Are faculty and staff in American higher education adequately paid?* New York: TIAA-CREF.

Bowen, H. R., and J. H. Schuster. 1986. *American professors: A national resource imperiled.* New York: Oxford University Press.

Bowen, W. G., and J. A. Sosa. 1989. *Prospects for faculty in arts and sciences.* Princeton, N.J.: Princeton University Press.

Bowie, N. E. 1994. *University-business partnerships: An assessment.* Lanham, Md.: Rowman and Littlefield Publishers, Inc.

Boyer, C. M., and D. R. Lewis. 1985. *And on the seventh day: Faculty consulting and supplemental income.* ASHE-ERIC Higher Education Research Report No. 3. Washington, D.C.: Association for the Study of Higher Education.

———. 1985. Maintaining faculty vitality through outside professional consulting. In *Faculty vitality and institutional productivity,* ed. S. M. Clark and D. R. Lewis, 177–97. New York: Teachers College Press.

Boyer, E. L. 1987. *College: The undergraduate experience in America.* New York: Harper and Row.

———. 1990. *Scholarship reconsidered: Priorities of the professoriate.* Princeton, N.J.: Carnegie Foundation for the Advancement of Teaching.

Branscomb, L. M. 1984. America's rising research alliance. *American Education* 20:43–6.

Breneman, D. W., and T. I. K. Youn. 1988. *Academic labor markets and careers.* New York: Falmer Press.

Brooks, H. 1984. Seeking equity and efficiency: Public and private roles. In *Public-private partnership: New opportunities for meeting social needs,* ed. H. Brooks, L. Liebman, and C. Schelling, 3–30. Cambridge, Mass.: Ballinger.

Business–Higher Education Forum. 1984. *Corporate and campus cooperation: An action agenda.* Washington, D.C.: Business–Higher Education Forum.

Cameron, K. 1978. Measuring organizational effectiveness in institutions of higher education. *Administrative Science Quarterly* 23:604–32.

Carnegie Foundation for the Advancement of Teaching. 1987. *A classification of institutions of higher education.* Princeton, N.J.: Carnegie Foundation for the Advancement of Teaching.

———. 1989. *The condition of the professoriate: Attitudes and trends, 1989.* Princeton, N.J.: Carnegie Foundation for the Advancement of Teaching.

Centra, J. A. 1983. Research productivity and teaching effectiveness. *Research in Higher Education* 18:379–89.

Chmura, T., J. Fairweather, and J. Melville. 1988. *From bystander to leader: Challenging higher education to join in building Baltimore's economic future.* Menlo Park, Calif.: SRI International.

Chmura, T., D. Henton, and J. Melville. 1988. *California's higher education system: Adding economic competitiveness to the higher-education agenda.* Menlo Park, Calif.: SRI International.

Choate, P. 1986. Business and higher education: Imperative to adapt. In *Issues in Higher Education and Economic Development,* 11–18. Washington, D.C.: American Association of State Colleges and Universities.

Clark, B. R. 1963. Faculty organization and authority. In *The study of academic adminis-tration*, ed. T. F. Lunsford, 37–51. Boulder, Colo.: Western Interstate Commission on Higher Education.

———. 1970. *The distinctive college: Antioch, Reed and Swarthmore*. Chicago: Aldine.

———. 1972. The organizational saga in higher education. *Administrative Science Quarterly* 17:178–84.

———. 1983. *The higher education system*. Berkeley, Calif.: University of California Press.

———. 1987. *The academic life: Small worlds, different worlds*. Princeton, N.J.: Carnegie Foundation for the Advancement of Teaching.

Clifford, G. J., and J. W. Guthrie. 1988. *Ed school: A brief for professional education*. Chicago: University of Chicago Press.

Cohen, M. D., and J. G. March. 1974. *Leadership and ambiguity*. Boston: Harvard Business School Press.

Cole, J. R. 1993. Balancing acts: Dilemmas of choice facing research universities. *Daedalus* 122:1–36.

Conrad, C. F., and R. T. Blackburn. 1985. Program quality in higher education: A review and critique of the literature. In *Higher education: Handbook of theory and research*, Vol. I, ed. J. C. Smart, 283–308. New York: Agathon.

Cook, E. P., P. Kinnetz, and N. Owens-Misner. 1990. Faculty perceptions on job rewards and instructional development activities. *Innovative Higher Education* 14:123–130.

Cresswell, J. W., and R. Roskens. 1981. The Biglan studies of differences among academic areas. *Review of Higher Education* 4:1–16.

Crimmel, H. H. 1984. The myth of the teacher-scholar. *Liberal Education* 70:183–98.

Cross, K. P. 1981. New frontiers for higher education: Business and the professions. In *Partnerships with business and the professions*, 4–7. Washington, D.C.: American Association of Higher Education.

Crosson, P. 1983. *Public service in higher education: Practices and priorities*. ASHE-ERIC Higher Education Research Report No. 7. Washington, D.C.: Association for the Study of Higher Education.

———. 1986. Encouraging faculty involvement in university economic development programs. In *Issues in higher education and economic development*. Washington, D.C.: American Association of State Colleges and Universities.

Curry, J., and M. Kenney. 1990. Land-grant university-industry relationships in biotechnology: A comparison with the non-land-grant research universities. *Rural Sociology* 55:44–57.

Daymont, T., and P. Andrisani. 1984. Job preferences, college major and the gender gap in earnings. *Journal of Human Resources* 19:408–28.

DeVries, D. L. 1975. The relationship of role expectations to faculty behavior. *Research in Higher Education* 3:111–29.

Diamond, R. M. 1993. Changing priorities and the faculty reward system. In *Recognizing faculty work: Reward systems for the year 2000*, ed. R. M. Diamond and B. E. Adam, 5–12. New Directions for Higher Education No. 81. San Francisco: Jossey-Bass.

Dickson, D. 1984. *The new politics of science*. New York: Pantheon Books.

Dillon, K. E., and K. L. Bane. 1980. Consulting and conflict of interest: A compendium of the policies of almost one hundred major colleges and universities. *Educational Record* 61:52–72.

Dillon, K. E., and H. W. Marsh. 1981. Faculty earnings compared with those of nonacademic professionals. *Journal of Higher Education* 52:615–23.

Dooris, M. J., and J. S. Fairweather. 1994. Structure and culture in faculty work: Implications for technology transfer. *Review of Higher Education* 17:161–78.

Dressel, P. 1987. Mission, organization, and leadership. *Journal of Higher Education* 58:101–9.

Ehrenberg, R., H. Kasper, and D. Rees. 1991. Faculty turnover at American colleges and universities: Analyses of AAUP data. *Economics of Education Review* 10:99–110.

Elman, S. E., and S. M. Smock. 1985. *Professional service and faculty rewards*. Washington, D.C.: National Association of State Universities and Land-Grant Colleges.

Eurich, N. P. 1985. *Corporate classrooms: The learning business*. Princeton, N.J.: Carnegie Foundation for the Advancement of Teaching.

Faia, M. A. 1976. Teaching and research: Rapport or mésalliance. *Research in Higher Education* 4:235–46.

Fairweather, J. S. 1988. *Entrepreneurship and higher education: Lessons for colleges, universities, and industry*. ASHE-ERIC Higher Education Research Report No. 6. Washington, D.C.: Association for the Study of Higher Education.

———. 1989. Academic research and instruction: The industrial connection. *Journal of Higher Education* 60:388–407.

———. 1990. Education: The forgotten element in industry-university relationships. *Review of Higher Education* 14:33–43.

———. 1991. Higher education and the economy: From social good to economic development to . . . Paper presented at the Annual Meeting of the Western Interstate Commission on Higher Education, Seattle, Wash.

———. 1995. Myths and realities of academic labor markets. *Economics of Education Review* 14:179–92.

Fairweather, J. S., and D. F. Brown. 1991. Dimensions of academic program quality. *Review of Higher Education* 14:155–76.

Fairweather, J. S., and M. P. Hancock. 1987. *Quality and recruitment desirability of selected programs in engineering, computer science, and business*. Menlo Park, Calif.: SRI International.

Fairweather, J. S., and D. M. Shaver. 1990. A troubled future? Participation in postsecondary education for youth with disabilities. *Journal of Higher Education* 61:332–48.

Feldman, K. A. 1987. Research productivity and scholarly accomplishment of college teachers as related to their instructional effectiveness: A review and exploration. *Research in Higher Education* 26:227–98.

Feller, I. 1984. Political and administrative aspects of state high technology programs. *Policy Studies Review* 3:460–6.

———. 1988. University-industry research and development relationships. Paper prepared for the Woodlands Center for Growth Studies Conference, Houston, Tex.

Finkelstein, M. J. 1984. *The American academic profession: A synthesis of social scientific inquiry since World War II*. Columbus, Ohio: Ohio State University Press.

Finnegan, D. E. 1992. Academic career lines: A case study of faculty in two comprehensive universities. Unpublished doctoral dissertation. University Park, Pa.: Penn State University.

Friedman, R. S., and R. C. Friedman. 1985. Organized research units in academe revisited. In *Managing high technology: An interdisciplinary perspective*, ed. B. W. Mar, W. T. Newell, and B. O. Saxberg, 75–91. New York: Elsevier.

Friedrich, R. J., and S. J. Michalak, Jr. 1983. Why doesn't research improve teaching? Some answers from a small liberal arts college. *Journal of Higher Education* 54:145–63.

Fulton, O., and M. Trow. 1974. Research activity in American higher education. *Sociology of Education* 47:29–73.

Gaff, J. G., and Associates. 1970. *The cluster college*. San Francisco: Jossey-Bass.

Gaff, J. G., and R. C. Wilson. 1971. The teaching environment. *AAUP Bulletin* 57:475–93.

Gappa, J. M., and D. W. Leslie. 1993. *The invisible faculty: Improving the status of part-timers in higher education*. San Francisco: Jossey-Bass.

Garvin, D. 1980. *The economics of university behavior*. New York: Academic Press.

Geiger, R. L. 1986. *To advance knowledge: The growth of American research universities, 1900–1940*. New York: Oxford University Press.

———. 1988. Milking the sacred cow: Research and the quest for useful knowledge in the American university since 1920. *Science, Technology and Human Values* 13:332–48.

———. 1990. Organized research units—Their role in the development of university research. *Journal of Higher Education* 61:1–19.

———. 1992. The ambiguous link: Private industry and university research. In *The economics of higher education*, ed. W. E. Becker and D. R. Lewis, 265–98. Boston: Kluwer.

Getz, M., and J. J. Siegfried. 1991. Costs and productivity in American colleges and universities. In *Economic challenges in higher education*, ed. C. J. Clotfelter, R. G. Ehrenberg, M. Getz, and J. J Siegfried, 261–392. Chicago: University of Chicago Press.

Gmelch,W., P. Wilke, and N. Lovrich. 1986. Dimensions of stress among university faculty: Factor-analytic results from a national study. *Research in Higher Education* 24:266–86.

Gold, G. G. 1981. Toward business-higher education alliances. In *Business and higher education: Toward new alliances*, New Directions for Experiential Learning No. 13, ed. G. G. Gold, 9–27. San Francisco: Jossey-Bass.

Golomb, S. W. 1979. Faculty consulting: Should it be curtailed? *National Forum: Phi Kappa Phi Journal* 69:34–7.

Gordon, N., and T. Morton. 1974. Faculty salaries: Is there discrimination by sex, race and discipline? *American Economic Review* 64:419–27.

Government-University-Industry Research Roundtable. 1986. *New alliances and partnerships in American science and engineering*. Washington, D.C.: National Academy Press.

Grant, G., and D. Riesman. 1978. *The perpetual dream: Reform and experiment in the American college*. Chicago: University of Chicago Press.

Gray, D., T. Gidley, and N. Koester. 1988. Outcomes of participation in industry-university cooperative research centers. Paper presented at the IUCDC Evaluators' Meeting, Arlington, Va.

Gray, P. J., R. C. Froh, and R. M. Diamond. 1991. Myths and realities. *AAHE Bulletin* 44:4–7.

Green, M. F. 1990. Why good teaching needs active leadership. In *How administrators can improve teaching*, ed. P. Seldin, 45–62. San Francisco: Jossey-Bass.

Haddad, J. A. 1986. New factors in the relationship between engineering education and research. In *The new Engineering Research Centers: Purposes, goals, and expectations*, 129–36. Washington, D.C.: National Academy Press.

Hambrick, R. S., Jr., and G. S. Swanson. 1979. The mobilization of expertise: The problems of managing applied research in a university. In *Linking science and technology to public policy: The role of universities*, ed. A. I. Baaklini, 115–42. Albany, N.Y.: New York State Assembly and State University of New York at Albany.

Hansen, W. L. 1985. Salary differences across disciplines. *Academe*, 71:6–7.

———. 1986. Changes in faculty salaries. In *American professors: A national resource imperiled*, ed. H. R. Bowen and J. H. Schuster, 80–112. New York: Oxford University Press.

———. 1988. Merit pay in higher education. In *Academic labor markets and careers*, ed. D. W. Breneman and T. I. K. Youn, 114–37. New York: Falmer Press.

Harry, J., and N. S. Goldner. 1972. The null relationship between teaching and research. *Sociology of Education* 45:47–60.

Hearn, J. C. 1992. The teaching role in contemporary American higher education: Popular imagery and organizational reality. In *The economics of higher education*, ed. W. E. Becker and D. R. Lewis, 17–68. Boston: Kluwer.

Hersh, R. 1983. Education and the corporate connection. *Educational Horizons* 62:5–8.

Hesseldenz, J. S. 1976. Personality-based faculty workload analysis. *Research in Higher Education* 5:321–34.

Hind, R. R., S. M. Dornbusch, and W. R. Scott. 1974. A theory of evaluation applied to university faculty. *Sociology of Education* 47:114–28.

Holmstrom, E. I., and J. Petrovich. 1985. *Engineering programs in emerging areas, 1983–84*. Higher Education Panel Report No. 64. Washington, D.C.: American Council on Education.

Houle, C. 1980. *Continuing learning in the professions*. San Francisco: Jossey-Bass.

Hoyt, D. P. 1974. Interrelationships among instructional effectiveness, publication record, and monetary reward. *Research in Higher Education* 2:81–9.

Huber, R. M. 1992. *How professors play the cat guarding the cream: Why we're paying more and getting less in higher education*. Fairfax, Va.: George Mason University Press.

Interuniversity Council of Ohio. 1970. *Faculty load study*. Columbus, Ohio: Interuniversity Council of Ohio.

Jacobsen, R. L. 1992. Colleges face new pressure to increase faculty productivity. *Chronicle of Higher Education* 38(April 15):1.

Jarvis, D. K. 1991. *Junior faculty development: A handbook*. New York: Modern Language Association of America.

Jauch, L. R. 1976. Relationships of research and teaching: Implications for faculty evaluation. *Research in Higher Education* 5:1–13.

Jencks, C. and D. Riesman. 1968. *The academic revolution*. Garden City, N.Y.: Doubleday.

Johnson, E. C., and L. G. Tornatzky. 1981. Academia and industrial innovation. In *Business and higher education: Toward new alliances*, ed. G. G. Gold, 47–63. San Francisco: Jossey-Bass.

Johnson, L. G. 1984. *The high-technology connection: Academic/industrial cooperation for economic growth*. ASHE-ERIC Higher Education Research Report No. 6. Washington, D.C.: Association for the Study of Higher Education.

Jones, L. V., G. Lindzey, and P. E. Coggeshall, eds. 1982. *An assessment of research-doctorate programs in the United States: Biological sciences*. Washington, D.C.: National Academy Press.

Kane, M., and J. S. Fairweather. 1988. *Issues in the preparation of special education teachers*. Washington, D.C.: Pelavin Associates.

Kasten, K. L. 1984. Tenure and merit pay as rewards for research, teaching, and service at a research university. *Journal of Higher Education* 55:500–14.

Katsinas, S. G., and V. A. Lacey. 1989. *Community colleges and economic development: Models of institutional effectiveness*. Washington, D.C.: American Association of Community and Junior Colleges.

Katz, D. A. 1973. Faculty salaries, promotion, and productivity at a large university. *American Economic Review* 63:469–77.

Katz, M. B. 1968. *The irony of early school reform: Educational innovation in mid-nineteenth century Massachusetts*. Cambridge, Mass.: Harvard University Press.

Keister, S. D., and L. G. Keister. 1989. Faculty compensation and the cost of living in American higher education. *Journal of Higher Education* 60:458–74.

Keller, G. 1983. *Academic strategy*. Baltimore: Johns Hopkins University Press.

Kenney, M. 1986. *Biotechnology: The university-industrial complex*. New Haven, Conn.: Yale University Press.

Kerr, C. 1982. *The uses of the university*. 3rd ed. Cambridge, Mass.: Harvard University Press.

Koch, J. V., and J. F. Chizmar. 1973. The influence of teaching and other factors upon absolute salaries and salary increments at Illinois State University. *Journal of Economic Education* 5:27–34.

Koehler, W. F. 1986. From evaluations to an equitable selection of merit-pay recipients and increments. *Research in Higher Education* 25:253–63.

Konrad, A. M., and J. Pfeffer. 1990. Do you get what you deserve? Factors affecting the relationship between productivity and pay. *Administrative Science Quarterly* 35:258–85.

Kreps, J. 1986. Maintaining the nation's competitiveness. In *Issues in higher education and economic development*, 4–10. Washington, D.C.: American Association of State Colleges and Universities.

Ladd, E. C., Jr. 1979. The work experience of American college professors: Some data and an argument. *Current Issues in Higher Education*. Washington, D.C.: American Association of Higher Education.

Ladd, E. C., Jr., and S. M. Lipset. 1975. *The divided academy*. New York: McGraw-Hill.
———. 1977. *Survey of the American professoriate*. Storrs, Conn.: University of Connecticut.

Lawrence, P. R., and J. W. Lorsch. 1967. *Organization and environment: Managing differentiation and integration.* Boston: Harvard University Press.

Lazerson, M., and U. Wagener. 1992. Rethinking how colleges operate. *Chronicle of Higher Education* 39(6):A44.

Lenth, C. S. 1990. *State priorities in higher education: 1990.* Denver: State Higher Education Executive Officers and the Education Commission of the States.

Leslie, L. L., and P. T. Brinkman. 1988. *The economic value of higher education.* New York: ACE/Macmillan.

Leslie, S. W. 1987. Playing the education game to win: The military and interdisciplinary research at Stanford. *Historical Studies in the Physical and Biological Sciences* 18:55–88.

Levin, H. M. 1991. Raising productivity in higher education. *Journal of Higher Education* 62:241–62.

Linsky, A. S., and M. Straus. 1975. Student evaluation, research productivity, and eminence of college faculty. *Journal of Higher Education* 46:89–102.

Logan, L. B., and J. O. Stampen. 1985. Smoke stack meets ivory tower: Collaborations with local industry. *Educational Record* 66:26–9.

Louis, K. S., D. Blumenthal, M. Gluck, and M. Stoto. 1989. Entrepreneurs in academe: An explanation of behaviors among life scientists. *Administrative Science Quarterly* 34:110–31.

Lozier, G. G., and M. J. Dooris. 1988. *Is higher education confronting faculty shortages?* Houston, Tex.: Institute for Higher Education Law and Governance.

Lynton, E. A., and S. E. Elman. 1987. *New priorities for the university.* San Francisco: Jossey-Bass.

Marsh, H. W., and K. E. Dillon. 1980. Academic productivity and faculty supplemental income. *Journal of Higher Education* 51:546–55.

Marver, J. D., and C. V. Patton. 1976. The correlates of consultation: American academics in the real world. *Higher Education* 5:319–35.

Matkin, G. W. 1990. *Technology transfer and the university.* New York: ACE/Macmillan.

McCullagh, R. D., and M. R. Roy. 1975. The contribution of noninstructional activities to college classroom teacher effectiveness. *Journal of Experimental Education* 44:61–70.

McKeachie, W. J. 1986. *Teaching tips: A guidebook for the beginning college teacher.* 8th ed. Lexington, Mass.: D.C. Heath.

Merton, R. K. 1957. *Social theory and social structure.* Glencoe, Ill.: Free Press.

Miles, M. B., and A. M. Huberman. 1984. *Qualitative data analysis: A sourcebook of new methods.* Beverly Hills, Calif.: Sage.

Millar, S. B., and J. S. Fairweather. 1992. *NSF Coalition: Report on the second year of activities: 1991–92.* University Park, Pa.: Center for the Study of Higher Education, Penn State University.

Millard, R. M. 1991. *Today's myths and tomorrow's realities.* San Francisco: Jossey-Bass.

Moore, K. M., and M. Amey. 1993. *Making sense of the dollars: The costs and uses of faculty compensation.* ASHE-ERIC Higher Education Research Report No. 5. Washington, D.C.: Association for the Study of Higehr Education.

National Research Council. 1985. *Engineering education and practice in the United States: Continuing education of engineers.* Washington, D.C.: National Academy Press.

————. 1985. *Engineering education and practice in the United States: Foundations of our techno-economic future.* Washington, D.C.: National Academy Press.

National Science Board. 1986. *Undergraduate science, mathematics and engineering education.* Washington, D.C.: National Science Board.

————. 1987. *Science and engineering indicators, 1987.* Washington, D.C.: National Science Board.

National Science Foundation. 1981. *Activities of science and engineering faculty in universities and 4 year colleges: 1978–79.* Washington, D.C.: National Science Foundation.

————. 1982. *University-industry research relationships: Myths, realities, and potentials.* Fourteenth Annual Report of the National Science Board. Washington, D.C.: National Science Foundation.

————. 1989. *National patterns of R&D resources: 1989.* Washington, D.C.: National Science Foundation.

Nelson, R. 1986. Institutions supporting technical advance in industry. *American Economic Review* 76:186–90.

Noble, D. F. 1977. *America by design: Science, technology, and the rise of corporate capitalism.* New York: Oxford University Press.

Office of Science and Technology Policy. 1986. *A renewed partnership: Report of the White House Science Council Panel on the health of U.S. colleges and universities.* Washington, D.C.: Office of Science and Technology Policy.

Orlans, H. 1962. *The effects of federal programs on higher education.* Washington, D.C.: Brookings Institute.

Parcel, T. L., and C. W. Mueller. 1983. *Ascription and labor markets: Race and sex differences in earnings.* New York: Academic Press.

Parnell, D., and R. Yarrington. 1982. *Proven partners: Business, labor, and community colleges.* Washington, D.C.: American Association of Community and Junior Colleges.

Parsons, T., and G. M. Platt. 1968. *The American academic profession: A pilot study.* Cambridge, Mass.: Harvard University Press.

Pascarella, E. T., and P. T. Terenzini. 1991. *How college affects students.* San Francisco: Jossey-Bass.

Perkins, J. A. 1966. *The university in transition.* Princeton, N.J.: Princeton University Press.

Peters, D. S., and J. R. Mayfield. 1982. Are there *any* rewards for teaching? *Improving College and University Teaching* 30:105–10.

Peters, L., and H. Fusfeld. 1983. Current U.S. university/industry research connections. In *University-industry research relationships: Selected studies,* 1–162. Washington, D.C.: National Science Foundation.

Pfeffer, J., and G. R. Salancik. 1978. *The external control of organizations.* New York: Harper and Row.

Powers, D. R., M. F. Powers, F. Betz, and C. B. Aslanian. 1988. *Higher education in partnership with industry: Opportunities for training, research, and economic development.* San Francisco: Jossey-Bass.

Public Policy Center, SRI International. 1986. *The higher education–economic development connection: Emerging roles for public colleges and universities.* Washington, D.C.: American Association of State Colleges and Universities.

Reynolds, A. 1992. Charting the changes in junior faculty: Relationships among socialization, acculturation, and gender. *Journal of Higher Education* 63:637–52.

Richter, M. N. 1985. Industrial funding of faculty research. *Humanity and Society* 9:459–85.

Rockhill, K. 1983. *Academic excellence and public service.* New Brunswick, N.J.: Transaction Books.

Rosenzweig, R. M., and B. Turlington. 1982. *The research universities and their patrons.* Berkeley, Calif.: University of California Press.

Rossman, J. E. 1976. Teaching, publication, and rewards at a liberal arts college. *Improving College and University Teaching* 24:238–40.

Russell, S. H., R. C. Cox, and J. M. Boismier. 1990. *A descriptive report of academic departments in higher education institutions.* Washington, D.C.: U.S. Department of Education.

Russell, S. H., J. S. Fairweather, R. S. Cox, C. Williamson, J. Boismier, and H. Javitz. 1990. *Faculty in higher education institutions.* Washington, D.C.: U.S. Department of Education.

Salthouse, T. A., W. J. McKeachie, and Y. Lin. 1978. An experimental investigation of factors affecting university promotion decisions. *Journal of Higher Education* 49:177–83.

Schuh, G. E. 1986. Revitalizing land grant universities: It's time to regain relevance. *Choices* (Second Quarter):6–10.

Schuh, G. E., and V. W. Rattan. 1992. The research and service missions of the university. In *The economics of higher education,* ed. W. E. Becker and D. R. Lewis, 69–87. Boston: Kluwer.

Seldin, P. 1990. Academic environments and teaching effectiveness. In *How administrators can improve teaching,* ed. P. Seldin, 3–22. San Francisco: Jossey-Bass.

Sheridan, H. W. 1990. Ichabod Crane dies hard: Renewing professional commitments to teaching. In *How administrators can improve teaching,* ed. P. Seldin, 165–80. San Francisco: Jossey-Bass.

Siegfried, J. J., and K. J. White. 1973. Teaching and publishing as determinants of academic salaries. *Journal of Economic Education* 4:90–8.

Slaughter, S. 1990. *The higher learning and high technology: Dynamics of higher education policy formation.* Albany, N.Y.: State University of New York Press.

Smart, J. C., and G. W. McLaughlin. 1978. Reward structures of academic disciplines. *Research in Higher Education* 8:39–55.

Smith, T. R., and M. Drabenstott. 1992. The role of universities in regional economic development. In *The economics of higher education,* ed. W. E. Becker and D. R. Lewis, 199–222. Boston: Kluwer.

Stankiewicz, R. 1986. *Academics and entrepreneurs: Developing university-industry relations.* London: Frances Pinter.

Stark, J., M. Lowther, and B. Hagerty. 1986. Faculty roles and role preferences in ten fields of professional study. *Research in Higher Education* 25:3–30.

Staton, A. Q., and A. L. Darling. 1989. Socialization of teaching assistants. In *Teaching assistants training in the 1990s,* New Directions for Teaching and Learning No. 39, ed. J. D. Nyquist, R. D. Abbott, and D. H. Wulff, 15–22. San Francisco: Jossey-Bass.

Stauffer, T. M. 1979. Expanding business-higher education cooperation on research and development. *Journal of the Society of Research Administrators* 11:41–6.

———. 1990. A university model for the 1990s. In *An agenda for the new decade,* New Directions for Higher Education No. 70, ed. L. W. Jones and F. A. Nowotny, 19–24. San Francisco: Jossey-Bass.

Study Group on the Conditions of Excellence in American Higher Education. 1984. *Involvement in learning: Realizing the potential of American higher education.* Washington, D.C.: U.S. Department of Education.

Swanson, D. H. 1986. Transferring technologies to industry. In *Issues in higher education and economic development,* 23–33. Washington, D.C.: American Association of State Colleges and Universities.

Tatel, D. S., and R. Guthrie. 1983. The legal ins and outs of university-industry collaboration. *Educational Record* 64:19–25.

Tierney, W. G., and R. A. Rhoads. 1993. *Enhancing promotion, tenure and beyond: Faculty socialization as cultural process.* ASHE-ERIC Higher Education Research Report No. 6. Washington, D.C.: Association for the Study of Higher Education.

Tornatzky, L. G., and M. Fleisher. 1990. *The process of technological innovation.* Lexington, Mass.: Lexington Books.

Trow, M. A. 1984. The analysis of status. In *Perspectives in higher education: Eight disciplinary and comparative views,* ed. B. Clark, 132–64. Berkeley, Calif.: University of California Press.

Tuckman, B. H. 1979. Salary differences among university faculty and their implications for the future. In *Salary equity: Detecting sex bias in salaries among college and university professors,* ed. T. R. Pezzullo and B. E. Brittingham, 19–36. Lexington, Mass.: D.C. Heath.

Tuckman, H. P. 1979. The academic reward structure in American higher education. In *Academic rewards in higher education,* ed. D. R. Lewis and W. E. Becker, Jr., 165–90. Cambridge, Mass.: Ballinger.

Tuckman, H. P., J. H. Gapinski, and R. P. Hagemann. 1977. Faculty skills and the salary structure in academe: A market perspective. *American Economic Review* 67:692–702.

Tuckman, H. P., and R. P. Hagemann. 1976. An analysis of the reward structure in two disciplines. *Journal of Higher Education* 47:447–64.

Turner, C. S. V., and J. R. Thompson. 1993. Socializing women doctoral students: Minority and majority experiences. *Review of Higher Education* 16:355–70.

Van Maanen, J. 1983. Doing new things in old ways: The origins of socialization. In *College and university organization: Insights from the behavioral sciences,* ed. J. L. Bess, 211–47. New York: New York University Press.

Veen, P. 1984. Characteristics of organizations. In *Handbook of work and organizational psychology,* ed. P. J. D. Drenth, H. Thierry, P. J. Williams, and C. J. de Wolff, 677–712. New York: John Wiley & Sons.

Watkins, C. B. 1985. *Programs for innovative technical research in state strategies for economic development.* Washington, D.C.: National Governors' Association Center for Policy Research and Analysis.

Webster, D. S. 1986. *Academic quality rankings of American colleges and universities.* Springfield, Ill.: Charles C. Thomas.

Weick, K. 1978. Educational organizations as loosely coupled systems. *Administrative Science Quarterly* 23:541–52.

Weimer, M. 1990. *Improving college teaching: Strategies for developing instructional effectiveness.* San Francisco: Jossey-Bass.

Weiner, C. 1982. Science and the marketplace: Historical precedents and problems. In *From genetic experimentation to biotechnology—The critical transition,* ed. W. J. Whelan and S. Black, 123–32. New York: John Wiley & Sons.

Winston, G. C. 1992. Hostility, maximization, and the public trust. *Change* 24:20–7.

Wofsy, L. 1986. Biotechnology and the university. *Journal of Higher Education* 57:477–92.

Wyer, J. C., and C. F. Conrad. 1984. Institutional inbreeding reexamined. *American Educational Research Journal* 21:213–25.

Yin, R. K. 1984. *Case study research: Design and methods.* Beverly Hills, Calif.: Sage.

Yuker, H. E. 1984. *Faculty workload: Research, theory, and interpretation.* ASHE-ERIC Higher Education Research Report No. 10. Washington, D.C.: Association for the Study of Higher Education.

Zemsky, R., W. F. Massy, and P. Oedel. 1993. On reversing the ratchet. *Change* 25:56–62.

APPENDIX 1

# Survey Design and Study Variables

Survey data were gathered from the 1987–88 National Survey of Postsecondary Faculty (NSOPF), sponsored by the National Center for Education Statistics. The survey examined a nationally representative sample of 11,071 faculty from 480 colleges and universities. Individuals who had at least some instructional duties during the 1987–88 academic year were eligible to participate. The institutional sample was stratified by Carnegie type,[1] source of control, and size (estimated number of faculty). The faculty sample was stratified by full- or part-time status and by program area. Of the original sample, 8,383 full- and part-time faculty from 424 institutions responded, a faculty response rate of 76 percent.[2]

## ANALYSIS PLAN

Analyses were carried out for *full-time, tenure-track* faculty from 4-year institutions ($n = 4,481$; weighted $n = 343,343$). Population estimates from survey data were based on weights derived from the inverse of the probability of a faculty member in a particular type of institution being selected. The probability of selecting a faculty member for the sample was a function of the odds of an institution's being selected from the universe of accredited postsecondary institutions, the probability of a faculty member's being selected from the population of faculty within his or her institution, and the sampling rate for employment status (full- or part-time) and program area.[3] Analyses for Chapter 2 (Faculty: The Focal Point) examined faculty workload and productivity by type of institution. These analyses take into account the importance of controlling for type of institution in analyses of faculty behavior.[4] In Chapter 3, the profiles of teaching-oriented and research-oriented faculty were examined by comparing faculty in the top quartile of these two activities, respectively, with their peers who spent less time on each activity.

In Chapters 3 and 4 (Subtle Messages: The Role of Pay in Faculty Rewards and Other Factors Influencing Faculty Teaching) the relationships between faculty activities in teaching and instruction, research and scholarship, administration, and service were first examined by breaking faculty activity variables into quartiles and comparing basic salary by quartile, by type of institution and program area. The distributions of some variables did not permit use of quartiles for analyses. So few faculty in 4-year institutions spent much time on service that the variable was split into two parts: those spending more than 5 percent of their time on service versus those who spent less than 5 percent. Finally, to study the combined relationships between faculty demographic characteristics, activities and workload, productivity, and compensation, in Chapter 3 multiple regression models were completed by type of institution, program area, and rank within institutional type.

In Chapter 8 (Traditional Knowledge and Technology Transfer) faculty consulting activity was first studied by the distribution of percent of time spent on consulting and on the percent of institutional income from consulting, by type of institution, program area, and academic rank. The correlates of percent of time spent on consulting with other faculty activities also were studied. Finally, faculty who spent the most time consulting (the top 10 percent) were compared with their peers on a number of indicators.

The same analyses were repeated for faculty who received research support from industry. In addition, the research dollar distribution for faculty who were principal investigators during Fall term 1987 was examined, including the percent of total research dollars received from industry.

Throughout the book, the criterion for minimally acceptable level of significance for statistical tests was $p < .05$. When multiple pairs were compared simultaneously, such as in the comparison of each program area mean with the overall average, the acceptable significance level was increased by the Bonferroni adjustment (i.e., dividing the level of significance by the number of multiple comparisons). The presentation of $t$-test results for mean differences or for differences between proportions is as follows: $t$(comparison/reference) = $t$-value, $p$-value (level of significance), where, for example, the comparison might be research universities versus comprehensive colleges and universities [referred to as $t$(res/comp)]. The relevant symbols are: res = research universities, doc = doctoral-granting universities, comp = comprehensive colleges and universities, lib = liberal arts colleges, other = other 4-year institutions. Only statistically significant differences are shown in the endnotes.

## NOTES

1. Carnegie Foundation for the Advancement of Teaching, *A Classification of Institutions of Higher Education* (Princeton, N.J.: Carnegie Foundation for the Advancement of Teaching, 1987).
2. S. H. Russell, J. S. Fairweather, R. S. Cox, C. Williamson, J. Boismier, and H. Javitz, *Faculty in Higher Education Institutions* (Washington, D.C.: U.S. Department of Education, 1990), 97–8.
3. Russell, Fairweather, Cox, Williamson, Boismier, and Javitz, *Faculty in Higher Education Institutions*, 99.
4. For example, see J. V. Baldridge, D. Curtis, G. Ecker, and G. Riley, *Policy Making and Effective Leadership* (San Francisco: Jossey-Bass, 1978).

APPENDIX 2

# Faculty Salaries
by Type of Institution,
Program Area, and
Demographic Characteristics

**TABLE A2.1  Basic Salary from Institution, by
Type of Institution**

|  | Basic Salary from Institution |
|---|---|
| All 4-Year Institutions | $42,498 |
| SE | 286 |
| Research | 49,648 |
| SE | 533 |
| Doctoral | 38,478 |
| SE | 528 |
| Comprehensive | 36,820 |
| SE | 335 |
| Liberal Arts | 30,628 |
| SE | 533 |
| Other 4-Year | 55,920 |
| SE | 2,403 |

Source: NSOPF 1988

**TABLE A2.2   Basic Income from Institution for Faculty in 4-Year Institutions, by Program Area**

|  | Basic Salary from Institution |
|---|---|
| Agriculture/Home Economics | $42,680 |
| SE | 977 |
| Business | 42,235 |
| SE | 1,005 |
| Education | 36,034 |
| SE | 576 |
| Engineering | 45,828 |
| SE | 934 |
| Fine Arts | 34,452 |
| SE | 542 |
| Health Sciences | 56,530 |
| SE | 1,756 |
| Humanities | 36,267 |
| SE | 372 |
| Natural Sciences | 41,825 |
| SE | 676 |
| Social Sciences | 38,212 |
| SE | 456 |
| Other Fields | 38,685 |
| SE | 942 |

Source: NSOPF 1988

**TABLE A2.3    Basic Salary from Institution, by Demographic Characteristics: 4-Year Institutions**

| | All 4-Year | Research | Doctoral | Comprehensive | Liberal Arts | Other 4-Year |
|---|---|---|---|---|---|---|
| | | | Mean ($) | | | |
| *Academic Rank* | | | | | | |
| Professor | 51,553 | 58,124 | 47,324 | 44,569 | 37,578 | 64,576 |
| SE | 440 | 732 | 797 | 437 | 966 | 4,214 |
| Associate | 39,307 | 45,939 | 36,913 | 33,742 | 29,981 | 52,172 |
| SE | 434 | 927 | 833 | 339 | 579 | 3,341 |
| Assistant | 32,302 | 37,303 | 29,526 | 29,038 | 23,365 | 43,561 |
| SE | 403 | 835 | 648 | 508 | 711 | 2,676 |
| *Age Group (years)* | | | | | | |
| < 30 | 28,604 | * | * | * | * | * |
| SE | 1,918 | * | * | * | * | * |
| 30–44 | 36,872 | 43,190 | 33,816 | 30,845 | 26,270 | 48,903 |
| SE | 423 | 757 | 923 | 506 | 634 | 2,852 |
| 45–54 | 44,348 | 51,924 | 38,941 | 38,366 | 32,901 | 65,831 |
| SE | 499 | 975 | 706 | 445 | 779 | 5,384 |
| 55–59 | 46,045 | 54,410 | 42,138 | 41,337 | 36,624 | * |
| SE | 615 | 1,075 | 1,334 | 698 | 1,914 | * |
| 60–64 | 51,820 | 59,000 | 49,454 | 46,084 | 34,938 | * |
| SE | 1,002 | 1,676 | 1,890 | 1,554 | 1,480 | * |
| 65 or more | 48,548 | 58,836 | 42,826 | 40,918 | * | * |
| SE | 1,479 | 3,057 | 3,074 | 1,369 | * | * |
| *Gender* | | | | | | |
| Female | 33,639 | 40,193 | 29,945 | 31,270 | 25,996 | * |
| SE | 430 | 983 | 762 | 481 | 802 | * |
| Male | 44,819 | 51,676 | 40,996 | 38,612 | 32,066 | 57,874 |
| SE | 334 | 597 | 610 | 402 | 636 | 2,609 |
| *Racial or Ethnic Minority* | | | | | | |
| Nonminority | 42,573 | 49,897 | 38,479 | 36,613 | 31,002 | 56,617 |
| SE | 305 | 563 | 562 | 355 | 557 | 2,655 |
| Minority | 41,527 | 46,918 | 38,651 | 38,739 | 25,710 | * |
| SE | 859 | 1,740 | 1,422 | 1,052 | 1,798 | * |
| *Highest Degree Awarded* | | | | | | |
| Doctorate/ Professional | 44,729 | 50,399 | 39,914 | 38,985 | 32,059 | 58,970 |
| SE | 320 | 550 | 577 | 404 | 661 | 2,644 |
| Other | 32,131 | 40,832 | 30,597 | 30,952 | 27,603 | 33,551 |
| SE | 455 | 1,894 | 1,024 | 435 | 809 | 2,544 |

Source: NSOPF 1988
* = Too few cases for reliable estimate.

**TABLE A2.4    Basic Salary from Institution, by Length of Service: 4-Year Institutions**

| | All 4-Year | Research | Doctoral | Comprehensive | Liberal Arts | Other 4-Year |
|---|---|---|---|---|---|---|
| | | | | Mean ($) | | |
| *Time in Rank* | | | | | | |
| < 3 years | 36,933 | 44,193 | 37,553 | 30,643 | 27,170 | 46,732 |
| SE | 613 | 1,328 | 1,419 | 616 | 900 | 3,248 |
| 3–5 years | 39,927 | 45,204 | 35,122 | 34,817 | 27,096 | 56,762 |
| SE | 549 | 871 | 938 | 580 | 976 | 5,236 |
| 6–11 years | 44,283 | 52,733 | 36,610 | 38,874 | 33,397 | 56,930 |
| SE | 593 | 1,122 | 783 | 783 | 802 | 4,516 |
| 12 + years | 47,966 | 55,037 | 44,369 | 41,237 | 38,138 | * |
| SE | 483 | 889 | 934 | 518 | 1,312 | * |
| *Years in Current Position at Institution* | | | | | | |
| < 4 years | 35,964 | 41,295 | 34,315 | 31,379 | 25,944 | 49,859 |
| SE | 568 | 1,062 | 1,074 | 775 | 1,024 | 3,803 |
| 4–7 years | 41,116 | 49,294 | 37,403 | 33,466 | 25,031 | * |
| SE | 873 | 1,646 | 1,679 | 818 | 1,201 | * |
| 8–14 years | 44,127 | 51,671 | 36,014 | 36,979 | 27,963 | 70,882 |
| SE | 775 | 1,227 | 1,095 | 985 | 721 | 7,084 |
| 15–19 years | 44,923 | 52,632 | 41,470 | 39,350 | 34,510 | * |
| SE | 549 | 1,120 | 1,217 | 602 | 821 | * |
| 20 + years | 46,200 | 52,674 | 44,071 | 41,442 | 39,289 | * |
| SE | 429 | 842 | 862 | 496 | 1,153 | * |

Source: NSOPF 1988
* = Too few cases for reliable estimate.

# APPENDIX 3

*Appendix 3 follows on pages 232–233.*

## Means and Variances: Study of Faculty Compensation

| | All 4-Year | | | Research Universities | | | Doctoral-Granting Universities | | |
|---|---|---|---|---|---|---|---|---|---|
| | Mean | SD | SE | Mean | SD | SE | Mean | SD | SE |
| Basic Income from Institution | $42,498 | 18,845 | 286 | 49,648 | 20,113 | 533 | 38,478 | 14,608 | 528 |
| *Demographic Characteristics* | | | | | | | | | |
| High Paying Field[*] | −.4 | .8 | .01 | −.1 | .8 | .02 | −.4 | .8 | .03 |
| Years Since Attained Highest Degree | 17.7 | 9.6 | .15 | 18.6 | 9.7 | .25 | 16.9 | 9.4 | .34 |
| Percent Minority | 10.40 | 30.6 | .46 | 10.4 | 30.5 | .80 | 7.2 | 25.9 | .93 |
| Percent Male | 79.2 | 40.6 | .61 | 82.5 | 38.0 | .98 | 77.6 | 41.7 | 1.49 |
| *Job History* | | | | | | | | | |
| Time in Rank (years) | 7.9 | 6.4 | .10 | 8.1 | 6.5 | .17 | 7.8 | 6.4 | .23 |
| Percent with Highest Degree–Doctorate | 83.4 | 37.2 | .56 | 93.4 | 24.8 | .65 | 85.9 | 34.8 | 1.26 |
| Years in Current Position | 12.4 | 8.7 | .13 | 12.4 | 8.7 | .23 | 11.9 | 8.7 | .31 |
| *Teaching* | | | | | | | | | |
| Percent of Time Spent on Teaching | 53.2 | 23.8 | .36 | 42.6 | 20.9 | .55 | 53.7 | 20.6 | .74 |
| Student Contact Hours (semester) | 322.3 | 496.3 | 7.60 | 322.9 | 656.0 | 17.7 | 303.5 | 386.2 | 14.10 |
| Number of Hours per Week Teaching in Class | 9.4 | 6.9 | .11 | 7.7 | 8.0 | .22 | 8.8 | 5.0 | .18 |
| Percent Who Taught Only Graduate Students | 11.7 | 32.1 | .48 | 20.1 | 40.1 | 1.04 | 6.5 | 24.6 | .88 |
| *Research* | | | | | | | | | |
| Percent of Time Spent on Research/Scholarship | 22.0 | 19.8 | .30 | 31.4 | 20.6 | .54 | 23.6 | 18.8 | .68 |
| Total Number of Publications during Career | 25.1 | 41.9 | .63 | 38.4 | 50.1 | 1.31 | 23.4 | 37.4 | 1.35 |
| Percent Who Were Principal Investigators on an Externally Funded Project | 24.7 | 43.1 | .64 | 40.2 | 49.0 | 1.27 | 22.3 | 41.6 | 1.49 |
| *Other* | | | | | | | | | |
| Percent of Time Spent on Administrative Activities | 14.0 | 15.2 | .23 | 14.6 | 15.1 | .40 | 13.4 | 14.9 | .54 |
| Percent of Time Spent on Community/Public Service | 2.0 | 4.0 | .06 | 1.6 | 4.0 | .10 | 2.2 | 3.9 | .14 |

Source: NSOPF 1988
NA = Not Applicable
[*] −1 = below average, 0 = average, 1 = above average
[**] No variance

| Comprehensive Universities | | | Liberal Arts Colleges | | | Other 4-Year | | |
| --- | --- | --- | --- | --- | --- | --- | --- | --- |
| Mean | SD | SE | Mean | SD | SE | Mean | SD | SE |
| 36,820 | 13,408 | 335 | 30,628 | 10,747 | 533 | 55,920 | 27,709 | 2,403 |
| −.5 | .7 | .02 | −.6 | .6 | .03 | 1.0 | ** | ** |
| 17.0 | 9.1 | .23 | 15.6 | 10.2 | .50 | 20.4 | 10.3 | .87 |
| 11.7 | 32.1 | .80 | 10.3 | 30.4 | 1.50 | 11.3 | 31.7 | 2.70 |
| 75.1 | 43.2 | 1.06 | 75.8 | 42.8 | 2.09 | 89.5 | 30.7 | 2.57 |
| 8.1 | 6.3 | .16 | 6.7 | 5.8 | .29 | 7.2 | 5.6 | .47 |
| 74.0 | 43.9 | 1.09 | 67.5 | 46.8 | 2.30 | 89.3 | 30.9 | 2.60 |
| 12.8 | 8.8 | .22 | 12.1 | 9.2 | .45 | 11.7 | 8.2 | .70 |
| 63.8 | 21.3 | .52 | 68.0 | 19.4 | .96 | 39.9 | 26.9 | 2.28 |
| 318.8 | 319.4 | 7.99 | 233.8 | 178.5 | 8.83 | 495.9 | 676.2 | 59.77 |
| 11.0 | 6.1 | .15 | 10.6 | 5.2 | .26 | 9.6 | 7.6 | .67 |
| 3.3 | 17.8 | .44 | NA | NA | NA | 32.9 | 47.0 | 3.94 |
| 12.6 | 13.2 | .33 | 10.5 | 12.7 | .63 | 27.5 | 23.3 | 1.97 |
| 11.4 | 27.1 | .67 | 8.1 | 15.3 | .75 | 45.1 | 51.7 | 4.36 |
| 10.7 | 30.9 | .76 | 8.5 | 27.9 | 1.36 | 34.1 | 47.4 | 3.98 |
| 13.4 | 15.6 | .39 | 13.8 | 14.6 | .72 | 15.4 | 14.2 | 1.20 |
| 2.4 | 4.1 | .10 | 2.3 | 3.7 | .19 | 1.3 | 3.9 | .33 |

APPENDIX 4

## Regression Equations for Basic Salary: Type of Institution

| | Research | Doctoral | Comprehensive | Liberal Arts | Other 4-Year |
|---|---|---|---|---|---|
| N | 1,259 | 700 | 1,465 | 366 | 114 |
| $R^2$ | .41 | .42 | .50 | .49 | .41 |
| | Beta | Beta | Beta | Beta | Beta |
| Intercept | 49388**** | 42706**** | 38954**** | 37686**** | 49736**** |
| *Control Variables* | | | | | |
| Source of Control | −3881**** | −2812** | 4516**** | NA | 0 |
| Seniority | 4068**** | 4948**** | 4900**** | 5553**** | 860 |
| Male | 2268**** | 1924**** | 1680**** | 1892**** | 4945 |
| Minority | 132 | 290 | 799*** | −930* | 403 |
| Highest Degree– Doctorate | 500 | 1993**** | 2092**** | 1951**** | 4440 |
| High Paying Field | 5847**** | 2614**** | 3795**** | 1516* | 0 |
| *Behaviors* | | | | | |
| Hours in Class/ Week | 1476*** | 957 | 646* | −1578** | −1543 |
| Student Contact Hours | 472 | −452 | 102 | 2686 | −264 |
| Taught Only Graduate Students | 1813**** | 3499**** | 5126**** | NA | −4904** |
| More Research/ Less Teaching | 1765*** | 1891*** | 1384**** | 3040**** | 320 |
| Publications, Career | 4596**** | 2573**** | 2948**** | 5439**** | 5954** |
| Principal Investigator | 266 | 1647*** | 136 | −320 | 5943** |
| % Time, Administration | 4585**** | 1090** | 2584**** | 569 | 11312**** |
| % Time, Public Service | 582 | 385 | 19 | −585 | −2274 |

Source: NSOPF 1988
NA = Not Applicable
**** = $p < .0001$; *** = $p < .001$; ** = $p < .01$; * = $p < .05$.

# APPENDIX 5

*Appendix 5 follows on pages 238–239.*

## Regression Equations for Basic Salary: Program Area

|  | Agriculture | Business | Education | Engineering |
|---|---|---|---|---|
| N | 171 | 167 | 365 | 152 |
| $R^2$ | .58 | .47 | .56 | .45 |
|  | Beta | Beta | Beta | Beta |
| Intercept | 44450**** | 46540**** | 36392**** | 44783**** |
| *Control Variables* |  |  |  |  |
| Source of Control | –3820 | –749 | 2831** | 508 |
| Seniority | 4505**** | 1766 | 5509**** | 3199**** |
| Male | 2740**** | 1552 | 1289*** | 1127 |
| Minority | –1091 | 806 | 642 | –991 |
| Highest Degree–Doctorate | 3462*** | 2517** | 1710**** | 469 |
| Doctoral Institution | –527 | 3143 | –113 | 386 |
| *Behaviors* |  |  |  |  |
| Hours in Class/Week | –1559 | –3105 | –1313* | –907 |
| Student Contact Hours | –710 | 1102 | 2871* | 335 |
| Taught Only Graduate Students | 1662 | 1269 | 944 | 1891 |
| More Research/Less Teaching | –1545 | 1040 | 548 | 3605** |
| Publications, Career | 2079* | 15382**** | 5928**** | 3738*** |
| Principal Investigator | 3428**** | –974 | 647 | 1643* |
| % Time, Administration | 3196**** | 144 | 1252** | 1227 |
| % Time, Public Service | –80 | –499 | 238 | 228 |

Source: NSOPF 1988
**** = $p < .0001$; *** = $p < .001$; ** = $p < .01$; * = $p < .05$.

| Fine Arts | Health Sciences | Humanities | Natural Sciences | Social Sciences | Other Fields |
|---|---|---|---|---|---|
| 274 | 218 | 1003 | 479 | 670 | 291 |
| .40 | .57 | .54 | .50 | .52 | .49 |
| *Beta* | *Beta* | *Beta* | *Beta* | *Beta* | *Beta* |
| 37568**** | 47996**** | 36902**** | 38555**** | 37248**** | 38726**** |
| 1662 | 1511 | 855 | 1867 | 90 | 705 |
| 4219**** | 3206 | 6034**** | 4752**** | 6142*** | 5480**** |
| 710 | 6068**** | 700** | 1528* | 512 | 1436 |
| 1720*** | 1728 | −20 | 684 | 109 | 601 |
| 1417*** | −1840 | 2221**** | 718 | 1663*** | 2569*** |
| 1035 | 2059 | −93 | −955 | 1340 | 5096** |
| −488 | 1131 | −3960**** | −354 | −1598* | −3728* |
| 1096 | 1068 | 5119**** | 13 | 545 | 6232*** |
| 1942* | 4521**** | 1884*** | 1460** | 127 | 2943** |
| 420 | 118 | 1127** | 1933** | 1129** | 2388* |
| 3582*** | 15003**** | 2105**** | 3540**** | 3386**** | 2888**** |
| 1771* | 651 | 1217** | 1559*** | 1337*** | 957 |
| 1842*** | 5241**** | 1834**** | 4481**** | 2172**** | 1095 |
| 67 | −10 | −1546**** | −410 | −331 | 1008 |

# APPENDIX 6

## Regression Equations for Basic Salary: Assistant Professors, by Type of Institution

|  | Research | Doctoral | Comprehensive | Liberal Arts |
|---|---|---|---|---|
| N | 273 | 171 | 354 | 102 |
| $R^2$ | .34 | .20 | .35 | .35 |
|  | **Beta** | **Beta** | **Beta** | **Beta** |
| Intercept | 37363**** | 32434**** | 34615**** | 41378**** |
| *Control Variables* |  |  |  |  |
| Source of Control | −898 | −1653 | 1215 | NA |
| Seniority | −3167* | 2464 | 2845**** | 3760* |
| Male | 1999*** | 831 | 833** | 305 |
| Minority | 829 | 1047 | 478 | −2087** |
| Highest Degree–Doctorate | 2024* | 948 | 1022** | 751 |
| High Paying Field | 5416**** | 2342** | 3173**** | 958 |
| *Behaviors* |  |  |  |  |
| Hours in Class/Week | 226 | −2158 | 283 | −2859** |
| Student Contact Hours | −318 | −274 | −1240 | 10029** |
| Taught Only Graduate Students | 1070 | −759 | 6460**** | NA |
| More Research/Less Teaching | 144 | 1522 | 1161* | 1786 |
| Publications, Career | 8604*** | −2397 | 3128 | 16187** |
| Principal Investigator | −1065 | 1351 | −981 | 527 |
| % Time, Administration | 2676** | −840 | −1891* | −53 |
| % Time, Public Service | 320 | −1474 | −297 | −761 |

Source: NSOPF 1988
NA = Not Applicable
**** = $p < .0001$; *** = $p < .001$; ** = $p < .01$; * = $p < .05$.

# APPENDIX 7

## Means and Variances: Study of Faculty Socialization

| Criterion | Junior Faculty | | | Senior Faculty | | |
|---|---|---|---|---|---|---|
| | Mean | SD | SE | Mean | SD | SE |
| Percent of Time Spent on Teaching | 56.8 | 23.1 | .72 | 51.4 | 23.7 | .41 |
| *Demographics* | | | | | | |
| Percent Male | 64.7 | 47.8 | 1.49 | 85.6 | 35.1 | .61 |
| Percent Minority | 13.6 | 34.2 | 1.07 | 9.2 | 28.9 | .51 |
| Time in Rank | 5.0 | 4.7 | .15 | 9.0 | 6.5 | .11 |
| *Early Socialization* | | | | | | |
| Highest Degree, Prestige | 2.3 | .8 | .03 | 2.5 | .7 | .01 |
| Percent Who Were a Teaching Assistant, Graduate School | 58.4 | 49.3 | 1.55 | 54.7 | 49.8 | .87 |
| *Current Socialization* | | | | | | |
| Satisfied with Activity Mix | 2.7 | .9 | .03 | 3.0 | .9 | .02 |
| Satisfied with Time for Students | 2.9 | .8 | .02 | 3.1 | .8 | .01 |

**Means and Variances: Study of Faculty Socialization**

| Criterion | Junior Faculty | | | Senior Faculty | | |
|---|---|---|---|---|---|---|
| | Mean | SD | SE | Mean | SD | SE |
| Agree That Publications Should Be the Criterion for Promotion | 2.3 | .9 | .03 | 2.4 | .9 | .02 |
| Would Leave Job to Reduce Pressure to Publish | 1.8 | .7 | .02 | 1.8 | .8 | .01 |
| *Work Allocation* | | | | | | |
| Hours in Class/ Week | 9.7 | 6.5 | .21 | 9.2 | 7.1 | .13 |
| Taught only Graduate Students | 11.4 | 31.8 | .99 | 11.8 | 32.3 | .56 |
| *Rewards* | | | | | | |
| Research Rewarded More than Teaching at Institution | 2.8 | 1.1 | .03 | 2.9 | 1.1 | .02 |
| Basic Salary | 32,201 | 12,762 | 403 | 46,459 | 18,838 | 332 |

Source: NSOPF 1988

# Index